The Complete
RESUME &
JOB SEARCH
Book for
College Students

by Bob Adams, Publisher of the *JobBank Series*
with Laura Morin

BOB ADAMS, INC.
PUBLISHERS
Holbrook, Massachusetts

Published by Bob Adams, Inc.
260 Center Street, Holbrook, MA 02343

ISBN: 1-55850-188-6

Printed in the United States of America

J   I   H   G   F   E   D   C   B   A

This publication is designed to provide accurate and authoritative information with regard to the subject matter covered. It is sold with the understanding that the publisher is not engaged in rendering legal, accounting, or other professional advice. If legal advice or other expert assistance is required, the services of a qualified professional person should be sought.

— From a *Declaration of Principles* jointly adopted by a
Committee of the American Bar Association and a
Committee of Publishers and Associations.

To your future.

Acknowledgments

This book would not have been possible without the encouragement and help of many people, including Christopher Ciaschini, who contributed his usual top-notch production work, Dawn Hobson, who met every deadline, and Brandon Toropov, who provided important insights and advice in the final stages.

Contents

Chapter 7

Mass mailings and phone calls • What kinds of companies should you contact? • Sources of company information • The best way to contact small and large companies • Following up with a phone call • What should a follow-up phone call sound like?

Chapter 8

Is networking an appropriate tool for college grads? • The key to networking • Tracking down leads • Name-dropping • What does a networking conversation sound like? • Overcoming uneasiness about talking to strangers over the telephone • The informational interview • Send a thank-you letter

Chapter 9

Starting early • Reading the trade literature • Adhering to your plan when appropriate—and reevaluating it when appropriate • Getting tips from other job-hunters • Using old newspaper ads • More networking? • Contacting the same firms twice • When all else fails . . . • What's next? • Sample letter for contacting the same firm twice

Chapter 10

Resume length • Paper size • Paper color • Paper quality • Typesetting • Computers, Word Processing, and Desktop Publishing • Typing • Printing • Proofreading is essential • Types of resumes • The chronological resume • The functional resume • Which type of resume is best for recent grads? • What comes first? • Show dates and locations • Avoid sentences and large blocks of type • Highlight relevant skills and responsibilities • Education • Should you include a job objective? • Personal data • References • Resume content

Chapter 11

Resume worksheet • Sample resume

Chapter 12

Five so-so resumes transformed into job-winning resumes!

Chapter 13

When to send a cover letter • Length of cover letter • Paper size • Paper color • Paper quality • Pre-printed stationery • Typing • Proofread your cover letter • Avoid messy corrections

Read This First

CONGRATULATIONS! You've just graduated from college or will soon do so. You've gone to a good school and worked hard to get your degree. Right now, you may be asking yourself, "I've gotten a good degree; I've gone to a good school; doesn't this mean that I'll get a good job?"

Unfortunately, in today's tough economy, the answer is no. There are approximately two million people who will be graduating from school this year—but there are not two million new jobs out there for them. There simply aren't enough jobs to go around. But don't lose hope! If you carefully follow the advice in this book, you can be the one who gets a good job—even if you're not a straight-A student.

It wasn't too long ago that getting a college degree set you apart from the vast majority of the competition and almost guaranteed you a good entry-level position in a professional career. Those days are past! Not only are companies curtailing their traditional on-campus recruiting programs, they have been cutting back on managerial and middle-level positions for some years now. At the same time, more and more people are earning their degrees, making the competition for good positions even tougher. There is a shortage of decent entry-level professional jobs. You face a very different job market than the job-seeker of only a few years ago.

In fact, the majority of today's college students will not have a job when they graduate. Worse, a large percentage won't have a job several months or even a year after graduation! On the other hand, the good news is that many students who graduate from college *will* land a terrific job—although it isn't always the same job they initially sought.

How can you be sure that you're going to get the best job possible? Are the grades you earned in college, your extra-curricular activities, or the school you went to enough to guarantee you a career? Absolutely not! *The quality of the position you obtain after graduation—and your ability to obtain a position at all—will be much more dependent on how much effort and energy you expend on a well-executed job-search strategy.*

You may be wondering if it is really worth it to put a great deal of time and effort into finding a good entry-level position. After all, how important could that first job after graduation be? Unfortunately, for most college students it is not very important at all—but it should be! Most college grads don't even stay with their initial job for one year. They are generally dissatisfied with their first position, which typically leads nowhere. However, you should know that if you do start out with a good job, a job you like, it can be a foundation for a terrific career.

The time, effort and energy you put into your job search campaign will probably come back to reward you many times more than the extra hours you may have spent studying and participating in extra-curricular activities. Really, looking for a job and going on interviews are like a final exam—only the consequences of this exam could very well affect your happiness for decades to come. This is one test you can't afford to fail!

Throughout this book, I'll detail all of the essential aspects of a successful job search campaign. If you really want to make sure your first job is a positive first step in a satisfying and rewarding career, then you need to put all of your effort into following the steps outlined in the pages ahead. I encourage you to go through this book thoroughly, review it again and again, and use it as a reference tool throughout your job search campaign.

So keep reading, and remember—you're on your way to a fabulous career!

CHAPTER ONE

What Every College Student Needs to Know Now About Job Hunting

AS A RULE, the best jobs do *not* go to the best qualified individuals; they generally go to the best job-hunters. This is a vitally important point, especially if you are competing for an entry-level position. Even though you may compete with people who have stronger credentials than you, you can still get the job you want if you're willing to put in the extra effort and energy necessary to outshine the competition.

WHAT TO EXPECT

A company will often consider scores if not hundreds of individuals for the typical entry-level position! Clearly, then, it is in your best interest to unearth every imaginable employment opportunity. You will need to dig up many, many companies at which to apply in order to turn the odds in your favor. Too many people study in school for seventeen years and then accept the first job offer that comes their way. You don't have to do that, especially if you are ready to put plenty of work into your job search campaign—and begin as soon as possible.

But be forewarned: getting even one job offer will be tough. Many graduating students enter the job market thinking that getting a job will be like applying to college. Perhaps you applied to only two or three top schools that you really wanted to get into, and to a couple of others that you considered "safety schools" or easy bets.

Applying to companies isn't like that at all. You might have to apply to one hundred companies just to get one interview. You might have to apply to two hundred to get a single job offer. But if you're really serious about job searching—if you're serious about your career—you'll probably have to go much further than that to win multiple job offers so that you can have your pick of the very best positions.

Success will not go to the job searcher who invests little effort, becomes discouraged, and takes the first job possibility that comes around. Remember, the time you put into your job search will be time well spent if you make sure all of that effort and energy is going in the right direction.

STANDING OUT FROM THE PACK

In addition to unearthing as many companies and job leads as possible, you can increase your chances of landing a great job by standing out from the pack. Most college students—regardless of their grades—have all of the basic requirements for the typical entry-level job. You must show why you stand out from the competition. You must demonstrate that in addition to fulfilling the basic requirements, there are some special reasons *you* deserve that extra consideration.

I'll show you how to do exactly that—and more—in the pages ahead.

CHAPTER TWO

What Are Employers Really Looking for?

YOU MAY BE surprised to learn that employers generally are not looking for just the best grade point average, the most clubs or the most athletic letters. One of the most important things that employers *are* particularly concerned with, however, is the answer to a simple question: How long will you stay with the company?

COMMITMENT

The average college grad only stays with his/her first employer for nine months. And remember, I'm only talking about an average; half of the people who are hired stay for less than nine months! Employers have concluded that most new young hires are unrealistic about what entry-level jobs entail and will soon leave in search of something "better." They're right.

This cycle costs companies a lot of money, because training new hires is very expensive. Some companies and large corporations might spend as much as $60,000 per new employee in training programs over the first six months. If you leave after nine months, the firm will lose on its investment. It's not surprising, then, that most companies—especially those with training programs—will be very interested in whether or not you are likely to remain in that position for a period of time.

How can you show a company that you won't move on too soon? Your grades and your athletic letters probably won't be a strong indication of this. You must display a true interest in the industry, in the job function itself, and particularly in that employer. Intelligently discussing current trends in the industry and showing that you are genuinely interested in the job are two great ways to communicate to an interviewer that you're a low-risk hire.

Another way to demonstrate this is to stress only a small number of extra-curricular activities that you pursued for an extended period of time: this shows that you didn't just participate in many different activities, jumping from one to the next. Although this may seem surprising, it may actually look better to an employer if you participated in only *one* activity during your college career than if you experimented with many. As long as the activity you highlight was something you spent a lot of time and energy doing, something you made progress in over the years, it will carry more weight than many activities that you were only nominally involved in. Remember, consistency is often more important to employers than excellence in school or outside activities.

Additionally, you should show the employer that you're likely to stay with the firm by making it clear that you know what you want. Although you probably don't know the precise title of the job you want, you must show the employer some particular interests and career direction. You should also show that you have a realistic feeling for what the job entails, that you understand what the pluses and minuses are in the position you are considering, and that you've decided, after making a realistic assessment of the job, that it's something you would enjoy doing for a substantial period of time.

MATURITY AND CONFIDENCE

Another factor that employers weigh heavily is maturity. Many young graduates, in one-to-one situations with older adults, simply don't come across being mature and confident enough for the professional world. Unfortunately, such judgments are often made based on a brief one-on-one interview. Your references could help you in some cases, but your interview is going to matter much more. Later on in this book, I'll talk about how you can prepare for your interviews, and how you can make sure that you project yourself as a candidate who is mature and ready to enter the business community.

PROFESSIONALISM

Employers will also want to know whether or not you have a professional demeanor. This demeanor is difficult to define, but it is perhaps best understood as the ability to "fit in with others" in a given work group, adhering to their standards of communication, dress, and conduct. Your professionalism is something you need to prove to employers as soon as you contact their firm. One of the ways you show a company this, of course, is by following a more or less accepted format for your resume. Your cover letter also needs to look professional. (We'll review all the details later in the book.) In terms of dress, it is important that you look like you will fit in at the company from the very first glimpse. In your answers and presentation at the job interview, you must convey that you know how to conduct yourself properly in a business setting.

ADAPTABILITY AND GROWTH

Proving you can do a certain job is not enough. Companies, especially those hiring for management training programs, also want to see that you are going to grow within the company. Employers hope to use these programs to groom potential future senior managers. You must assure them that you are capable of adapting to new positions within the company and that you can handle a good deal of responsibility.

BUT THAT'S NOT ALL!

Punctuality is a sign of responsibility. It follows that you've got to be on time for the interview. (Many students aren't.) What's more, you will have to project the image of a business-oriented person by showing an interest in the industry and in the business world in general. To be sure, employers also want to see that you can perform the job function with a reasonably high degree of certainty. But because most students applying for an entry-level position aren't going to be able to prove their capabilities by citing previous professional work experience, elements such as punctuality and business orientation are so crucial in applying for that first job.

In short, employers are looking for applicants who are likely to stay with their company for a reasonable length of time, have some career direction, and are interested not only in the job itself, but the industry as well. Recruiters seek applicants who are realistic about the job they're applying for; they like to see people who are mature, confident, responsible, and professional. Lastly, employers seek applicants who are ready and eager to enter the business world and who will grow within their company and contribute to its success.

So much for the qualities companies are looking for. You may feel the temptation at this point to pick up the phone or mail letters in hopes of securing the interviews at which you can project these qualities. Before you do, however, you will need to focus your search . . . and you will need to take a good look at the specific "package" you will offer the employer.

CHAPTER THREE

Where to Start

BEFORE YOU CONTACT prospective employers, you must focus your job search. You should decide on the industry, job function, and geographic location of greatest value to you. One reason to do this is that it makes your job search manageable; if you try to pursue too many different avenues, your job search will most likely become frustrating and unproductive. You should remember that employers like job candidates who have real interests and a clear direction. They know that if you are interested in a particular industry, company, or job, you are more likely to enjoy that position, excel in it, and stay with the company for a good period of time. Recruiters do *not* like to hear that you aren't at all discriminating—that you'll take whatever job they have available.

TAKING INVENTORY OF YOUR INTERESTS AND ABILITIES

There are many ways to focus your interests and choose which field you would like to work in. One way to do this is by taking an interest-inventory test. These are multiple choice tests designed to assess your likes and dislikes and determine which jobs are best for you. (Your placement office probably has a test you can review.) You might find out some interesting things by taking such an exam. I remember taking one test while I was at business school that showed that I should be either an army general or a store clerk! Of course, the difference between the two is extreme enough to cast some doubt on the whole exercise. This is not to say that an interest-inventory test can't be helpful to you; if you take such tests, though, you should keep in mind that they should be only one of many different factors in your decision-making process.

CONSIDERING THE DAILY TASKS

I feel that a better way to approach this issue of interests and abilities is to consider the daily tasks of a number of jobs that you are considering. Look at the daily tasks of each entry-level position and the daily tasks of the positions that it might lead to. Ask yourself if you really find the duties of that job interesting and if you would like to perform them on a daily basis.

MAKING A GOOD MATCH

Keep in mind that, on a daily basis, you will spend about as much time in your job as you do sleeping—so it's important to know that you'll enjoy the work before you decide on a particular type of employment. For instance, if you are thinking about becoming an elementary school teacher, you must first be sure that you enjoy spending a great deal of time with small children. If you want to be an accountant, you should first ask yourself if you are very meticulous and like detail-oriented work. If you want to work for a daily newspaper, you must be sure that you can handle a fast-paced, high-pressure environment. Take advantage of the many books and other resources that detail what it's like to work in a particular career on a day-to-day basis. You may also wish to phone or write companies before making a formal application to request a written job description. (Also, see the Appendix for a detailed listing of great job options for college grads of the 90's.)

Bear in mind, too, that you are choosing not just a job but a lifestyle. If you decide, for example, that your goal is to be a management consultant for an international firm, chances are you will be spending a great deal of your time in an airplane—so you'd better like to fly! Similarly, you should think about geography. Do you want a career that would require you to live in a large city, such as an urban engineer? Or would you rather live in a less populated, rural area? Consider such issues closely before you commit yourself to any one profession.

Think about what the compensation possibilities are—not necessarily for the entry-level position, but for the positions it might lead to. Which do you feel is more important: to make a lot of money or to be fulfilled by your work? Think about your work schedule. If you want a job where you have a flexible schedule, this will have a big impact on the type of job you can choose. If you are very ambitious and achievement-oriented, that's likely to mean that you will spend some time "burning the midnight oil." How fast do you want to advance to your next job? In some careers and in some companies, there's a much greater chance that you will be able to advance quickly to a higher position than in other careers, companies, and positions. In some fields, the opportunities for advancement are virtually nonexistent.

OTHER IMPORTANT CONSIDERATIONS

You must also ask yourself whether the industry you are interested in is flourishing or dying. This isn't to say that you should jump into a particular field just because it's doing well, but the growth in a given field will probably have a major impact on your career prospects some years down the road. If the industry is flourishing, it could mean many more exciting challenges and better opportunities will be available to you—but it could also mean that you have chosen a much less stable profession, and will have to jump from one company to the next throughout your career. Sometimes it's a good idea to consider careers in industries that are slowing down or maturing—because they are more likely to have greater opportunities for advancement than industries that are booming and flooded with very talented young applicants.

Take into consideration whether the job function itself is flourishing or dying. Will the demand be increasing for the job, or is it slowing down? Again, you've got to consider not only what the competition will be like to get the job, but also what the competition will be like to advance.

BEING REALISTIC

Most importantly, make sure that your career plans are realistic. Accept that most entry-level positions are usually lower-paying, less-than-glamorous jobs. It will probably take you a number of years to achieve your career goals and advance to your ideal job. It is important to set realistic goals, particularly in a difficult economic climate.

Today's job market is tough, and as a job seeker you face many challenges.

However, if you recognize this fact and keep putting sufficient effort and energy into your job search day after day, you will greatly increase the number of opportunities that are open to you and ultimately find the top-notch job you deserve. After all, your job search can itself be considered your first full-time assignment. Treat it as such, and you will reap rewards.

CHAPTER FOUR

Beyond the Classifieds—The Best and Worst Ways to Find Jobs

YOU MAY BE surprised to learn that some of the most popular job-search methods are quite unsuccessful for most of the people who use them. In this chapter, you'll have a chance to take a look at the real value of the major techniques at your disposal.

ON-CAMPUS RECRUITERS

Many college students and their parents assume that they can focus their job-hunting plans solely on those companies that recruit on campus. Approaching a job search campaign in this way is a bad idea; there simply aren't enough companies recruiting on college campuses to provide an ample source of jobs for interested students. Those companies that do recruit on campus typically visit a large number of colleges and receive many more job inquiries than they are able to interview people for, let alone hire people for. It is not uncommon for firms to receive as many as 300 applications for every job opening. The competition is so fierce that a typical student's chances of actually getting a job through the on-campus recruitment process are comparable to the chances of winning a state lottery—it's certainly not *impossible*, but it's very tough.

Nevertheless, it is true that some of the very best positions for college students are offered by companies that recruit on campus. The starting positions at these companies might not seem that much better than jobs you could find by using other job-search methods, but many of these companies offer fast-track training programs; the management training programs in particular offer terrific opportunities. If you decide to pursue on-campus recruiting opportunities, however, make sure that you don't spend all of your time and effort in this area.

One of the most overlooked avenues for jobs is companies that don't actually visit college campuses, but do post notices that they are interested in receiving applications from candidates. Many companies try to cut their overhead costs by limiting or eliminating recruiting visits—but are still interested in hiring people. These companies are not as easily visible to college students as the firms that actually visit campuses, but they can be an even better source of job possibilities due to decreased competition for job openings.

INTERNSHIPS

There are many benefits to internships, the most important of which is that internships sometimes lead directly to job opportunities. If a company needs to fill an entry-level position, it will most likely consider its intern before any outside applicants because (1) the intern already is familiar with the company and how it operates and (2) the company already knows whether or not the intern would be a good hire, based on previous work done there.

There are other reasons you should consider an internship. If you aren't sure about what you want to do after graduation, an internship will give you a good idea of what it would be like to work in a particular field. Internships also strengthen your resume and can provide you with some valuable business contacts.

COLLEGE CAREER PLANNING AND PLACEMENT OFFICES

Your college placement office can help you find a job by matching your qualifications with appropriate job openings. You can also get counseling, testing, and job search advice—and you can take advantage of the school's career resource library. As I noted earlier, your college placement office can help you identify and evaluate your interests, work values, and skills. They offer workshops on such topics as job search strategy, resume writing, letter writing, and effective interviewing or job fairs for meeting with prospective employers.

JOB COUNSELING SERVICES

The job counseling services offered by your city or town, which can be found in the Yellow Pages of your local phone directory, are another useful option. The National Board for Certified Counselors will provide you with a listing of certified career counselors in your area. Write:

> National Board for Certified Counselors
> 3D Terrace Way
> Greensboro, NC 27403
> (919) 547-0607

You may also wish to consult *The JobBank Guide to Employment Services*, which lists career counseling services as well as executive search firms, employment agencies and temporary help services located throughout the United States. This guide may be found in your local library or your college career office.

PROFESSIONAL EMPLOYMENT AGENCIES

Should you work with professional employment agencies? Unfortunately these agencies tend to focus on either secretarial or administrative positions or on highly specialized professional openings intended for people with a great deal of professional experience. Chances are, then, that employment agencies won't be able to help you find the professional position you want. It might be possible that an agency would have a few jobs appropriate for college grads, but it isn't very likely.

What's more, many people who use employment agencies wind up in a job that they really didn't want in the first place. You should know that virtually all employment agencies are paid for by the employer. It's not surprising, then, that the employment agency is going to be much more responsive to the needs of the employer than to your needs.

Very few recent college grads find professional positions through employment agencies; I strongly suggest that you spend your time pursuing other, more productive avenues.

COMMUNITY AGENCIES

Many non-profit organizations offer counseling, career development, and job placement services. Often these services are targeted to a particular group, for example women, minorities, the blind, and the disabled. Many cities and towns have commissions that provide services for these special groups. The following national organizations provide information on career planning, training, or public policy support for specific groups.

Women:

> U.S. Department of Labor
> Women's Bureau
> 200 Constitution Avenue NW
> Washington, DC 20210
> Phone: (202) 523-6652
>
> Catalyst
> 250 Park Avenue South
> 5th Floor
> New York, NY 10003
> Phone: (212) 777-8900
> (Ask for the free referral pamphlet, *Career Development Resources*.)
>
> Wider Opportunities for Women
> 1325 G Street NW
> Lower Level
> Washington, DC 20005
> Phone: (202) 638-3143

Minorities:

> National Association for the Advancement of Colored People (NAACP)
> 4805 Mount Hope Drive
> Baltimore, MD 21215-3197
> Phone: (301) 358-8900
>
> National Urban League
> Employment Department
> 500 E. 62nd Street
> New York, NY 10021
> Phone: (212) 310-9000
>
> National Urban League
> Washington Operations
> 1111 14th Street NW
> 6th Floor
> Washington, DC 20005
> Phone: (202) 898-1604

The blind:
> Job Opportunities for the Blind Program
> National Federation for the Blind
> 1800 Johnson Street
> Baltimore, MD 21230
> Phone: (800) 638-7518

The disabled:
> President's Committee on Employment of People with Disabilities
> 1331 F Street NW
> Third Floor
> Washington, DC 20004
> Phone: (202) 376-6200

PUBLIC EMPLOYMENT SERVICE

Your state employment service, sometimes called the Job Service, operates in coordination with the Labor Department's U.S. Employment Service. The service has about 1,700 local offices (also called employment service centers), nationwide, which help match job-seekers with appropriate job openings free of charge. The Job Service also offers counseling and testing to help you choose a career by determining your occupational aptitudes and interests.

NEWSPAPER ADS

Are newspaper ads a good source of opportunities for those entering the job market after graduation? Unfortunately, the answer is no. For *anyone* trying to find a job at *any* point in their career, newspaper ads are not a great way to find a job. Department of Labor statistics show that most people do not get their jobs through newspaper ads.

One of the reasons newspapers are not a good source for job opportunities is that once a company advertises a job opening in a newspaper, it is deluged with hundreds of applications. This is often quite disruptive; a company will typically try anything and everything to fill a job opening before resorting to listing it in the classified section. This means that there are very few job openings listed in the newspaper relative to the actual number of jobs available at any given time.

There's more bad news. By the time a job is listed in the classified ads, there's a good chance the position has already been filled or is close to being filled. Even if the position is still available by the time the company receives your resume, the competition will be so fierce that your chances of getting an interview will be quite small.

For all of these reasons, relying solely on newspaper ads is usually a very tough way to get a job. This is not to say that you should ignore promising opportunities you see advertised, but you certainly shouldn't make scanning the want ads your primary research activity.

Think of your job search campaign as a military campaign—you have to follow every avenue possible to win, but some avenues are likely to be more productive than others. It's hard to say which avenue is going to pan out for you, so you shouldn't rule out any possibilities. At the same time, however, you can't afford to spend too much time in any area that is unlikely to be productive. That means newspaper ads should be a secondary line of attack at best.

DIRECT CONTACT

Among the best ways for a college grad to find a job is the direct contact method. Direct contact means contacting potential employers directly and on your own. This method of finding a job will be discussed in detail in Chapter Seven.

NETWORKING

Another excellent method is networking, which means a method of finding a job by developing a network of "insider" contacts. This is a great approach to use even if you don't have any professional contacts. Networking takes many forms; with a little skill and a lot of effort, it can be a very productive tool for you. In Chapter Eight, I'll take you through the networking process step by step.

CHAPTER FIVE

Making a Job-Search Plan

IT'S VITALLY IMPORTANT to have a job-search plan so that you can pace yourself and monitor your progress against predetermined goals. Having a plan will also help you to keep up the vigorous pace of the job-search process and help keep you from becoming frustrated or unmotivated. If your plan is not an effective one, you will be able to see problems more clearly and tackle them head-on by changing direction or using different techniques.

CHOOSE A CAREER PATH

As I noted earlier, you must select an industry and job category as your first step. If you have trouble deciding on just one career path, you should do more research on the fields you are most interested in. Try your local library and your college's career center—they're both great sources of information about different professional occupations. Speak with people who work in the different industries you are interested in. If, after all of this, you still can't decide which is best for you, a good option is simply to pick one field from the group and focus your job-search efforts on it exclusively. If you don't find any job leads after an appropriate interval of time, then you can look into a different field or a different position.

DEVELOP A STRATEGY

Your job search plan should take into consideration many different job-finding strategies. Decide who you plan to get in touch with initially for networking; find out which sources of company listings will best suit your needs; decide whether or not you will participate in on-campus recruiting; decide which newspapers are worth monitoring. Then predict how much time you are going to spend pursuing these different avenues and set up a schedule for yourself. It's very important to plan out your job search in this way; you'll be less likely to fall behind. You'll also find that it's easier to put that extra effort and energy into job hunting if you can actually see the progress you're making as you go along.

A JOB-HUNTING PLAN FOR YOUR SENIOR YEAR

If it's at all possible, begin your job search campaign early in your senior year—it will give you an edge over the competition. Here is a general outline for a job-hunting plan for your senior year:

September/October   Decide on which industry or job function you are interested in. After you've reviewed Chapters Ten through Fifteen, put your resume together and practice writing cover letters. Buy any stationery that you will need (including paper and envelopes for your resume and cover letters).

November Develop a comprehensive job search plan. If you decide that on-campus recruiting is a good option for you, decide which on-campus recruiters you'd like to talk to. Express your interest in those companies you choose with a letter and perhaps a follow-up phone call as well.

December Start to contact those companies who *won't* be coming to your campus, beginning with those companies who expressed interest through your school in receiving applications from college students. Then start contacting other companies that you learned about through other resources such as library listings and the JobBank series of local employment guides.

January After you have reviewed Chapter Eight, start networking.

February Set aside time for interviewing, both on and off-campus.

March Begin to review help-wanted advertisements in newspapers.

April Start to focus your efforts on the job-search method that has been most productive for you so far. If you are not sure of which technique to use, I would suggest either contacting companies on your own or networking. These are probably the two most dependable methods for finding a job.

HOW MANY STUDENTS LAND A JOB BEFORE THEY GRADUATE?

Most students won't have jobs by the time they graduate. So if you fall into this category, don't be dismayed—you're not alone! Don't sell yourself short, you went to school to get an education—and you did. But finding a job is a completely separate endeavor.

A JOB-HUNTING PLAN FOR AFTER GRADUATION

Ideally, for the first few months after graduation, you should try to look for a job full-time. If you're able to do this, be sure to work from a vigorous, intense job-search plan that allows you to invest about 40 hours per week.

Vary your activities a little bit from day to day—otherwise it will quickly become very tedious. For example, every Sunday you can look through the classified ads and determine which jobs are appropriate for you. On Monday, follow up on these ads by sending out your resume and cover letter and perhaps making some phone calls as well. For the rest of the week I would suggest that you spend your time doing other things besides following up specific job openings. On Tuesday, for instance, you might decide to focus on contacting companies directly. On Wednesday, you can do more research to find listings of other companies you can contact. Thursday and Friday might be spent networking, as you try to set up appointments to meet with people and develop more contacts.

Every few weeks, you should evaluate your progress and fine-tune your search accordingly. If you find that, after putting in a great deal of effort over a period of several months, you aren't even close to getting a job, then it's probably time to reconsider your options. Is the job you want realistic for you? Are the opportunities for getting this position greater in another city?

At this point you should probably think about changing your job search techniques, moving to another city, or focusing on a different job or industry—but there is always the possibility that you need to be more aggressive in your job-search efforts. The key is knowing when to persist in the current direction that your job hunt is taking and when to give up what you're doing and start anew. It isn't easy. Often, talking with other job hunters and knowing the current state of the job market in your industry of interest will help you to draw this fine line.

HOW MUCH EFFORT AND ENERGY SHOULD A JOB SEARCH TAKE?

Finding a job is not easy. It takes a lot of energy and a tremendous amount of effort. If you are looking for a job full-time after graduation, your job search will probably last from three to six months. If the economy is in particularly bad shape, however, you should be prepared to search for a year or more.

Note: If you still don't seem close to finding a job after two or three months of searching full-time, you should consider finding a part-time position. (Financially, this will probably be something of a necessity at this point.) With a part-time job, you will earn some money and gain a valuable sense of personal accomplishment. After several months of tedious searching, you will probably have dealt with your share of stress; a part-time job will help to break up your routine a bit and help keep you motivated and enthusiastic about your job search campaign. Working part-time also displays initiative and a good work ethic, which is something that recruiters always like to see.

If you think that you might be having trouble finding a job because you have no experience in a particular field, consider doing an internship while you are job-hunting. Although internships are often not paid, they can, as we have seen, provide valuable experience, numerous business contacts, and sometimes even job opportunities.

CHAPTER SIX

Avoiding Common Pitfalls

BEFORE LOOKING AT the specifics of contacting potential employers, let's examine some of the common pitfalls that stall job searches.

FOLLOWING THE PACK

Don't let yourself get caught up in what everyone else is doing! If you know that a large number of people are trying to interview with just a few highly sought-after companies, don't spend all of your time doing the same. Instead, try to interview at the companies others may have overlooked. Try something different, and you'll be likely to come across several job openings before your competition does.

RELYING ON EMPLOYMENT AGENCIES

One of the problems with employment agencies is that they often try to steer you in a direction you're not interested in. You should know, too, that employment agencies often place college graduates in clerical positions. While it is true that clerical work can sometimes be an effective inroad to a professional career, you should not rely on this path unless you are having great difficulty securing a professional position.

USING EMPLOYMENT MARKETING SERVICES

Employment marketing services are very different from employment agencies. Whereas employers pay agencies, *you* pay an employment marketing service (often thousands of dollars) to help you find a job. These companies will send out letters, make phone calls for you, and basically do the things you should be doing in your job search. Their results are usually nothing to write home about. My advice is, don't pay anyone to help you find a job! Go out and do it yourself—not only will you save a great deal of money, but you'll gain some important experience—and probably make invaluable contacts.

If you feel that you really need help finding a job and don't know where to turn, try your college placement office before you sign on with a marketing service. (Most colleges will assist you in your job search even if you've graduated some time ago.)

CALLING 900 NUMBERS

Job-hunting services with 900-prefix numbers are a relatively new phenomenon. Most are scam operations. These companies boast that they have many terrific job openings, and that all you have to do is call to be on your way to a great career. My advice is, *don't call*! Usually the services list only a few job leads, most of them for positions already filled. Despite the low quality of the leads, these calls can be very expensive—often $10 to $20 each.

RUNNING LOW ON ENERGY

Another trap you should avoid is letting yourself believe that job searching is easier for everyone else than it is for you. It is all too easy to become frustrated when you aren't seeing immediate results from all your hard work. At this stage in the job-hunting process, it is normal for you to begin to have self-doubts. But you mustn't let your doubts overwhelm you. Believe me, job searching is *not* easy for everyone else!

Job searching is tough, whether you are a recent college grad or someone who's been in the work place for many years. It will get easier each time you do it, but it will always challenge you, particularly when you're job searching for the first time. You aren't used to it. Remember, if it's tough for you, it's tough for other people—and just about everybody goes through the process. Stay with it, work hard, have confidence and you will get the right job!

CHAPTER SEVEN

Contacting Companies Directly

MASS MAILINGS AND PHONE CALLS

CONTACTING COMPANIES ON your own does not mean sending out mass mailings or making a barrage of hurried phone calls. Direct contact means making a professional, personal approach to a select group of companies. As discussed earlier, you need to focus on a particular field or a particular job function for your job search to be effective, and nowhere is that more true than in contacting potential employers directly.

WHAT KINDS OF COMPANIES SHOULD YOU CONTACT?

Aren't the largest, most successful companies the best places to look for a job? Don't they offer the most security? Contrary to what many believe, this is not always the case. In recent years, some of the largest and most successful companies in America have been dramatically downsizing their work force. These companies are *not* necessarily secure places to work. Furthermore, these giants are the very companies that are deluged with resumes and job applications. For example, some of the largest banking corporations receive as many as 3,000 resumes every day!

There are many more moderate-size companies, with only several hundred employees and not well known to the general public, that you should contact. These companies are a much better source of jobs: they are large enough to have a number of job openings at any given time, but they are small enough that they are often overlooked by other job hunters. This means that there will be less competition for openings and a greater chance that you will find a job at a company of this size.

The best source of job opportunities for college students or recent grads, however, is small companies—especially those with under fifty employees. These companies are not very visible at all and although there will be fewer job openings per company than at larger firms, there will also be much less competition. Another significant advantage of working for a small firm is that there will probably be significant room for career growth there. At the same time, however, smaller companies are typically less stable than larger firms, and offer less job security and fewer benefits. Nevertheless, most job openings today exist within these small companies—and these are the opportunities that are most often overlooked by college students and recent graduates.

SOURCES OF COMPANY INFORMATION

So—how do you find out which companies you should contact? Well, as discussed earlier, you should know which fields you are most interested in. Do some research and put together a list of the companies in these fields. You should research a number of companies; if you just focus on one company at a time you will soon become very frustrated. Helpful hint: rather than going into great detail in your search, you should get a little bit of information about many different companies.

Where should you go to get this information? One of the obvious sources is the *JobBank* series, a group of employment directories listing almost all companies with 50 or more employees in larger cities and metropolitan areas in the U.S. Each *JobBank* is a complete research tool for job-hunters, providing up-date information including:

- ☐ Full name, address, and telephone number of firm
- ☐ Contact name for professional hiring
- ☐ Listings of common positions, educational backgrounds sought, and fringe benefits offered
- ☐ A section on the region's economic outlook
- ☐ The addresses of professional associations, chambers of commerce, and executive search and job placement agencies

The series covers 37 different industries, from Accounting to Utilities. The number of employers listed in each book ranges from several thousand for smaller cities to almost 20,000 for metro New York or Los Angeles. These books are available for the following regions: Atlanta; Boston; Chicago; Dallas/Fort Worth; Denver; Detroit; Florida; Houston; Los Angeles; Minneapolis/St. Paul; New York; Ohio; Philadelphia; Phoenix; San Francisco Bay Area; Seattle; St. Louis; and Metro Washington D.C.

There are other resources you can use to find listings of companies. For example, there are many directories available, such as *Dun & Bradstreet's Million Dollar Directory* and *Standard & Poor's* investment guide, which lists basic information about companies such as the name of the president and a brief description of the company's products and/or services. These directories, as well as many state manufacturer listings, can be found in your local library. The advantage that the *JobBank* series has over these directories is that they list typical entry-level positions for each firm and include the name of the person you should contact.

Remember, your aim is to learn a little about many companies. You do not need a tremendous amount of information before you contact a firm, particularly if you're up to speed with what's going on in the industry.

THE BEST WAY TO CONTACT SMALL AND LARGE COMPANIES

How you go about contacting a company depends upon the size of the firm. At small firms, such as those with under 50 employees, you should contact the president directly. Out of the 50 people who might work at a small company, there are approximately 5–7 professional people working there. These firms hire professional employees on an irregular basis and it's likely that the president of the company him/herself will the highly involved in the recruitment process.

As a general rule, you should always *try* to contact a department head or the president of a company—even for moderate-size companies with several hundred employees and large companies with over 1,000 employees. But as you apply to larger and larger companies, you will find yourself more and more often bumped back to the personnel office. Do not let this discourage you. The personal office is where a great deal of hiring is done; it can be a very valuable resource. There are many books on the market that tell you to avoid personnel offices like the plague, but you'll find that many department heads will not want to interview even a very strong candidate who is a recent college grad.

The first step you should take in contacting a company directly is sending out your resume with a cover letter. The letter should be addressed to a specific person; try to avoid sending letters to "To whom it may concern", "To the Personnel Office", etc. (Chapters Ten through Fifteen explain how to create a job-winning resume and how to write terrific cover letters.)

After you have sent your letter and allowed sufficient time for the person to receive it, you should call. The idea is to call that person one or two days after your resume arrives so that you will be more likely to be remembered.

Can you call the company to see if there are any job openings *before* you make the effort of sending your resume? If you are unusually confident and articulate on the phone, you may have success with this approach. Such calls are especially effective if you are contacting smaller companies since you are more likely to reach a key decision-maker directly, rather than being blocked by a secretary. However, at larger companies you will find that simply sending a resume and cover letter is a much more effective method.

FOLLOWING UP WITH A PHONE CALL

After you've sent your resume and cover letter, you should always follow up with a phone call. What you should say on the phone is important, but so is *how* you say it. You need to speak with an aura of confidence—even though there may not be a job opening available at a certain company, you need not be apologetic for making a call. All companies hire at some point, and each has, at least in theory, a responsibility to be courteous when an outsider makes a call inquiring about potential job openings.

Will all of your calls be answered courteously? No. Some will be answered very abruptly—often you'll be calling somebody who is very busy. But you must project confidence on the phone. Remember, one of the most important things that companies are looking for in entry-level hires is maturity and confidence. One of the ways you can express these qualities is by sounding confident on the phone.

It is extremely important that you be succinct and to the point on the phone. One good way to do this is by writing out a short script for yourself before you call. You should be sure not to sound as if you're reading this script, but do become very familiar with it—so you won't forget what you want to say even if you're nervous. You need to make three points:

1. Why you're calling
2. Why you'd be a strong candidate for hiring
3. What kind of position you're interested in

You should do this very briefly—in twenty seconds or less. At the same time, however, you must be sure to speak clearly and slowly enough to be understood.

WHAT SHOULD A FOLLOW-UP PHONE CALL SOUND LIKE?

Let's say you're calling a very small bank, perhaps a bank that has one office and employs thirty people. Because the bank is so small, you should try to speak with the president. Here is an example:

Receptionist: Good morning, Main Street Bank. Can I help you?

> *You:* Good morning! I'd like to speak with Mr. Smith, please.

Mr. Smith being the president of the bank. Your call is then transferred to his office.

> *Secretary:* Mr. Smith's office.
> *You:* Good Morning! This is Bob Adams calling. Is Mr. Smith available?

I would not suggest that you tell the secretary at this point that you are calling about a job, because the secretary might then block your call. Instead, you want to sound professional and businesslike, as if there is a good reason why you are calling Mr. Smith—which there is. However, if you are asked why you would like to speak to Mr. Smith, you will have to try to sell the secretary on the idea of you working for that firm, just as if you were talking to Mr. Smith.

> *Secretary:* Mr. Smith is very busy. Can I tell him what this is regarding?
> *You:* Yes, my name is Bob Adams. I just graduated with honors from City University with a degree in English. I am seeking an entry-level position at your bank as a loan officer.
> *Secretary:* We don't have any openings at this point in time.
> *You:* Well, that's very good—I understand that might be the case. But I would like to have a couple of minutes to speak with Mr. Smith anyway, in case something might come up in the future. I know he's very busy—I only need to speak with him for a moment.

With a little luck, the secretary will then put your call through to Mr. Smith. If appropriate, you should also indicate that you already sent in a resume and that you live in the same town the company is located in (local roots can help your cause.) It is very important that you try to speak with the Mr. Smith even if you are told that there aren't any jobs available. If you do and if a job opportunity arises in a couple of months , you might have a chance to interview for the position before it is advertised. Don't take "no openings at this time" to mean "no openings ever"—it doesn't!

Be polite but aggressive in your job search. Show that you are genuinely interested in the firm. If you are talking to a department head or the president of the company, that person may be in a position to create a job for you.

If your call gets rerouted through personnel try to use this same strategy: get the decision-making person on the phone, briefly explain why you're calling, demonstrate that you're a strong candidate for hiring, and request an interview.

If you are successful in getting Mr. Smith (or any decision-maker) on the phone, the conversation might go like this:

> *Mr. Smith:* Hello?
> *You:* Hi! Is this Mr. Smith?
> *Mr. Smith:* Yes, this is he.
> *You:* Mr. Smith, my name is Bob Adams and I've lived in this town for the last ten years (or: I'm a member of such-and-such local organization). I've just graduated from City University with a degree in English and I very much want to pursue a career in banking. I'm interested in becoming a loan officer and I know that you may not have any openings at this time, but I would like to come by and talk

to you for a couple minutes about the opportunities that might be available in banking. I sent you a resume and cover letter last week. Did you receive my letter?

One of the reasons you want to ask if Mr. Smith has received your letter is because you're trying to get a conversation started. Mr. Smith might respond by saying, "Yes, I read your letter, I saw that you've done such and such . . . " If he does not recall your letter, briefly summarize its contents. Avoid saying something like, "Mr. Smith, do you have a job there now?" It's very easy for Mr. Smith to say no—and end the conversation. Instead ask if he's received your letter, get a polite, upbeat conversation started, and request an interview.

But what if the call doesn't go so smoothly? Here is an example of one way to handle tougher calls:

> *Mr. Smith:* Hello?
>
> *You:* Mr. Smith?
>
> *Mr. Smith:* Yes, this is he.
>
> *You:* Mr. Smith, my name is Bob Adams. I've just graduated from City College.
>
> *Mr. Smith:* Bob, I did get your letter and I want to thank you for thinking of our bank. I think you have some very strong credentials and I'm sure you're going to do very well, but we don't have any job openings at the moment.
>
> *You:* I understand that you might not have any job openings right now. I've lived in this area for a while, and as I've indicated, I very much want to pursue a career in banking here. I'd like to have a chance to meet with you just for a couple of minutes anyway, just to see if you could tell me a little bit about the banking industry in this town and a little bit about the opportunities one might expect at those places that might be hiring. Would this be possible?

This way, you're showing Mr. Smith some important things: You're a confident, professional individual; you're courteous; you're *not* demanding a job, but you would like to have the opportunity to talk with him briefly.

CHAPTER EIGHT

Networking Your Way to a Job

NETWORKING IS THE process of exchanging information, contacts, and experience for professional purposes. One reason so many people use networking is that it's a great method for finding a new or better job.

IS NETWORKING AN APPROPRIATE TOOL FOR COLLEGE GRADS?

Traditionally, networking is used by people with a great deal of work experience. But you can use it even if you have no experience whatsoever.

Perhaps you're asking yourself, "Don't I have to know people who are in a position to hire to be able to network? Don't I have to know a lot of people in general, or in a specific geographic area, to get a job through networking?" The answer to both questions is no. You don't have to know anybody at all—you just have to *get to know* people.

THE KEY TO NETWORKING

One of the secrets of networking is knowing what you want—or at least appearing to know what you want. For instance if, when you are making networking calls, you tell your contacts that you are interested in the industry they work in, and if you sound only somewhat knowledgeable about that industry, that makes you more or less an industry insider. If you show that you intend to become part of the industry, that you are going to start an important career in their area, your contacts will probably conclude that you could be an important contact some years down the road. Industries are social entities; once you've shown that you are an industry insider, that you are committed to an industry, you become part of that social circle. Of course, you won't have access to everybody in the industry. But you will find some open doors.

So—how do you start? Keep up to date with the industry. Read the trade publications. These are specialized journals and magazines that address the concerns of professionals in a given industry; virtually every type of business has at least one. The motion picture and entertainment industry's chief trade publication is *Variety*; publishers subscribe to *Publishers Weekly* to keep track of the major events in their field. Go to the library and find the magazine, journal, or newsletter that claims as its readers the people who work in the industry you have selected. Then read the publication(s) regularly. In addition, you should keep an eye out for information about your chosen industry that appears in the mainstream media: your daily newspaper, magazines like *Time* and *Business Week*, news broadcasts, books, and other sources. Lastly, you should make a point of getting out and talking to people about developments in your industry, even at social events such as parties or community gatherings where you would not expect to find "insiders." Before long, you will come across as someone genuinely interested in the field, and you will get much better results from your networking efforts.

TRACKING DOWN LEADS

Who should you contact? Some of the obvious sources are friends, relatives, and neighbors. Alumni directories are particularly important resources you can access through your college, grad school, or prep school—will have alumni directories. Even a small school graduating only about 1,000 people yearly can be a significant source of industry contacts. Over the years, the numbers add up so that such a school could potentially have 50,000 graduates in the workplace—people who might be very willing to talk with you about their industry.

Friends, relatives, and neighbors can be important contacts, as well. They might not work in the industry you're interested in, but they could very well know someone you should contact. Someone who knows someone who . . . you get the idea. At first, you might not think you have many contacts at your disposal—but if you think carefully you'll realize you do. Let's say that, between your friends, relatives, neighbors, and academic contacts, there are thirty-five people you can contact. Let's assume none of these thirty-five people work in the industry you're interested in. They may, as a group, know forty people who do work in that industry, work in a related industry, or are in a position to know someone who works in the industry. That's a lot of people. You probably have access right now to many different potential contacts in the industry of your interest.

Your goal in contacting so many people is not to win a job, but to get referrals. You want people to refer you to other people until you come across job leads. Contact your initial base of people; tell them that you just graduated, that you want to pursue a career in such-and-such a field, and that you're eager to talk to anyone who could give you some background information. This is a much better approach than stating that you want a job; you'll get more information, learn more about the industry, and become more of an insider. If you do contact someone who has a position available, you'll sound less threatening if you say you want to come in and talk rather than if you say you're looking for a job.

NAME-DROPPING

Be sure to drop names; it's one of the most important ways to get ahead in the business world. ("Jane Phillips suggested I call you.") As you continue networking, you will find yourself dropping names of people you have met only by phone. If you are uncomfortable with this, you shouldn't be; this is the way it's done. Someday you may be in a position to help other job-hunters in this way, but right now you need to do everything you can to increase *your* chances of finding a job.

WHAT DOES A NETWORKING CONVERSATION SOUND LIKE?

Here's a sample of what your networking conversations should sound like:

> *You:* Hi Uncle Joe! It's Bob. As you might have heard, I just graduated from college and I want to pursue a career in banking. Is there anyone you can think of who might be willing to talk to me about the banking industry, to fill me in on some background information?

Relative: I really can't think of anyone in the banking industry—but why don't you call up my attorney, Don Silva. He's not a real close friend, but I deal with him every month or so. He knows a lot of business people, not necessarily in the banking industry, but you never know. Why don't you call him and see if he can be of any help. His number is 555-1212.

You: Thanks a lot, Uncle Joe!

You then call the attorney, immediately identifying who referred you:

You: Mr. Silva, my name is Bob Adams and my uncle, Joe Adams, suggested that I call you. I'm interested in a career in banking and I wondered if you might know anyone in that field who might be able to talk to me about the industry for a little bit.

Attorney: Well, I'm not really sure. Let me think about it a little bit and I'll get back to you.

Keep the momentum on your side by offering to follow up yourself.

You: That's fine. Why don't you think about it for a couple of days and I'll call you back. If there's someone in the industry who you can refer me to or someone who might know somebody else in the industry, I'd really appreciate it.

If a networking contact seems reluctant, you could redirect the conversation in this way:

Attorney: Gee, I do know a few people in the industry, but they're probably not hiring now . . .

You: That's fine. I just want to talk to someone for a few minutes to find out what's going on in the industry. If you'd like, I can stop by for a few minutes at your convenience so we can meet, and in the meantime maybe you could think of some other names that you'd feel comfortable referring me to.

That way, if your contact is hesitant to give any names out without seeing in person that you're a polished, professional individual, you may be able to overcome some of that reluctance by setting up a face-to-face meeting. This technique also gives your contact the opportunity to think of some more names of people he can refer you to.

The attorney example is a good one; you should consider meeting with people who service others in your chosen industry. If the contact is still unwilling to meet with you, don't be overly insistent. Instead, ask the contact to recommend someone else for you to call. Eventually, you should network your way to someone who works within your chosen industry.

Remember, you don't want to scare your contacts off. If for some reason you suspect a particular contact is in a position to hire, you should *not* specifically ask about a job. Ask about the industry, relay that you are interested in pursuing a career in that field, and try to set up a time to meet briefly so you can get some background information.

Let's suppose that you know for a fact that a certain contact has an opening available that you'd be suitable for—perhaps you saw the ad in the classifieds. Should you mention it in your conversation with this person? Absolutely not. Remember, you earned this contact through networking, not by reading a classified ad. You want to position yourself as an industry insider who is networking around, not as just another person responding to an ad. Follow this advice and you'll be taken a lot more seriously than other people who may call as a result of a newspaper ad. What's more, your contact will feel more comfortable talking to you. This is one of the reasons networking is among the best ways to learn about job openings.

OVERCOMING UNEASINESS ABOUT TALKING TO STRANGERS OVER THE TELEPHONE

Many college students and recent grads are uneasy talking to strangers on the phone. They're not alone. Most people are, at first, a little uncomfortable calling people they don't know and asking for contact names and interviews. But you must realize that while networking by phone is not likely to be rated one of life's most enjoyable activities, it does get easier the more you do it.

You'll be nervous the first few times, but with practice you'll feel much more comfortable and confident making calls. The key is to think about what you're going to say in advance, pick up that phone and just do it. No one else can network for you. Once you gain some confidence, you'll find that your calls will make a big difference in your job search campaign.

THE INFORMATIONAL INTERVIEW

Informational interviews are extremely important. Not only do they build your network, but they can lead to valuable information and contact sources. Do not, however, approach an informational interview as though it were a job interview. Stick to gathering information and leads and see what happens.

Here are some good questions to ask during an informational interview:

- ☐ How did you get started in this business?
- ☐ What do you like the most about your job, your company, and your industry?
- ☐ What do you dislike the most about your job, your company, and your industry?
- ☐ What are the current career opportunities for college grads in the industry?
- ☐ What are the basic requirements for an entry-level position in the industry?
- ☐ Is there a trade association or a trade publication that might aid me in my job search?
- ☐ Where do you see the industry heading in the near future?
- ☐ What advice would you give a college grad looking for a job in the industry?
- ☐ Could you recommend someone else for me to contact in the industry?
- ☐ Is there anything else I should know about the industry?

SEND A THANK-YOU LETTER

If a networking contact has been particularly helpful to you, by all means send a thank-you note. Not only is this courteous, it keeps your contacts current. That person may be an important business contact for you for years to come—especially if the individual is active in your industry.

CHAPTER NINE

How to Get That Extra Edge Over the Competition

THE DIFFERENCE BETWEEN finding a terrific job in a relatively short period of time and suffering through a prolonged job-hunting campaign can be a little extra effort. This chapter examines some of the ways you can get that "extra edge" and outshine the competition.

START EARLY

One important way to get that "extra edge" in your job hunting campaign is to start as soon as you can. It bears repeating that the beginning of your senior year is an ideal time to begin; by the time graduation comes along, you will be well into your search and have several possibilities in mind that you are prepared to take action on. If you have already graduated, don't panic—there are plenty of other steps you can take to distinguish yourself.

READING THE TRADE LITERATURE

As noted earlier, you should make a habit of reading the trade literature of the industry you are focusing on; you should also read some background books about the field. Remember, your aim is to sound like an industry insider; you'll need to be familiar with industry-related topics while you're networking and interviewing.

ADHERING TO YOUR PLAN WHEN APPROPRIATE—AND REEVALUATING IT WHEN APPROPRIATE

Another key to job searching is staying with the plan you made, even if it doesn't seem to be working at first. Of course you will need to reevaluate every once in a while to make sure that your chances of getting the job you want are realistic. If everyone you speak to tells you that the industry is in bad shape, that there are layoffs at companies of all sizes, that the outlook for newcomers is bleak—maybe you should look into a different field. If everyone you speak to tells you that you are underqualified, perhaps you need to look into firms where the competition for positions is not as fierce—or consider a position where your qualifications are more suitable. You may decide to try another field entirely.

GETTING TIPS FROM OTHER JOB-HUNTERS

Meet and talk with other job-hunters from time to time. Seek out job-hunters who, like you, are creative and innovative in their search; share leads, insights, and techniques with each other. Doing this on a regular basis will yield fresh ideas and help keep up your morale.

USING OLD NEWSPAPER ADS

Instead of calling only current newspaper ads, try calling the old ones too. If you respond to a newspaper ad that's six months old, it's possible the person who was hired to fill the position didn't work out. In a situation like this, there won't be hundreds of other people responding to that ad when you call. By the same token, a company that had a job opening six months ago is likely to have a different position opening up now that hasn't been advertised yet. There is often a long interval between the time a manager first starts thinking about filling a position and the time an opening is publicized. You may find old newspapers to be more useful than new ones in terms of unearthing realistic job opportunities

MORE NETWORKING?

Go back and call once again those people you already contacted for leads several months ago. Such a conversation might sound like this:

> *You:* You know, I'm still interested in a career in banking. I know that we talked a few months ago, but I wondered if any other people might have possibly come to mind with a background in banking.

You may be pleasantly surprised. It is not uncommon to catch a contact in a different frame of mind and learn of someone new. Or perhaps, since the last time you spoke with your contact, new leads have arisen, but you haven't heard about them due to a hectic schedule.

CONTACTING THE SAME FIRMS TWICE

Similarly, you can call some of the firms you contacted a few months previously. You could say:

> *You:* My name is Bob Adams and I contacted your firm several months ago about an entry-level position in banking. I'm particularly interested in working for your company. I've been talking with other firms and I'm very much committed to this industry; I recently saw your firm mentioned in the paper, and I'm more convinced than ever that this is a terrific place to work. I feel I have a lot to offer you. I know you didn't respond to me but I'd like you to reconsider my application.

This approach shows that you are genuinely interested in the firm, and will certainly make you stand out in the contact's mind.

The technique works especially well when you contact firms you interviewed with. Only a fraction of those applying for a position get to the interview stage; if you were one of them, the firm was obviously impressed with your qualifications. Chances are good that you would still be considered for another position at that company.

You don't have to telephone, of course; you might prefer to write a letter. At the end of this chapter is a sample of a letter you could send to a company that interviewed you but did not offer you a position.

WHEN ALL ELSE FAILS . . .

If you find, as time goes by, that you aren't getting very far in your job search, consider trying another type of position, a different industry, and/or another city. The ideal way to apply for a job in another city is to move there first and start applying there. Of course, this is not a viable option for everyone. Job searching long-distance is possible, though, but you should explain immediately that you are willing to relocate to that particular area.

WHAT'S NEXT?

At last—you have a good idea of what your battle plan looks like. Before you head for the trenches, however, you'll need plenty of top-notch ammunition—and that means developing the best possible resume and cover letter. In the next two chapters, you'll learn how to do just that.

Sample Letter for contacting the same firm twice

81 Sandypine Road
Joppa, Maryland 20707
(301) 555-1551

October 27, 1993

Mr. Henry Stanhope
Personnel Manager
Lisa Fleischman Associates
2125 Wisconsin Avenue NW
Suite 202
Washington, DC 25507

Dear Mr. Stanhope:

As you may recall, I interviewed with you back in March for an
Advertising Assistant position. I very much enjoyed meeting with you
and was impressed by your organization.

I realize that you have filled that particular opening, but I am
contacting you now because I am still quite interested in obtaining a
position with Lisa Fleischman Associates. Perhaps you have an
appropriate position available currently or anticipate an opening soon.

In case you no longer have my resume on file, I am enclosing another
copy for your consideration. As you can see, I graduated from Colgate
University this past May with a Bachelor of Science degree in
Marketing. In addition to my degree, I have experience working in both
marketing and sales.

I would like to be considered for any appropriate job openings that
may arise. I may be reached at the above listed phone number between 9
am and 5 pm for an interview at your convenience. Again, thank you for
your time.

Sincerely,

Rosemary L. Brandenburg

enc.

CHAPTER TEN

Writing Your Resume

WHEN FILLING A position, a recruiter will often have 100 or more applicants, but time to interview only the five or ten most promising ones. So the recruiter will have to reject most applicants after a brief skimming of their resumes. You could say that the resume is more the recruiter's tool for eliminating candidates than the candidate's tool for gaining consideration.

Unless you have phoned and talked to the recruiter—which you should do whenever you can—you will be chosen or rejected for an interview entirely on the basis of your resume and cover letter. Because of this, your resume must be outstanding. Yet a resume is no substitute for a job search campaign. It is only one of many tools that you must use in order to find a job.

RESUME LENGTH

College students or recent grads should never submit a resume of more than one page in length. If you must squeeze more information in than would otherwise fit, use a smaller typeface or wider page margins.

PAPER SIZE

Use standard 8½" x 11" paper. Recruiters handle hundreds of resumes; if yours is on a smaller sheet, it is likely to be lost in the pile, and if it is oversized, it may get crumpled and have trouble fitting in a company's files.

PAPER COLOR

White and ivory are the only acceptable paper colors for resumes and cover letters.

PAPER QUALITY

Standard, inexpensive office paper (20# bond) is perfectly acceptable. Some job seekers use more expensive stationery papers such as ivory laid, but for a college student or recent graduate, such papers may appear pretentious. They could actually hurt your chances of getting a job interview.

TYPESETTING

Modern photocomposition typesetting gives you the clearest, sharpest image, a wide variety of type styles and effects such as italics, bold facing, and book-like justified margins. Typesetting is the best resume preparation process, but is also the most expensive.

COMPUTERS, WORD PROCESSING, AND DESKTOP PUBLISHING

The most flexible way to type your resume is on a computer or word processor. This will allow you to make changes almost instantly, and to store different drafts on disk. Word processing and desktop publishing systems also give you many different options that a typewriter does not, such as boldfacing for emphasis, different "fonts" or typefaces, justified margins, and clear, sharp copies.

The end result, however, will be largely determined by the quality of the printer you use. A dot matrix printer is completely unacceptable for a resume because the type is much rougher than that of a typewriter. You need at least "letter quality" type. (Do no use a "near letter quality" printer.) Laser printers will generally provide the best quality lettering from a computer. This level of quality will not be as high as a photo-typesetting system, but it should be fine for virtually all graduating college students' resumes.

TYPING

Household typewriters and office typewriters with nylon or other cloth ribbons are not acceptable for typing the resume you will have printed. If for some reason you decide against word processing or typesetting, hire a professional with a high quality office typewriter with a plastic ribbon (usually called a "film ribbon").

PRINTING

Find the best quality offset printing process available. *Do not* make your copies on an office photocopier. Only the personnel office may see the resume you mail; everyone else may see only a copy of it. Copies of copies quickly become illegible. Some professionally maintained, very high-quality photocopiers are of adequate quality, if you are in a rush. But top quality offset printing is best.

PROOFREADING IS ESSENTIAL

Whether you typed it yourself or paid to have it produced professionally, mistakes on resumes can be embarrassing, particularly when something critical (such as your name) is misspelled. No matter how much money you paid to have your resume written or typeset, you are the only one who will lose if there is a mistake. So proofread it as carefully as possible. Get a friend to help you—read your draft aloud as your friend checks the proof copy. Then have your friend read aloud while you check. Next, read it word by word to check spelling and punctuation.

If you are having your resume typed or typeset by a resume service or a printer, and you can't bring a friend or take the time during the day to proof it, pay for it and take it home. Proof it there and bring it back later to have it corrected and printed.

If you wrote your resume on a word processing program, use that program's built-in spelling checker to double-check for spelling errors. Most quality word processors include this convenient feature; however, a spelling checker is *not* a substitute for proofreading your resume—it must still be proofread to ensure that there are no errors. (Bear in mind that a spelling checker cannot flag errors such as "to" for "two," or "belt" for "bell."

TYPES OF RESUMES

There are two basic types of resumes. The most common is the chronological resume; the other is the functional resume.

The Chronological Resume

A chronological resume is actually a reverse chronological resume—items are listed in reverse chronological order, with your most recent schooling or job first. On a chronological resume, education and work experience are always grouped separately.

The Functional Resume

Far less common is a functional resume. A functional resume lists your capabilities and your qualifications, but does not list your work history or education in chronological order.

The main purpose of a functional resume is to better the chances of candidates who might look like a weak job candidate on a chronological resume—or who are in the midst of a career change and wish to deflect attention from recent employment experience. For example, an army officer, a teacher or a homemaker seeking a position at a large corporation might choose a functional resume.

WHICH TYPE OF RESUME IS BEST FOR RECENT GRADS?

Corporate recruiters prefer chronological resumes, especially when evaluating recent grads. Many corporate recruiters will immediately assume that there is a hidden negative aspect of your work or school history if you use a functional resume. Accordingly, I recommend that you use a chronological resume.

WHAT COMES FIRST?

Your education should appear first—and should be outlined in detail. Experience should only be listed first when you have at least two years of full-time career work experience. After your education, list your job experience in reverse order, with your most recent job first and the rest going back in time.

SHOW DATES AND LOCATIONS

Clearly show the dates and locations of your employment and education on your resume. List the dates of your employment and education on the left of the page; put the names of the companies you worked for and the schools you attended a few spaces to the right of the dates. Lastly, align the city and state where you studied or worked with the right margin.

AVOID SENTENCES AND LARGE BLOCKS OF TYPE

Your resume will be scanned, not read. Short, concise phrases are much more effective than long-winded sentences. Consider the difference between these two examples:

Long-winded

```
Over the course of the months of December 1993 and January
1994, I completely redid the inventory system at my place of
employment, which ended up resulting in a final savings of a
great deal of money—perhaps $10,000. It was also considerably
easier to perform office tasks efficiently under the new ar-
rangement, not only for myself, but also for others who worked
with me at the store.
```

Clear and concise

```
Winter, 1993:  Designed and implemented new inventory system, resulting in
               a cost savings of approximately $10,000 and increased employee
               efficiency.
```

Make sure that everything is easy to find. Avoid paragraphs longer than six lines and never go ten or more lines in a paragraph. If you have more than six lines of information about one job or school, rewrite the material into two or more paragraphs.

HIGHLIGHT RELEVANT SKILLS AND RESPONSIBILITIES

Be specific. Slant your past accomplishments toward the type of position that you hope to obtain. Do you hope to supervise people? If so, state how many people, performing what function, you have supervised.

EDUCATION

Mention degrees received and any honors or special awards. Note individual courses or research projects that might be relevant for employers. For instance, if you are a liberal arts major, be sure to mention any courses you may have taken in such areas as accounting, statistics, computer programming, or mathematics—even if these do not reflect your main interests at school.

SHOULD YOU INCLUDE A JOB OBJECTIVE?

The best advice is to omit any reference to a job objective. Even if you are certain of exactly the type of job you want, the inclusion of a job objective might eliminate you from consideration for other positions. You may end up with a job that is quite different than the one that you initially wanted (Most recent college grads do!).

You may wish to use a job objective heading at the top of your resume to express a general interest in the industry you have selected, but you should not designate a particular job. Even if you have made up your mind to settle for only one job function, it may appear presumptuous to specify this on your resume.

Therefore, if you feel you must list a job objective, you should list it in general terms. For example, "Objective: an entry-level position in the banking industry" or "Objective: to pursue a career in book publishing".

PERSONAL DATA

It is not imperative that you include personal data, but if you do, keep it very brief—two lines maximum. A concise reference to commonly practiced activities such as golf, skiing, sailing, chess, bridge, tennis, etc. can prove to be an interesting conversation piece during an interview. Do not include your age, weight, height, marital status, or any similar item.

REFERENCES

Simply write "References available upon request." This enables you to change your references and to know when they are going to be contacted.

RESUME CONTENT

Be factual. In many companies, inaccurate information on a resume or other application will be grounds for dismissal as soon as the inaccuracy is discovered. Protect yourself.

Be positive. You are selling your skills and accomplishments in your resume. If you achieved something, say so, and put it in the best possible light. Don't hold back or be modest—no one else will. At the same time, however, *don't* exaggerate to the point of misrepresentation.

Be brief. Include the relevant and important accomplishments, but do it in as few words as possible. A vigorous, concise resume will be examined more carefully than a long-winded one.

Emphasize relevant experience. Highlight continued experience in a particular type of function or continued interest in a particular industry. De-emphasize any irrelevant positions.

Stress your results. Elaborate on how you contributed to your past employers. Did you increase sales, reduce costs, improve a product, implement a new program? Were you promoted?

CHAPTER ELEVEN

The Resume Worksheet

THIS CHAPTER WILL take you step by step through the resume writing process. You will need plenty of paper; feel free to work with a typewriter or computer in developing your resumes or to enter your answers by hand. You may keep notes separately or enter your responses on the worksheets here.

Name

Write your name, in capital letters, as you wish it to appear on your resume. Center it horizontally on the page, about one inch from the top. Use your formal name, even if no one ever calls you by it. Use a middle name or initial if possible—it adds prestige.

<u>Example</u>

STEVEN M. PHILLIPS

Address/Phone

Enter your school address on the left-hand margin and your permanent address on the right-hand margin, two or three lines beneath your name.

Even if you do not plan to move back home, you should list your permanent address. This gives employers a chance to leave a message for you if they are unable to reach you for any reason.

(*Note:* If you live on campus, you may wish to buy or borrow an answering machine, assuming yours is a private phone. Do not leave frivolous recordings on the machine for potential employers to hear.)

School address:

Street _____

Apartment, dormitory,
or mail box# _____

Name of school
(if living on-campus) _____

City, state, zip _____

Phone _____

Permanent address:

Street _____

Apartment # (if any) _____

City, state, zip _____

Phone _____

Example

School Address:
1015 Commonwealth Avenue
Apartment 16
Boston, Massachusetts 02145
Phone: 617/555-1483

Permanent Address:
507 North 6th Street
Houston, Texas 77024
Phone: 713/555-2341

Education

Next, list your education (unless you have two or more years of full-time relevant career experience).

If you have not yet graduated and are currently working toward a degree (either full-time or part-time), you should begin with the phrase "Candidate for the degree of . . .".

If you have already graduated, you should begin "Awarded the degree of."

If you did not graduate and are not currently pursuing your degree, you should simply list the dates you attended and the courses studied. For example, "Studied mathematics, physics, chemistry, and statistics."

Not yet graduated:

Candidate for the degree of _____

in (month/year), _____

majoring in _____.

Already graduated:

Awarded _____

degree in (month, year), _____

majoring in _____.

Did not graduate, not currently pursuing degree:

Studied (list key courses or subjects) _____

and other courses (or subjects) from (dates) _____.

Courses

Then list from one to six courses, particularly emphasizing ones that might be relevant for positions you might be applying for. If none are relevant, you should list courses that might indicate an ability to excel at work assignments. You may also list courses that simply sound impressive.

Courses include _____ , _____

_____ , _____

and _____ .

Grade point average

Next, you should list your grade point average (GPA) — but only if it will be viewed positively by recruiters. Grade point average is only one aspect that recruiters evaluate; if they are extremely concerned about it, they will probably ask for a transcript anyway. How impressive your grade point average appears and whether or not you should include it on your resume depend upon the institution where you received your degree, the nature of your course load, and the competition for the particular position you are seeking. In any event, you should not include a GPA below 3.0 on a 4.0 scale or a B- on a letter scale.

_____ grade point average.

If your GPA in your major field of study is much higher than your overall GPA, you should include this information with or without your overall GPA.

_____ grade point average in major.

Notable academic honors

Now you should list any special academic awards, honors, or competitive scholarships.

Example

```
education
1989-1993  BOSTON UNIVERSITY                    BOSTON, MASSACHUSETTS
           Candidate for the degree of Bachelor of Arts in June 1993,
           majoring in mathematics. Courses include statistics and com-
           puter programming. Thesis topic: "New Applications of Co-Lin-
           ear Coordinates." 3.4 grade point average. Awarded the Elliot
           Smith Scholarship in 1991.
```

Class Rank

If you ranked extremely high in your class (generally within the top ten), you should include it in your resume.

I ranked _____ in a class of

_____ students.

Academic achievements, special projects, thesis, etc.

Especially if you are unable to list a notable academic honor, it is a good idea to list a special project that you may have worked on. It may be a project that required only a few days of your time, but it could be important if it shows initiative in the academic area that has been the main focus of your college career.

Example

```
Conducted an independent research study on the effect of
television on pre-adolescent children.
```

If you did not perform a special project, you may wish to list your senior thesis, if you wrote one, or your minor field of study. Make it clear to the reader of your resume that even though you didn't necessarily graduate at the top of your class, you were a quick study and an eager participant in the academic process.

Example

```
Thesis topic: "New Application of Co-Linear Coordinates."
```

List your academic achievements, awards, special projects, thesis topic, etc. here:

_____

_____

_____

_____

Extracurricular Activities

Even if you have glowing academic credentials, it is essential to list some extracurricular activities. This demonstrates that you are sociable, get along well with people, and that you will easily adjust to the many different people you might encounter in the work place. Extracurricular activities help a recruiter perceive you as a "low-risk" hire.

At the same time, by carefully choosing the extracurricular activities you list, you can help set yourself apart from the competition and move closer to the job you want.

The key is selectively choosing and developing a limited range of activities. (You may want to choose only one activity.) Avoid simply listing many sports or clubs haphazardly. This might give the impression that you start many projects with enthusiasm but don't finish them. Furthermore, in the small space available on your resume, you will only have room to describe a few items. If you include too many, you will give no indication of the depth of interest in any one activity. (Interests that you choose not to include under extracurricular activities can be included toward the bottom of your resume under the heading "Personal Background.")

Extracurricular activity #1: _____

" " activity #2 (optional): _____

" " activity #3 (optional): _____

" " activity #4 (optional): _____

Example

```
Treasurer of the Mathematics Club. Responsible for $7,000.00
annual budget. Co-chairperson of Boston University's semi-an-
nual symposium on "The Future of Mathematics". Exhibitor and
prize-winner at local photography shows. Helped to establish
university darkroom.
```

High School

Including high school information on your resume is optional. If you have made exceptional achievements in college and in your summer or part-time jobs, you should probably include these in your resume and omit your high school information. Most college graduates don't include their high school information on their resumes, but there are sometimes good reasons to do so.

If you do decide to include your high school achievements on your resume, describe them more briefly than your college achievements. Even if they are very impressive, putting too much emphasis on your high school years may give the impression that your highest performance days were in the past.

Name of high school _____

Location (city, state) _____

Date of graduation: _____

GPA: _____

Class Rank: _____

Notable academic honors (list one to three): _____

_____

_____

_____

Academic achievements, special projects, etc. (list one to three): _____

_____

_____

_____

Extracurricular activities (list one to three): _____

_____

_____

_____

Example

```
1985-1989  HOUSTON PUBLIC HIGH SCHOOL                    HOUSTON, TEXAS
           Received diploma in June 1989. Achieved Advance Placement
           Standing in calculus and physics. Academic Honors all terms.
           Assistant Editor of school yearbook.
```

Work Experience

Work experience of some kind is an essential part of any resume. Recruiters want to see some kind of work history because it demonstrates that you have a good work ethic. Remember, volunteer work and unpaid internships are almost as important to recruiters as paid work is. Be sure to include such activities on your resume in the same format as your work experience.

If, during college, you spent a summer traveling, studying or performing some other enlightening or substantive activity rather than working, be sure to include this information. Recruiters hate to see gaps in resumes. They might assume that you sat on the beach for the entire summer—or even fear that you have a medical or other personal problem that will interfere with your ability to work.

List your experience in straight, reverse chronological order. Alternatively, you may group your summer positions together, listing them in reverse chronological order and then listing your part-time positions in reverse chronological order.

While it is important to show jobs or other substantive activities for each summer during your college years, you do not need to list summer jobs or part-time jobs that you held during your high school years unless they make a positive contribution to your resume. In fact, you should not list any jobs that you held for a very short duration. For example, if you held two different positions during a summer vacation, you should only list the job of longer duration. While you may be able to explain during a job interview a very good reason why you switched jobs in the middle of the summer, you may never get to the interview stage in the first place if you list jobs of short duration.

Always be truthful on your resume. In addition to the ethical arguments, more and more companies are checking resumes these days. Remember, false information on a resume is often considered grounds for dismissal. This can happen even if the falsehood is discovered years after you are hired. Nonetheless, your resume is essentially an advertisement for yourself, and you have every right to put your best foot forward and show your strongest points.

Choosing which positions to list and highlight on your resume is an important part of creating a positive advertisement for yourself. Unless your part-time positions are significantly more impressive than your summer positions, you should list your summer positions first.

If you have any full-time career-related internships, you should list them even before your summer positions, as they could be a significant advantage in getting the position you desire.

In the left column, list your dates of employment with each company. For summer positions, the word "summer" followed by the year is sufficient. For part-time work, you may list the year(s) or starting and ending month and year.

In the main column, list the company name. In the right column, list the location (by city and state). Be sure that the spelling of the employer is exactly right; the recruiter may recognize the firm or wish to verify your employment.

Next, list your job title. In the case of a large corporation, list the department you worked for—but only if this is to your advantage. For example, if you are seeking a career position as a salesperson and your summer work has been as a typist, it would be a definite plus if you worked as a typist in the sales department. The assumption is that even if you did not gain sales experience, at least you gained an understanding of the sales process at the company in question.

Describe the duties and responsibilities of your position. If you are listing several summer positions and several part-time positions, space constraints dictate that you either be very brief in describing each position or that you only list job titles for less significant positions.

Rather than list a perfunctory job description for each position, go into more detail on the more impressive, relevant, or interesting positions. Remember, your resume is an advertisement for yourself to open doors for interviews. It is not an exam. You should focus on presenting those aspects of your position that speak most positively of your experience. Do not feel compelled to summarize the entire position or even to list your major duties as though you were writing a formal job description.

An even better idea than listing job duties is to focus on accomplishments or achievements, even if they are only small ones. For example, for a summer lifeguard position, a brief summary of your duties might read: "Supervised waterfront for busy public beach; responsible for safety of bathers, maintaining public order and cleanliness of the beach and parking areas." But is this enough?

While this description of your work might, at first glance, make the position of lifeguard sound more impressive than simply writing "Lifeguard at public beach", it does nothing to distinguish you from any other person who worked as a lifeguard. It would be much more effective to list an on-the-job accomplishment or achievement—even a minor one. For example, if you set up a box beside the trash can to collect paper or bottles and cans for recycling, you could replace the previous job description with, "Established recycling program for bottles and cans." This shows motivation, effort, and initiative beyond the basic duties of the position.

Summer Jobs Held During College Summers:

Date of employment (summer, year): _____

Company name: _____

Company location (city, state): _____

Job title (and department, if relevant): _____

_____

Job description and/or accomplishments: _____

_____

_____

_____

_____

Date of employment (summer, year): _____

Company name: _____

Company location (city, state): _____

Job title (and department, if relevant): _____

_____

Job description and/or accomplishments: _____

_____

_____

_____

_____

Date of employment (summer, year): _____

Company name: _____

Company location (city, state): _____

Job title (and department, if relevant): _____

_____

Job description and/or accomplishments: _____

_____

_____

_____

_____

Date of employment (summer, year): _____

Company name: _____

Company location (city, state): _____

Job title (and department, if relevant): _____

_____

Job description and/or accomplishments: _____

_____

_____

_____

_____

Example

```
summer 1993  DATA PUNCH ASSOCIATES, INC.              NEW YORK, NEW YORK
             Mail Clerk and Courier for Accounting Department. Reorganized
             mail distribution and sorting system in the department. De-
             livered sensitive documents to the executive department.

summer 1992  TOWN OF FALMOUTH                      FALMOUTH, MASSACHUSETTS
             Lifeguard at busy public beach. Established recycling program
             for bottles and cans.

summers 1990,
        1991 SAM'S BEEFBURGERS                          CHICAGO, ILLINOIS
             Began work as dishwasher. Was promoted to short order cook.
```

Next, you can list summer jobs you held in high school. You should list high school jobs only if *both* of the following apply: (1) your college summer work experiences are not particularly outstanding; and (2) there is no part-time work experience that you can list. (If, however, you find that you have too much material at the end of this process for your one-page resume, you should delete summer jobs held in high school.)

Summer Jobs During High School:

Date of employment (summer, year): _____

Company name: _____

Company location (city, state): _____

Job title (and department, if relevant): _____

_____

Job description and/or accomplishments: _____

_____

_____

_____

Date of employment (summer, year): _____

Company name: _____

Company location (city, state): _____

Job title (and department, if relevant): _____

_____

Job description and/or accomplishments: _____

_____

_____

_____

Date of employment (summer, year): _____

Company name: _____

Company location (city, state): _____

Job title (and department, if relevant): _____

_____

Job description and/or accomplishments: _____

_____

_____

_____

Example

```
summer 1988  Town of Lake Forest                        Lake Forest, Illinois
             Tutored emotionally disturbed grade schoolers for basic arith-
             metic in remedial summer school program.
```

Part-time Jobs

Next, list your part-time positions. You should include only part-time jobs you held for at least six months. You want to avoid appearing like a job-hopper, so it's a good idea not to list more than four part-time positions. It is not necessary to have a part-time position listed for each year. In fact, many students have no part-time positions to list at all.

Be selective in the part-time positions you list. Stress those that are the most relevant to your career: those that show initiative, those that are interesting, or those you held for the longest period of time.

Generally, you'll want to devote little space to part-time positions in comparison to summer positions—unless the part-time positions are unusually significant experiences, such as work in the industry of your choice.

Part-time positions should be described in a format similar to summer positions—but somewhat briefer. First list the date of employment (on the left), the employer (in the center), and the city and state (on the right). Then list the job title and department, if relevant. For particularly important part-time jobs, you may wish to include a brief job description or (better yet!) specific accomplishments.

Part-time positions:

Date of employment (summer, year): _____

Company name: _____

Company location (city, state): _____

Job title (and department, if relevant): _____

_____

Job description and/or accomplishments: _____

_____

Date of employment (summer, year): _____

Company name: _____

Company location (city, state): _____

Job title (and department, if relevant): _____

_____

Job description and/or accomplishments: _____

_____

Date of employment (summer, year): _____

Company name: _____

Company location (city, state): _____

Job title (and department, if relevant): _____

_____

Job description and/or accomplishments: _____

_____

Example

```
part-time
1990-1991  Boston University Bookstore                Boston, Massachusetts
           Floor and Stockroom Clerk. Responsibilities included arranging
           merchandise displays, customer service and checking packing
           slips against shipments.
```

Alternative for Part-Time Jobs

If your summer jobs are fairly impressive, or if you are short on space, you can simply list a number of part-time positions without individual job descriptions. Nonetheless, you should not list any part-time jobs held for less than six months; a recruiter might ask you for the specific dates that you held each part-time position. You should not list more than four positions. For some jobs listed in this manner, you may also wish to add the name of the employer.

Part-time positions include: _____ , _____ ,

_____ , and _____ .

Example

```
part-time
1989-1992  Part-time positions include Floor and Stockroom Clerk at Uni-
           versity Bookstore, Short-order Cook, and Tutor in mathematics.
```

Alternatively, you may wish to list noteworthy part-time positions separately from the other part-time positions. In this case, you would include the noteworthy positions with your other work experience under the heading "experience." You would then simply list your other part-time jobs in the same format, under the heading "other part-time positions."

Interim Jobs

Today's tough economy means that recent college graduates will probably have to spend many months job hunting before they find a suitable career position. This means that many graduates will secure a temporary job or "interim" job to provide some income while they search for a permanent professional position.

Should you list such positions on your resume? It really depends on how strong your other work experiences are. You should not list an interim job if you have been out of school less than six months. Otherwise, it's acceptable to include one on your resume—but do not list more than one.

Job Titles

The best rule to follow here is simplify, simplify, simplify! It is better to use titles that are universal enough to be understood by all who read your resume than to use confusing titles that reflect exactly what you were called by a particular employer. If, at a particular job, you were called "First-level Pascal Programmer II", simply write this as "Computer Programmer."

Do not exaggerate your job title. If you worked in an office greeting clients and answering phones, simply write "Receptionist" on your resume. Do not try to impress potential employers by describing this position as, for example, "Inter-Communications Specialist." If you do, it will become clear that you've misrepresented yourself when the recruiter asks about your job experience at the interview.

At the same time, you are trying to put your best foot forward and "sell" yourself to the recruiter. The best way to do this is to make the most of the job description following your job title. (But remember: keep it relatively brief! You can elaborate on your work experiences once you get to the interview.)

Personal Background

While not the most important part of the resume, you should always include some personal background. This section shows that you are an interesting person—and it gives the interviewer something to start a conversation with during the interview. Perhaps the interviewer will even share some of your interests!

List different areas of personal interest without embellishment—unless there is an unusually significant personal accomplishment in this category that will help you get a job. If this is the case, you should keep the details very brief. Don't list too many items—it is better to list only a few that you are particularly interested in. This way you will have more to talk about if the recruiter asks you about any particular one. Also it implies more depth of interest than a listing of many activities.

Generally you will want to list three or four activities.

Personal background:

Interest/Activity #1: _____

Interest/Activity #2: _____

Interest/Activity #3: _____

Interest/Activity #4: _____

Example

```
    personal
    background  Enjoy photography, reading, science fiction, and playing
               bridge.
```

References

The last item on the resume should read:

```
references  Personal references available upon request.
```

You should not list references on the resume for two reasons: it looks less professional, and it's good for you to know beforehand when a reference will be called. Not listing them on your resume also enables you to change or vary the references.

That's it! You should now have the text for a completed resume that looks great. Don't forget to check it for spelling errors and accuracy—then double-check it with a friend.

Sample resume

STEVEN M. PHILLIPS

School Address:
1015 Commonwealth Avenue
Apartment 16
Boston, Massachusetts 02145
Phone: 617/555-1483

Permanent Address:
507 North 6th Street
Houston, TX 77024
Phone: 713/555-2341

education

1989-1993 BOSTON UNIVERSITY   BOSTON, MASSACHUSETTS
Candidate for the degree of Bachelor of Arts in June 1993, majoring in mathematics. Courses include statistics and computer programming. Thesis topic: "New Applications of Co-Linear Coordinates." 3.4 grade point average. Awarded the Elliot Smith Scholarship in 1991.

Treasurer of the Mathematics Club. Responsible for $7,000.00 annual budget. Co-chairperson of Boston University's semi-annual symposium on "The Future of Mathematics." Exhibitor and prize-winner at local photography shows. Helped to establish university darkroom.

1985-1989 HOUSTON PUBLIC HIGH SCHOOL   HOUSTON, TEXAS
Received diploma in June 1989. Achieved Advance Placement Standing in calculus and physics. Academic Honors all terms. Assistant Editor of school yearbook.

experience

summer 1992 DATA PUNCH ASSOCIATES, INC.   NEW YORK, NEW YORK
Mail Clerk and Courier for the Accounting Department. Reorganized mail distribution and sorting system in the department. Delivered sensitive documents to the executive branch.

summers 1990, 1991 HARVEY'S BEEFBURGERS, INC.   HOUSTON, TEXAS
Began work as a dishwasher. Was promoted to short-order cook.

part-time BOSTON UNIVERSITY   BOSTON, MASSACHUSETTS
One of six students invited to tutor for The Department of Mathematics. Also graded student papers and worked as a Research Assistant in Theoretical Calculus.

part-time
1989-1990 BOSTON UNIVERSITY BOOKSTORE   BOSTON, MASSACHUSETTS
Floor and Stockroom Clerk. Responsibilities included arranging merchandise displays, customer service and checking invoices against shipments.

personal background Enjoy photography, reading science fictions, and playing bridge. Published two articles in mathematics journals.

references Personal references available upon request.

CHAPTER TWELVE

Resume Make-Overs

WHILE A GOOD resume can open doors for you, a bad resume can close them just as easily.

In this chapter, we include five not-so-great resumes and point out some of their most glaring flaws. After some rewriting and rearranging, we've transformed them into interview-winning resumes. You can see the difference for yourself . . .

Before

> Resume lacks definition and is difficult to read at a glance.

Janet Dubois
1312 Liberty Street
Lowell, MA 01854
(617) 555-5208

EDUCATION Brown University, Providence, RI.
Bachelor of Arts degree received May 1993
Major: English Literature GPA: 3.10

Internship, Boston Literacy Program, Boston, MA.
Assisted in reading program, teaching illiterate children
and adults reading skills.

EXPERIENCE Editorial Assistant, The Bostonian Journal
June 1993-August 1993
Edited articles, features, and illustrations for monthly
publication.

Editor-in-Chief, Brown U. Newspaper
September 1992-May 1993
Selected submissions, edited and wrote headlines for submissions and columns, laid out page, dealt with public, recruited columnists, trained associates.

Associate Editor, Brown U. Newspaper
January 1991-May 1992
Trained for Editor-in-Chief position; assisted in selecting
submissions, edited and wrote headlines for submissions
and columns, laid out page, miscellaneous other tasks.

Copy Editor, Brown U. Newspaper
Edited news stories, wrote headlines, assisted with layout
of page, occasionally solicited advertising and helped
with distribution.

COMPUTER
SKILLS Word Processing - Working knowledge of WordPerfect and Microsoft Word.
Spreadsheets - Familiar with all aspects of creating and
using a spreadsheet using Lotus 1-2-3.

ACTIVITIES Senior Class Secretary, Dean's List

After

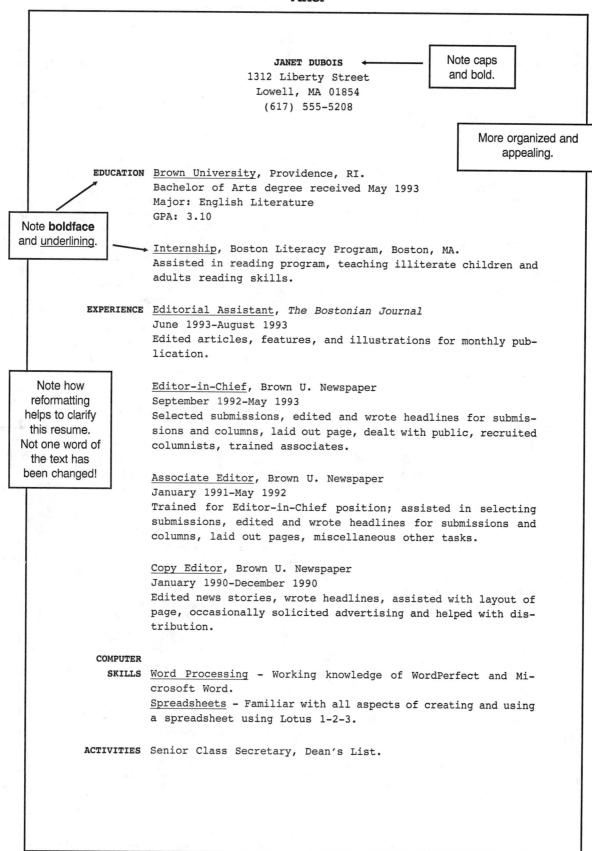

JANET DUBOIS ← Note caps and bold.
1312 Liberty Street
Lowell, MA 01854
(617) 555-5208

More organized and appealing.

Note **boldface** and underlining.

EDUCATION <u>Brown University</u>, Providence, RI.
Bachelor of Arts degree received May 1993
Major: English Literature
GPA: 3.10

<u>Internship</u>, Boston Literacy Program, Boston, MA.
Assisted in reading program, teaching illiterate children and adults reading skills.

EXPERIENCE <u>Editorial Assistant</u>, *The Bostonian Journal*
June 1993-August 1993
Edited articles, features, and illustrations for monthly publication.

Note how reformatting helps to clarify this resume. Not one word of the text has been changed!

<u>Editor-in-Chief</u>, Brown U. Newspaper
September 1992-May 1993
Selected submissions, edited and wrote headlines for submissions and columns, laid out page, dealt with public, recruited columnists, trained associates.

<u>Associate Editor</u>, Brown U. Newspaper
January 1991-May 1992
Trained for Editor-in-Chief position; assisted in selecting submissions, edited and wrote headlines for submissions and columns, laid out pages, miscellaneous other tasks.

<u>Copy Editor</u>, Brown U. Newspaper
January 1990-December 1990
Edited news stories, wrote headlines, assisted with layout of page, occasionally solicited advertising and helped with distribution.

COMPUTER SKILLS <u>Word Processing</u> - Working knowledge of WordPerfect and Microsoft Word.
<u>Spreadsheets</u> - Familiar with all aspects of creating and using a spreadsheet using Lotus 1-2-3.

ACTIVITIES Senior Class Secretary, Dean's List.

Before

Recruiters probably won't even read this resume.

Too long & wordy. Hard to read.

Too much detail about work experience, not enough detail about education.

Frank Hamilburg
1334 23rd St., #104
New York, NY 10022
212/555-5512

EDUCATION
New York University, Manhattan
Bachelor Degree in Management
Date of Graduation: June 1992

EXPERIENCE
John D. MacDougall, Inc., 55 East 10th St., New York NY
Executive Assistant - Assistant to the President and Senior Vice President, responsible for providing extensive and highly confidential administrative assistance and support. Due to my highly visible and important role within the organization, I ensured that top company executives were constantly kept abreast of situations, problems, etc. that arose within the company, as well as within the industry. Responsible for the complete coordination of semi-annual company meetings consisting of 250 guests; which included the site selection, attainment of desired atmosphere, planning and arranging of speakers/guests, hotel accommodations and land and air transportation, as well as ensuring the successful attainment of budgeted costs. Also coordinated company social functions including dinners, parties, and holiday celebrations; which included the initiating ideas for these functions, selection of the location of the function, coordination of all details such as reservations, transportation, etc., and also ensuring attainment of budgeted costs. Heavy involvement with the Young Executive Program; reviewed personnel reports for content, personal and professional objectives, kept records of job performance over time, and made recommendations of salary adjustments based on overall rating. Acted as the on-site computer resource with respect to the explanation and solving of all company computing problems. Working knowledge of WordPerfect and dBase programs. May 1991 to September 1991.

Tecchi Management Corporation, 833 Fifth Avenue, New York NY
Administrative Assistant/Coordinator - Assistant to the President as well as the Accounting Manager. Constantly updated my supervisor on their employees' absenteeism, tardiness, performance appraisals and disciplinary actions needed to be taken. Responsible for the orientation of new employees on all company benefits and policies; taught employees company procedures for using technical equipment such as the fax machine, typewriters, computers, copy machines, phone system, etc. Intense amount of communication with high level staff and outside agencies. Performed customer service functions, including the resolving of all consumer and agency complaints and problems. May 1990 to September 1990.

Avenue Investments, 1323 Avenue of the Americas, New York NY
Administrative Assistant - In charge of confidential communications including typing company documents, correspondence, generation of charts and data, and filing. Associate in charge of outside communications via the telephone and switchboard. Completely responsible for the travel arrangements of 10 company executives, including scheduling, coordination, and budgeting. Coordinated office supply inventory and responsible for maintaining and reordering supplies including letterhead stationary and computer disks. June 1989 to September 1989.

After

Easy and quick to read. Only relevant details are included.

```
            Frank Hamilburg
           1334 23rd St., #104
           New York, NY 10022
              212/555-5512
```

Expanded section on educational background.

EDUCATION

New York University, Manhattan
Bachelor of Science degree awarded in June 1992, majoring in Management. Courses include Physics, Biochemistry, Economics and Statistics. 3.4 grade point average in major. Honors: Dean's List.

Student member of the American Management Association. Props assistant for College Theatre. Co-captain of Intramural Volleyball Team. Actively involved in Students Against Drunk Driving.

EXPERIENCE

Executive Assistant

John D. MacDougall, Inc., 55 East 10th St., New York NY   (Summer 1991)
- Responsible for providing extensive and highly confidential administrative assistance and support to the President and Senior Vice President
- Heavy involvement with the Young Executive Program; reviewed personnel reports for content, personal and professional objectives, kept records of job performance over time, and made recommendations of salary adjustments based on overall rating
- Acted as the on-site computer resource with respect to the explanation and solving of all company computing problems
- Coordinated company social functions and very large semi-annual company meetings

Administrative Assistant/Coordinator

Tecchi Management Corporation, 833 Fifth Avenue, New York NY   (Summer 1990)
- Assistant to the President and the Accounting Manager
- Responsible for the orientation of new employees on all company benefits policies, and procedures
- Extensive communication with high level staff and outside agencies
- Performed customer service functions, including the resolving of all consumer and agency complaints and problems

Administrative Assistant

Avenue Investments, 1323 Avenue of the Americas, New York NY   (Summer 1989)
- Extensive typing and filing
- Generated charts and data
- Operated switchboard
- Responsible for the travel arrangements of 10 company executives, including scheduling, coordination, and budgeting

COMPUTER SKILLS
- Working knowledge of WordPerfect and dBase programs

Before

Too many different typefaces distract the reader.

LINDA McFARLANE

School Address:
167 South Union Street
Burlington, VT 05401
Phone: 802/555-3354

Permanent Address:
756 Maple Street
Manchester, NH 03104
Phone: 603/555-0856

education
1988-1992 UNIVERSITY OF VERMONT   BURLINGTON, VERMONT
Bachelor of Arts degree, May 1992. Major: Women's Studies.
Minor: Art. 3.5 grade point average.

experience
summer 1991 OFFICE OF THE PUBLIC DEFENDER   BURLINGTON, VERMONT
Summer Intern. Performed research, attended court sessions,
posted bail for defendants. Liaison with District Attorney's Office.

Information is too brief.

summers
1989-1990 SWEETWATER'S RESTAURANT   BURLINGTON, VERMONT
Began work as hostess, promoted to waitstaff. Also relief
bartender.

part-time
1989-1992 ACADEMIC COMPUTING SERVICES   UNIVERSITY OF VERMONT
Computer counselor for campus computer lab. Hardware main-
tence and software troubleshooting.

part-time
1988-1989 UNIVERSITY BOOKSTORE   UNIVERSITY OF VERMONT
Cashier/Clerk. Acted as cashier, stocked shelves, and miscellaneous other duties.

interests Painting, sculpture, and aerobics.

references Personal references available upon request.

After

LINDA McFARLANE

School Address: Permanent Address:
167 South Union Street   756 Maple Street
Burlington, VT 05401   Manchester, NH 03104
Phone: 802/555-3354   Phone: 603/555-0856

education
1988-1992 **UNIVERSITY OF VERMONT**   **BURLINGTON, VERMONT**

> Shows initiative and motivation.

Awarded Bachelor of Arts degree in May 1992, majoring in Women's Studies, minoring in Art. Courses include Economics, Statistics, Political Science and Public Speaking. Thesis topic: The Political Economy of Our Domestic Health Care System. 3.5 grade point average. Awarded the Bailey-Howe Scholarship in 1990.

Contributing editor for campus newspaper, The Cynic. Member of the Outing Club. Member of Varsity Crew Team. Designed and painted university-sponsored mural with the theme of cultural diversity.

experience
summer 1991 **OFFICE OF THE PUBLIC DEFENDER**   **BURLINGTON, VERMONT**

> Emphasizes valuable experience.

Summer Intern working with five attorneys. Performed extensive research to support court cases and attended court sessions. Handled confidential documents and paperwork. Liaison with District Attorney's Office.

summers
1989-1990 **SWEETWATER'S RESTAURANT**   **BURLINGTON, VERMONT**

Began work as hostess, promoted to waitstaff. Also relief bartender.

part-time
1989-1992 **ACADEMIC COMPUTING SERVICES**   **UNIVERSITY OF VERMONT**

> Stresses accomplishments

Computer counselor for campus computer lab. Maintained hardware and worked on network and mainframe. Performed extensive troubleshooting for students and faculty regarding software, hardware, and printing problems. Instituted "Freshman Orientation Session" for new lab users.

part-time
1988-1989 **UNIVERSITY BOOKSTORE**   **UNIVERSITY OF VERMONT**

Cashier/Clerk. Acted as cashier, stocked shelves, and miscellaneous other duties.

personal
background Enjoy painting, sculpture, aerobics, and camping. Member of the National Organization of Women.

references Personal references available upon request.

Before

> Ho-hum . . . Drab language, needs action.

DANIEL R. PAPPAS

School Address: Permanent Address:
121 University Terrace, Room 402   4 Squirrel Drive
University of North Carolina   Sarasota, FL 34234
Chapel Hill, NC 27510   Phone: 813/555-2955
Phone: 919/555-5581

education

1990-1992 **UNIVERSITY OF NORTH CAROLINA   CHAPEL HILL, NORTH CAROLINA**
Associates degree of Engineering; June 1992. Concentration in Mechanical Power Engineering Technology. Winner of the Newton Award for Engineers for research in magnetic fields in 1992.

Member of University Engineering Association. Member of cross-country track team.

1986-1990 **MEMORIAL HIGH SCHOOL   SARASOTA, FLORIDA**
Given High School Diploma in 1990. Got Advance Placement Standing in Calculus and Physics. High Honor roll. Varsity member of spring, winter, and cross-country track.

experience

summer 1991 **QUEEN CITY ELECTRIC   SARASOTA, FLORIDA**
Intern for the power generation service division. Was helper in the overhaul, maintenance and repair of large generators and auxiliary equipment. Worked to increase energy conservation by studying projects.

summer 1990 **J.R. COLEMAN COMPANY   MEMPHIS, TENNESSEE**
Intern for production division. Helped make conveyors and elevators better. Helped to conduct study to make more profits. Resulting data was used to make group more efficient.

part-time

1990-1992 **R & W NUCLEAR SERVICE COMPANY   CONCORD, NORTH CAROLINA**
Worked in tools division. Put on training sessions for fellow engineers so they could learn Computer Aided Design.

skills   Know Computer Aided Design (VERSACAD). Programming in GW Basic, Pascal, and Fortran.

references Personal references available upon request.

After

Attention-grabbing resume.

DANIEL R. PAPPAS

School Address:
121 University Terrace
Room 402
University of North Carolina
Chapel Hill, NC 27510
Phone: 919/555-5581

Permanent Address:
4 Squirrel Drive
Sarasota, FL 34234
Phone: 813/555-2955

Dynamic language. →

education
1990-1992 **UNIVERSITY OF NORTH CAROLINA   CHAPEL HILL, NORTH CAROLINA**
Awarded an Associates degree of Engineering in June 1992, concentrating in Mechanical Power Engineering Technology. Winner of the Newton Award for Engineers for research in magnetic fields in 1992.

Member of University Engineering Association. Member of cross-country track team.

1986-1990 **MEMORIAL HIGH SCHOOL   SARASOTA, FLORIDA**
Awarded High School Diploma in 1990. Achieved Advance Placement Standing in Calculus and Physics. High Honor roll. Varsity member of spring, winter, and cross-country track.

experience
summer 1991 **QUEEN CITY ELECTRIC   SARASOTA, FLORIDA**

Focus on accomplishments →

Intern for the power generation service division. Assisted in the overhaul, maintenance and repair of large generators and auxiliary equipment. Analyzed energy conservation projects for the maximization of energy management system and for interior lighting reduction.

summer 1990 **J.R. COLEMAN COMPANY   MEMPHIS, TENNESSEE**

Exciting action verbs.

Intern for production division. Assisted in redesign of conveyors and elevators. Conducted study to reduce manufacturing labor while maintaining product quality. Modified and improved existing system using resulting data; increased group efficiency as measured by time and quantity parameters by 33%.

part-time
1990-1992 **R & W NUCLEAR SERVICE COMPANY   CONCORD, NORTH CAROLINA**
Designed and tested tools used in nuclear power plants. Developed processes for using tools designed. Conducted computer training sessions for engineers using Computer Aided Design.

skills and
abilities Working knowledge of Computer Aided Design (VERSACAD). Programming in GW Basic, Pascal, and Fortran.

references Personal references available upon request.

Before

Phone number is missing.	**SHARON L. O'CONNELL** 72 Oak Street, #3A Seattle, Washington 92013

education
1989-1993   **BATES COLLEGE**   **LEWISTON, MAINE**
Candidate for the degree of Bachelor of Sciences, majoring in Biology, minoring in Horticulture. Courses include Biochemistry, Anatomy & Physiology, Chemistry, Physics, Computer Science and Advanced Calculus. 3.77 grade point average. Awarded the Biological Sciences Society Award for Outstanding Students of Biology. I ranked 4 in a class of 276.

Unnecessary information. Better to specify "summer."

Failing to list extracurricular activities might result in your being labeled a high-risk hire.

experience
May-August
1992   **MAINE STATE PARKS AND RECREATION**   **MAINE STATE**
Volunteer for State of Maine Summer Clean-Up Program. Trash and litter removal, landscaping, repairs and maintenance of state buildings, signs, and benches.

June-August
1991   **TUFTS UNIVERSITY**   **MEDFORD, MASSACHUSETTS**
Staff Assistant for the New England Environmental Newsletter. Provided administrative support to the Director of Environmental Affairs.

Time gaps make a poor impression on recruiters.

part-time
Sept 1990-
May 1993   **BATES COLLEGE LIBRARY**   **LEWISTON, MAINE**
Front desk clerk. Processed books, restacked shelves, answered phones, and assorted other duties.

personal
background   Enjoy gardening, reading, and scuba diving.

references   Personal references available upon request.

After

SHARON L. O'CONNELL
72 Oak Street, #3A
Seattle, Washington 92013
703/555-9998

education
1989-1993   **BATES COLLEGE**   **LEWISTON, MAINE**
           Awarded a Bachelor of Sciences degree in May 1993, majoring
in Biology, minoring in Horticulture. Courses include Biochemistry, Anatomy & Physiology, Chemistry, Physics, Computer Science and Advanced Calculus. 3.77 grade point average. Awarded
the Biological Sciences Society Award for Outstanding Students
of Biology. Class rank: 4/276.

Founded the Bates College Greenhouse. Member of E.A.R.T.H. for
Students. Weekend disc jockey for WBTS, college radio station.
Created and hosted the "Earth Talk", radio program for dis-
cussing environmental issues.

> **Highlights great activities; shows motivation and initiative.**

experience
summer 1992   **MAINE STATE PARKS AND RECREATION**   **PORTLAND, MAINE**
           Volunteer for State of Maine Summer Clean-Up Program. Removed
trash and litter from state grounds, landscaped state and local parks, repaired and repainted state buildings, signs, and
benches. Promoted recycling and other environmental programs.
Established new state garden at Old Orchard Beach.

summer 1991   **TUFTS UNIVERSITY**   **MEDFORD, MASSACHUSETTS**
           Staff Assistant for the New England Environmental Newsletter.
Wrote and edited articles. Provided administrative support to
the Director of Environmental Affairs.

> **Filled-in time gaps make resume much stronger.**

summer 1990   **PURITAN ICE CREAM PARLOR**   **SEATTLE, WASHINGTON**
           Counter Person/Ice Cream Scooper. Invented new hit ice-cream
flavor, Rain Forest Pecan.

part-time
1990-1993   **BATES COLLEGE LIBRARY**   **LEWISTON, MAINE**
           Front desk clerk. Processed books, restacked shelves, answered
phones, and assorted other duties.

personal
background   Enjoy gardening, reading, and scuba diving. Published feature
article in *American Horticulture*.

references   Personal references available upon request.

> **If you can't think of any major accomplishments you've made, stress small ones!**

CHAPTER THIRTEEN

Cover Letters

WHILE YOUR RESUME is a summary of your credentials, your cover letter should essentially be a sales pitch. Your aim is to demonstrate why you and your background make a perfect match for the position you're applying for.

The cover letter is not the place to summarize your background—you have already done this on your resume. Remember, the corporate recruiter typically receives dozens if not hundreds of applications for each job opening. You must stand out from the crowd in a positive way.

The best way to distinguish your application from others is to highlight one or two of your accomplishments or abilities that show you are an above-average candidate for this position. Stressing only one or two unique attributes will increase your chances of being remembered by the recruiter and getting to the interview stage, where you can elaborate on the rest of your accomplishments.

You can gain the extra edge in your cover letter by showing that you know a little bit about the company and the industry. This shows that you are genuinely interested in the job you are applying for—and that you are not blindly sending out hundreds of resumes. More importantly, the recruiter will view your interest as an indication that you will stay with the company for a period of years if you are hired.

WHEN TO SEND A COVER LETTER

Always mail a cover letter with your resume. Even if you are following up an advertisement that reads simply "send resume," or you are following up a phone call with a hiring executive who requests you to "send a resume," be sure to include a cover letter. It is not professional to send a resume without one.

LENGTH OF THE COVER LETTER

Four short paragraphs (on one page) is an ideal length for a recent college graduate's cover letter. A letter any longer than that is unlikely to be read. (Most recruiters have hectic schedules and prefer cover letters that are short and succinct.)

PAPER SIZE

Use standard 8½" x 11" paper for your cover letter. If you use a smaller size, the correspondence will appear more personal than professional; a larger size would simply look odd.

PAPER COLOR

White and ivory are the only acceptable paper colors for resumes and cover letters.

PAPER QUALITY

As with resumes, standard, inexpensive office paper (20# bond) is perfectly acceptable. Stay away from the more expensive stationery papers such as ivory laid.

PRE-PRINTED STATIONERY

Avoid using pre-printed stationery—even if you have a ready supply. Only a senior executive with many, many years of experience should use such paper. For a college student or recent graduate, pre-printed stationery can actually put you at a disadvantage.

TYPING

Your best options are to use a high-quality office typewriter, a word processor with letter-quality type or a word processing program on a computer with a letter-quality printer.

However, the quality of the type on your cover letter is not as crucial as it is on your resume. A good, clean home typewriter is a satisfactory alternative for your cover letter. On the other hand, a dot matrix printer or a home typewriter that does not produce clear, crisp letters is unacceptable.

PROOFREAD YOUR COVER LETTER

It's very easy to make mistakes on your cover letters—particularly when you're writing many in succession. But it is also very easy for a corporate recruiter to reject out of hand *any* cover letter that contains errors. Why hire someone who doesn't appear to take care with such an important piece of correspondence? As with your resume, you must proofread your cover letters carefully—and have a friend proofread them as well.

AVOID MESSY CORRECTIONS

Try to avoid using correction fluid or making any messy corrections. It's always a better idea to take the time to retype the letter perfectly.

CHAPTER FOURTEEN

The Cover Letter Worksheet

Return Address and Date

Your return address should appear in the top right hand corner, without your name, followed by the date. As a general rule, you should avoid abbreviations in the addresses on the cover letters, although abbreviating the state is increasingly common in all business correspondence.

Return Address:

Your street address: _____

Apartment # (if appropriate): _____

City, state, and zip code: _____

_____

Date (write out): _____

<u>Example</u>

                                              312 Main Street
                                              Houston, Texas 77031

                                              January 3, 1993

The Addressee

Always try to find the name and proper title of the addressee before you send out a cover letter. Two lines beneath the date, list the full name of the addressee preceded by Mr. or Ms. (It is safest to avoid using Miss or Mrs.) On the next line, list the individual's formal title; on the subsequent line, list the name of the company. This is followed by the company's address, which generally takes two lines. Occasionally, the individual's full title or the company name and address will be very long, and can appear awkward on the usual number of lines allocated. In this case, you may prefer using an extra line.

Addressee:

Mr./Ms. (full name of addressee): _____

Full title of addressee: _____

Full company name: _____

Street address, suite number (if appropriate): _____

_____

City, state, and zip code: _____

Example

```
Ms. Suzanne Lee Waters
Vice President, Corporate Personnel
Rockport Insurance Companies, Inc.
437 Coastal Highway, Suite 312
Boston, Massachusetts 02100
```

The Salutation

The salutation should be typed two lines beneath the company's address. It should begin with "Mr." or "Ms.", followed by the individual's last name and a colon. A colon appears more business-like than a comma.

Even if you have previously spoken with an addressee who has asked to be called by first name, you should never use a first name in the salutation.

Dear Mr. (Ms.) _____:

Example

```
Dear Ms. Waters:
```

Content

The body of the letter will be determined by a four-paragraph formula that will be examined in detail in a moment.

General Guidelines for The Body of The Letter

There is considerably more latitude in what is considered acceptable content for a cover letter than there is for a resume. Nonetheless, all cover letters from college students or recent graduates should adhere to the following principles:

- ☐ Use proper English and avoid abbreviations and slang. Use short sentences and common words. Make your letter more interesting by using action verbs such as "designed," "implemented," and "increased."
- ☐ Personalize each letter. *Do not* send form letters!
- ☐ In the first paragraph, state immediately and concisely which position or what type of function you wish to be considered for.
- ☐ In the last paragraph, either specifically request an interview or mention

that you will be calling to request an interview.
- ☐ Be sure the entire letter fits onto a single page. (Actually, the letter should give the appearance of being half a page long.)

First Paragraph

Immediately explain why your background makes you the best candidate for the position that you are applying for. Keep the first paragraph short and hard-hitting.

Example

```
Having majored in Mathematics at Boston University, where
I also worked as a Research Assistant, I am confident that
I would make a very successful Research Trainee in your
Economics Research Department.
```

Second Paragraph

Detail what you could contribute to this company. Show how your qualifications will benefit this firm. Remember, be brief! Few recruiters will read a cover letter longer than half a page.

Example

```
In addition to my strong background in mathematics, I also
offer significant business experience, having worked in a
data processing firm, a bookstore, and a restaurant. I am
sure that my courses in statistics and computer program-
ming would prove particularly useful in the position of Re-
search Trainee.
```

Third Paragraph

Describe your interest in the corporation. Subtly emphasize your knowledge about this firm (the result of your research effort) and your familiarity with the industry. It is common courtesy to act extremely eager to work for any company where you apply for a position.

Example

```
I am attracted to City Bank by your recent rapid growth
and the superior reputation of your Economic Research De-
partment. After studying different commercial banks, I
have concluded that City Bank will be in a strong competi-
tive position to benefit from upcoming changes in the in-
dustry, such as the phasing out of Regulation Q.
```

Final Paragraph

In the closing paragraph, specifically request an interview. Include your phone number and the hours when you can be reached. Alternatively, you might prefer to mention that you will follow up with a phone call within the next several days to arrange an interview at a mutually convenient time.

Example

```
        I would like to interview with you at your earliest conven-
        ience. I am best reached between 3 and 5 pm at 555-1483.
```

The Closing

The closing should begin two lines beneath the body of the letter and should be aligned with your return address and the date (towards the right of the page). Keep the closing simple—"Sincerely" suffices. Four lines underneath this, and aligned with the "Sincerely," type in your full name, preferably with a middle name or middle initial.

Sign above your typed name in black ink. *Don't forget to sign the letter!* As silly as it sounds, people often forget to sign their cover letters. This creates the impression that you don't take care with your work.

Example

```
                          Sincerely,

                          John R. Smith

                          Jason R. Smith
```

The Enclosure Line

You will help the employer to see you as a meticulous, detail-oriented professional if you include an enclosure line at the bottom of the letter.

Example

```
    Enc.: Resume
```

Sample Cover Letter

1015 Commonwealth Avenue
Apartment 16
Boston, MA 02145

May 12, 1993

Mr. Clark T. Johnson
Vice-President/Human Resources
Boston City Bank Corporation
110 Milk Street
Boston, Massachusetts 02114

Dear Mr. Johnson:

Having majored in Mathematics at Boston University, where I also worked as a Research Assistant, I am confident that I would make a very successful Research Trainee in your Economics Research Department.

In addition to my strong background in mathematics, I also offer significant business experience, having worked in a data processing firm, a bookstore, and a restaurant. I am sure that my courses in statistics and computer programming would prove particularly useful in the position of Research Trainee.

I am attracted to City Bank by your recent rapid growth and the superior reputation of your Economic Research Department. After studying different commercial banks, I have concluded that City Bank will be in a strong competitive position to benefit from upcoming changes in the industry, such as the phasing out of Regulation Q.

I would like to interview with you at your earliest convenience. I am best reached between 3 and 5 pm at 555-1483.

Sincerely,

Steven M. Phillips

Steven M. Phillips

Enc.: Resume

CHAPTER FIFTEEN

Sample Resumes and Cover Letters

THIS CHAPTER INCLUDES forty excellent sample resumes with their corresponding cover letters. The resumes and cover letters are those of fictional college students and recent grads. Use them as a guide for writing your own job-winning resumes and cover letters.

The resumes included in this chapter cover most college majors. The majors covered are as followed:

Accounting
African-American Studies
Anthropology
Art History
Biology
Business Administration
Chemistry
Classical Civilization
Classics
Communications
Computer Science/Programming
Earth Science/Forestry
Economics
Education
Electrical Engineering
English
English Literature
Finance
Food Science
Geography

German/Italian Language
Government
International Relations
Linguistics
Management
Management Information Systems (MIS)
Marketing
Mathematics
Mechanical Engineering
Philosophy/World History
Physics
Psychology
Quantitative Analysis
Sociology
Speech
Statistics
Theatre
Western Civilization
Women's Studies

Accounting Major

19 Kellock Drive
Quincy, IL 60601

June 18, 1992

Ms. Amy Bauer
Accounting Manager
Deloit & Holt Associates
324 Main Street
Quincy, IL 60622

Dear Ms. Bauer:

Thank you for taking the time to speak with me on the phone today. As I mentioned, I would like to be considered for your opening for an Accounting Assistant.

I graduated last month from Wheaton College with a Bachelor's degree in Accounting. Particularly valuable to me in my studies were courses that I took in Finance, Bookkeeping, Business Law, and Computer Science. I did extremely well in school, having graduated summa cum laude with a GPA of 3.9.

In my Junior year, I founded the Wheaton College Student Credit Union, a credit union run solely by and for college students, which has been very successful to date. During my senior year, I also acted as the Treasurer of the Senior Class Council and was responsible for a $18,000 budget.

In addition to having worked as a Research Assistant and an Office Assistant at Wheaton, I served as an Intern for a local accounting firm . In this position I handled some accounts payable, resolving over 32% of the company's past due accounts. I also made deposits, performed data entry, and other clerical duties.

I would like to meet with you to further discuss this position. You may reach me between 9 AM and 6 PM at 312/555-2401. I look forward to hearing from you!

Sincerely,

Monica Duvalier

Monica Duvalier

enc. resume

Accounting Major

MONICA DUVALIER
19 Kellock Drive
Quincy, Illinois 60601
312/ 555-2401

Education

WHEATON COLLEGE, Wheaton, Illinois

Bachelor of Sciences Degree in Accounting awarded in May 1992. Course work included Finance, Bookkeeping, Business Law, and Computer Science. 3.9 grade point average on a 4.0 scale. Graduated summa cum laude.

Founder of the Student Credit Union, a credit union run solely by and for college students. Treasurer of the Senior Class Council. Member of Women's Rugby Team.

KNOX COLLEGE, Galesburg, Illinois

Studies included political science, sociology, and economics. Fall 1987 through spring 1988.

Internship

HOWE & HOWE ASSOCIATES, Wheaton, Illinois

Accounting Intern for the Vice President of the company. Handled accounts receivable, made deposits, performed data entry, and some clerical. Cleared up over 32% of the company's past due accounts. Summers 1990 and 1991.

Work Experience

WHEATON COLLEGE, Wheaton, Illinois

Office Assistant for the Career Development Office. Assisted students with career objectives, including writing resumes and cover letters, mapping out job searching strategies, processing referral requests, phone calls, and general clerical. Part-time from 1988 to 1990.

WHEATON COLLEGE, Wheaton, Illinois

Research Assistant for political science professor. Researched, prepared summary reports, compiled statistical and journalistic evidence of political dimensions of U.S. and Japanese economic relations for the professor's upcoming book. Summer 1989 and part-time through spring 1990.

Special Skills

Familiar with IBM and MacIntosh computers. Experience using Lotus 1-2-3, dBase, EXCEL, SAS, and SPSSX. Typing 90 wpm. Speak fluent French.

African-American Studies Major

13 Marilyn Drive
Cedar City, Utah 84725
(801) 555-8420

April 4, 1993

Ms. Sharon L. Conn
McKensie and Conn
Attorneys-at-Law
1355 Park Street South
Salt Lake City, Utah 85560

Dear Ms. Conn:

Justice Joanna Smith, of the City of Provo Courthouse, suggested that I contact you regarding an opening you may soon have for a Legal Assistant.

I will be graduating this May from Brigham Young University with a BA in African-American Studies. In addition to my core studies, I studied in a variety of areas including Business Administration and Computer Applications. In 1991, I was awarded the prestigious Lieberman Scholarship.

I also offer a strong background in law, having worked in a variety of legal settings throughout my college years. I was a volunteer for Brigham Young's Student Legal Aid, helping students with a variety of legal problems. I worked part-time over the past three years as a Volunteer Probation Officer for the City of Provo Juvenile Court. And in addition to being an Outside Media Contact for a Provo Outreach Unified Neighborhood Team, I spent one summer as a Research Assistant for the Chief County Clerk of the City of Provo.

All of these positions have given me a strong sense of the law and the American legal system. Moreover, this experience convinced me that I would like to pursue the law for a career. Justice Smith highly recommends your firm as one which might be a good match for my goals and qualifications.

Enclosed is my resume. I will contact you within the week for us to discuss further the possibilities of securing this position. Thank you for your time.

Sincerely,

William Hough

William Hough

Encl. Resume

African-American Studies Major

WILLIAM HOUGH

13 Marilyn Drive
Cedar City, Utah 84725
(801) 555-8420

Education
1989-1993 **BRIGHAM YOUNG UNIVERSITY**   **PROVO, UTAH**

Candidate for the degree of Bachelor of Arts in May 1993, majoring in African-American Studies. Other course work includes Marketing, Business Administration, and Computer Applications. Awarded the Lieberman Scholarship.
Volunteer for Student Legal Aid. Participant in SAFE Escort Program for Students.

Experience
summer 1992 **WBYU-FM RADIO**   **PROVO, UTAH**

Promotion Intern for college radio station. Assisted Promotion Manager in writing copy and creatively planning promotional tactics for clients. Participated in promotional campaigns and live broadcasts. Responsible for the successful completion of many promotional events.

summer 1991 **CITY OF PROVO COURTHOUSE**   **PROVO, UTAH**

Research Assistant. Assisted Chief County Clerk in analyzing efficiency of various departments, reviewing budgets and recommending areas for improvement. Collected, organized, and evaluated data.

summer 1990 **OUTREACH UNIFIED NEIGHBORHOOD TEAM**   **PROVO, UTAH**

Outside Media Contact. Responsible for raising community awareness of activities and fundraisers. Participated in the organization and implementation of various programs benefitting the Provo community.

part-time
1990-present **PROVO JUVENILE COURT**   **PROVO, UTAH**

Volunteer Probation Officer. Trained in court procedures and served as a role model for juveniles on probation. Worked with probation officer to discuss and prepare probation reports on the juvenile's progress.

References Available upon request

Anthropology Major

1297 High View Road
Bar Harbor, Maine 04608
(207) 555-5599

July 5, 1993

Ms. Andrea Lamb
Lobster Hut Corporate Headquarters
11 Cain Street
Portland, Maine 04581

Dear Ms. Lamb:

I read with interest your advertisement in the <u>Portland Gazette</u> for an Assistant Manager. Enclosed is my resume for your review and consideration.

I graduated in 1992 from Colby College with a Bachelor of Arts degree in Anthropology. I also studied intensely in such areas as Mathematics and Computer Science which, in addition to my minor in Economics, gave me an excellent sense of business.

In the year since I graduated, I have been working as an Assistant Manager of a busy local restaurant. Here I oversaw food preparation and cooking, in addition to hiring and training new employees. I was also responsible for selecting daily and evening specials, ordering supplies, evaluating quality of food, maintaining and repairing equipment, waste removal and pest control. During busy periods, I never hesitated to roll up my sleeves and help with the cooking, clearing of tables, and other tasks.

I believe that my qualifications would be beneficial to Lobster Hut Corporation. I would appreciate the opportunity to discuss the Assistant Manager position with you. I can be reached at the above address and phone number for an interview at your convenience.

Thank you for your consideration of my application.

Sincerely yours,

Peter Wallerham

Peter Wallerham

Enc.

Anthropology Major

PETER WALLERHAM

1297 High View Road
Bar Harbor, Maine 04608
(207) 555-5599

Education
1988-1992   COLBY COLLEGE   WATERVILLE, MAINE
Awarded the degree of Bachelor of Arts in June 1992, majoring in Anthropology. Minor in Economics. Courses include Mathematics and Computer Science. 3.1 grade point average. Senior Scholar.

President of the local chapter of the Disabled Students Union. Responsible for increased accessibility of the campus to physically handicapped students, including more wheelchair ramps, designated parking spaces, and special class scheduling.

Experience
1992-present   THE MARBLE ROOM   BAR HARBOR, MAINE
Assistant manager of busy local restaurant. Responsible for selecting daily and evening specials, ordering supplies, evaluating quality of food, maintaining and repairing equipment, waste removal, and pest control. Oversaw food preparation and cooking, responsible for hiring and training new workers. During busy periods, assisted with cooking, clearing tables, and other tasks. Resolved customer complaints about food, quality, and service.

summers
1991-1992   MR. TED'S ICE CREAM PARLOR   BANGOR, MAINE
Waitperson for busy seasonal ice cream parlor. Served ice cream and food to customers, operated cash register, cleared tables, assisted in cleaning. Assisted in making the ice cream itself; suggested new flavors. Began as busperson; promoted to waitstaff.

summer 1989   R. JANINE APPAREL   BAR HARBOR, MAINE
Sales Associate. Assisted in layout of store merchandise, stocking and inventory control. Trained new staff members. Two-time winner of employee sales contests.

References   Available upon request.

Art History Major

                                        566 Beacon St., #3A
                                        Boston, MA 02254
                                        January 14, 1992

Mr. John R. Mercier
Museum Director
Boston Museum of Fine Arts
465 Huntington Avenue
Boston, MA 02254

Dear Mr. Mercier:

    I am a recent graduate from Emerson College with a well-rounded
Art History background, both through education and practical
experience. I would like to put my skills and knowledge to use in an
entry-level position at your prestigious museum, perhaps as an
Assistant Director or as an Apprentice to the Curator.

    As my resume indicates, I participated in an exclusive summer
program for Art History majors at Le Louvre in Paris. Here, I studied
some of the most significant works in European art and attended a very
interesting seminar about the workings of the Louvre itself. I also
worked for two summers at the Fuller Museum of Art in Brockton, where
I worked as a Museum Assistant at the Information Booth. My coursework
in African-American Art, Modern Art, and Museum Science has also
prepared me well for an entry-level position in a fine arts museum.

    I have long been a lover of art and likewise art museums. I have
been going to your museum ever since I was a small child and would be
thrilled at the opportunity to become a part of your excellent staff.

    I have included my resume for your consideration. I may be reached
at (617) 555-4458 after 3 P.M. and on weekends. I hope to hear from
you soon.

                                    Sincerely,

                                    Olivia J. Abbot

                                    Olivia J. Abbot

Enc. resume

Art History Major

OLIVIA J. ABBOT

566 Beacon St., #3A
Boston, MA 02254
(617) 555-4458

558 Lakeview Terrace
Apartment 24
Barrington, RI 44329
(416) 555-1479

EDUCATION:

1987-1991 **EMERSON COLLEGE**   **BOSTON, MASSACHUSETTS**
Bachelor of Fine Arts degree in Art History awarded in December 1991.
Concentration: History of African and African-American Art. Courses include:
New Trends in Modern Art, Introductory Museum Science, Public Speaking,
and Business Management, 3.7 grade point average.

Vice President of Student Arts League. Member of the Walker Museum Advisory Committee. Helped organize exhibition of artwork by minority art students. Representative in Senior Class Counsel.

INTERNSHIP:

summer 1991 **LE LOUVRE**   **PARIS, FRANCE**
Participated in exclusive program for Art History majors. Studied hundreds
of the world's most famous paintings and their history, including the Mona
Lisa. Attended special seminar on the Louvre itself, its history, administration, and management.

EXPERIENCE:

**summers
1989, 1990** **FULLER MUSEUM OF ART**   **BROCKTON, MASSACHUSETTS**
Worked as Museum Assistant at the Information Booth. Distributed headsets and museum maps for self-guided tours, provided wheelchair assistance when necessary, answered phones, and assisted visitors with their questions and/or problems.

summer 1988 **JABOT DEPARTMENT STORE**   **QUINCY, MASSACHUSETTS**
Cosmetics Associate for Lancome Cosmetics. Advised customers on the use and application of cosmetics. Assisted in customer make-overs. Arranged counter displays. Operated cash register.

**part-time
1987-present** Part-time positions include Courier, Sales Clerk, and stable hand.

INTERESTS: Painting, drawing, and horse-back riding.

REFERENCES: Personal references available upon request.

Biology Major

72 Oak Street, #3A
Seattle, WA 92013

June 24, 1993

Mr. John Reese
Department of Parks and Recreation
344 Cobb Street
Seattle, WA 92044

Dear Mr. Reese:

I would like to apply for the Park Reservationist position
advertised in yesterday's <u>Seattle Post</u>.

As you can see from my resume, I fulfill all of the
qualifications listed in your advertisement. I offer detailed knowledge
of horticultural principles and, equally important, a desire to clean
up and protect the earth's natural environment.

I graduated from Bates College in May with a Bachelor of Sciences
degree in Biology and Horticulture. In addition to my studies, I
founded the Bates College Greenhouse and was an active member of
E.A.R.T.H. for Students. I created and hosted an educational college
radio program, called "Earth Talk", which provided a format for
students to discuss their questions and concerns about the
environment. And earlier this spring, I was awarded the Biological
Sciences Society Award for Outstanding Students of Biology.

As for work experience, last summer I was a volunteer for the
State of Maine Summer Clean-up Program, which is designed not only to
clean up the environment, but prevent it from future destruction
through recycling and other environmental programs. I also served as a
Staff Assistant for the New England Environmental Newsletter, published
by Tufts University in Massachusetts.

As I will be out of town next week, a message can be left for me
at (703) 555-9998. I look forward to hearing from you. Thank you for
your consideration.

Sincerely,

Sharon L. O'Connell

enc.

Biology Major

SHARON L. O'CONNELL
72 Oak Street, #3A
Seattle, Washington 92013
703/555-9998

education
1989-1993 BATES COLLEGE   LEWISTON, MAINE
Awarded a Bachelor of Sciences degree in May 1993, majoring in Biology, minoring in Horticulture. Courses include Biochemistry, Anatomy & Physiology, Chemistry, Physics, Computer Science and Advanced Calculus. 3.77 grade point average. Awarded the Biological Sciences Society Award for Outstanding Students of Biology. Class rank: 4/276.

Founded the Bates College Greenhouse. Member of E.A.R.T.H. for Students. Weekend disc jockey for WBTS, college radio station. Created and hosted the "Earth Talk", radio program for discussing environmental issues.

experience
summer 1992 MAINE STATE PARKS AND RECREATION   MAINE
Volunteer for State of Maine Summer Clean-Up Program. Removed trash and litter from state grounds, landscaped state and local parks, repaired and repainted state buildings, signs, and benches. Promoted recycling and other environmental programs. Established new state garden at Old Orchard Beach.

summer 1991 TUFTS UNIVERSITY   MEDFORD, MASSACHUSETTS
Staff Assistant for the New England Environmental Newsletter. Wrote and edited articles. Provided administrative support to the Director of Environmental Affairs.

summer 1990 PURITAN ICE CREAM PARLOR   SEATTLE, WASHINGTON
Counter Person/Ice Cream Scooper. Invented new hit ice-cream flavor, Rain Forest Pecan.

part-time
1990-1993 BATES COLLEGE LIBRARY   LEWISTON, MAINE
Front desk clerk. Processed books, restacked shelves, answered phones, and assorted other duties.

personal
background Enjoy gardening, reading, and scuba diving. Published feature article in *American Horticulture*.

references Personal references available upon request.

Business Administration Major

26 Mountain View Drive
Ladysmith, Wisconsin 54891
715/555-6605

April 14, 1993

Mr. Frederick Gillette, Manager
Janston Athletic Gear Company
1022 Rodeo Drive
Salinas, CA 92004-1879

Dear Mr. Gillette:

The Campus Career Center at the University of Wisconsin suggested that I contact you regarding your management-training program.

I will be graduating next month with a Bachelor of Science degree in Business Administration. I have studied Marketing, Industrial Relations, Finance, Management, Accounting, Business Law, Economics, and Computer Applications, all of which I am confident will help me succeed in the world of business. I worked very hard in school and received a variety of academic honors and awards, including a Certificate of Award for Outstanding Business Administration Graduates.

As my resume indicates, I have worked as a Data-Entry Clerk for the order department of a busy mailing list company. In this position, I gained experience processing orders on a computer, controlling inventory, handling customer inquiries and problems, and packing and shipping. As the Office Assistant to a local shoe store owner, I learned all aspects of running a small retail store, including sales, accounting, inventory control, and advertising. When the store's owner went on vacation for two weeks, I successfully co-managed the store.

I am particularly interested in working for a sports-related company, as I have always been very athletic. I founded and directed the League of Women's Soccer in Madison and I teach and choreograph aerobics at a local fitness club. In 1989, I received the Wisconsin Times Scholar Athlete Award, which is given to the most outstanding female student athlete in Green County.

I feel that the combination of my business background and my athletic lifestyle makes me an excellent match for your company. If you agree, please give me a call. I am looking forward to meeting you.

Sincerely,

Alisia Petersham

Alisia Petersham

enc.

Business Administration Major

ALISIA PETERSHAM

School Address: Permanent Address:
301 Temple Hall   26 Mountain View Drive
University of Wisconsin at   Ladysmith, Wisconsin 54891
Madison 53201   715/555-6605
414/555-5711

education
1989-1993   UNIVERSITY OF WISCONSIN   MADISON, WISCONSIN
             Candidate for the degree of Bachelor of Science in May 1993,
             majoring in Business Administration. Courses include Mar-
             keting, Industrial Relations, Finance, Management,
             Accounting, Business Law, Economics, and Computer Applica-
             tions. 3.4 grade point average.

             Golden Key Society, Wisconsin University Fellowship, Cer-
             tificate of Award for Outstanding Business Administration
             Graduates. Varsity Soccer.

experience
summer 1992 GOODELL & HITE ASSOCIATES   MADISON, WISCONSIN
             Data entry clerk for order department. Responsibilities in-
             cluded order processing, customer service, inventory
             control, and some packing and shipping.

summer 1991 HIERLAND SHOES   LADYSMITH, WISCONSIN
             Office Assistant for local shoe store. Assisted in all as-
             pects of running store, including sales, accounting,
             inventory control, advertising, and maintenance. Co-managed
             store while owner was on vacation for two weeks.

summer 1990
and part-time
1990—present ISLAND FITNESS HEALTH CLUB   MADISON, WISCONSIN
             Aerobics instructor and choreographer. Voted "Best Instruc-
             tor" by members and staff.

activities Founder and Director of League of Women's Soccer in Madison.
             Recipient of *Wisconsin Times* Scholar Athlete Award, awarded
             to the most outstanding female student athlete in Green
             County.

references Personal references available upon request.

Business Administration Major

409 Birch Road
Peru, Nebraska 68492
(402) 555-8466

May 3, 1993

Mr. Anthony Peretti
Employment Manager
CompuServe Incorporated
5000 Arlington Centre Blvd.
PO Box 20212
Columbus, OH 43220

Dear Mr. Peretti:

Please accept this letter as application for your opening for an Account Representative, as advertised through the Career Development Center at University of Nebraska. I have enclosed my resume for your review.

I will be graduating next week from the University of Nebraska at Lincoln with a Bachelor of Sciences degree in Business Administration. Throughout my college career, I was consistently recognized for academic excellence and was made President of the local chapter of the National Honor Society in Business Administration. In addition to my core studies, I feel confident that my course work in marketing, statistics, calculus, and computer applications, will become invaluable to me as an Account Representative for your company.

Because I am experienced not only with computers but with working in representation, I feel that I am especially well-suited for this position. I offer a strong computer background and am familiar with a wide variety of software packages. I worked for two summers as a Sales Associate for Super Computer Store, which greatly enhanced my knowledge of computer software and hardware. I also have experience working as a Junior Client Service Representative for an investment firm, which has prepared me well for future work in consulting and representation.

It would be my pleasure to discuss with you positions that are available or are expected to become available with your company in the near future. I can be reached during business hours at (402) 555-1121, or a message can be left for me with my home telephone. I look forward to that opportunity.

Sincerely yours,

Mary H. Sciratti

Mary H. Sciratti

enc.

Business Administration Major

MARY H. SCIRATTI

409 Birch Road
Peru, Nebraska 68492
(402) 555-8466

Education
1988-1993   UNIVERSITY OF NEBRASKA   LINCOLN, NEBRASKA
Candidate for the degree of Bachelor of Science in Business Administration, to be awarded in May 1993. Courses include Marketing, Statistics, Calculus, and Computer Applications. 3.8 grade point average in major, 3.6 overall grade point average.

President of local chapter of National Honor Society in Business Administration. Dean's List all semesters. Varsity letter in tennis.

Internship
summer 1992   KEYBROOK INVESTOR RESOURCE CENTER   LINCOLN, NEBRASKA
Junior Client Service Representative. Served as principal contact for various brokerage firms. Trained and checked work of six other staff members. Provided tax information to shareholders, prepared daily and monthly financial reports, handled correspondence with shareholders, and processed financial transaction requests.

Experience
summers
1990-1991   SUPER COMPUTER STORE   LINCOLN, NEBRASKA
Sales Associate for large computer store chain. Advised customers on a variety of computer software. Cashier and quality control. Promoted from Stock Person.

summer 1989   BIG X DRUGSTORE   PERU, NEBRASKA
Merchandiser. Checked stock in, took inventory. Operated cash register.

part-time
1990-present   UNIVERSITY OF NEBRASKA   LINCOLN, NEBRASKA
Archival Research Assistant. Catalogued and reproduced documents and photographs and archival collection, cleaned and repaired damaged documents, transcribed oral history projects, located and acquired historic material, and coordinated with local archival organizations.

Personal   Willing to relocate and travel

References   Available upon request.

Chemistry Major

24 School Street
Norfolk, Virginia 23507
804/555-9855

March 2, 1993

Human Resources Manager
Brauman Industries
555 Industrial Park Drive
Fairfax, Virginia 22035

To the Human Resources Manager:

I am writing and enclosing my resume to apprise you of my interest in working for your Chemical Research Department.

I have just graduated from Radford University with a Bachelor of Sciences degree, majoring in Chemistry, minoring in Biology, and concentrating in Biochemistry. I am confident that my course work in such areas as Anatomy & Physiology, Environmental Studies, Chemical Research, and Modern Laboratory Technology, as well as my independent study on marine pollutants, gives me an excellent basis to begin a career in laboratory technology.

I have solid laboratory research experience as well, having worked as a Laboratory Assistant for the Chemical Research Department of a local fabrics manufacturer and as the assistant to the Head of the Chemistry Department at Radford, conducting research on non-combustible fuels. At Peller Laboratories, I developed a new fabric dye that is now being tested for use.

I have been recognized for academic excellence on several occasions. In 1990, I received the Curie Scholarship for Promising Students of Life Sciences. My independent study was recognized for excellence by the National Foundation for Scientific Research and was published in *Environment Today*.

It would be my pleasure to discuss with you any appropriate positions that are available or are expected to be available at your company in the near future. I can be reached during business hours at (804) 555-8881, or a message can be left for me at my home telephone. I hope to hear from you soon!

Sincerely,

Martin H. Ericson

Martin H. Ericson

enc.

Chemistry Major

MARTIN H. ERICSON

24 School Street • Norfolk, Virginia 23507 • 804/555-9855

Objective To obtain a challenging position in laboratory technology.

EDUCATION
Radford University, Radford, Virginia.
Bachelor of Science degree in Chemistry awarded in December 1992. Minor in Biology with a concentration in Biochemistry. Courses include Anatomy & Physiology, Environmental Studies I-IV, Introductory Chemical Research, and Modern Laboratory Technology. 3.3 grade point average. Awarded the Curie Scholarship for Promising Students of Life Sciences.

Member of Students for Environmental Protection. Organized students into a clean-up crew and combed city for litter and trash. Established campus/city program for recycling paper, plastics, and aluminum cans. Recycled over 50 tons of materials in first year alone.

INDEPENDENT STUDY
Topic: The Effects of Petroleum-Based Pollutants on Crustacean Life and the Food Chain on the Mid-Atlantic Coast. Published in Environment Today. Recognized for excellence by the National Foundation for Scientific Research. Fall 1992.

RELATED WORK EXPERIENCE
Peller Laboratories, Norfolk Virginia.
Laboratory Assistant for Chemical Research Department of fabrics manufacturer. Assisted in research for development of new synthetic fabrics. Independently developed new red dye that won't fade or bleed, which is currently being tested for use. Summer 1992.

Chemistry Department, Radford University.
Assistant to Department Head for government-commissioned research on non-combustible fuels. Conducted experiments, recorded and analyzed data, and redesigned flawed experiments. Spring-Summer 1991.

UNRELATED WORK EXPERIENCE
Unrelated work experience includes Sales Clerk, Delivery Person, Warehouse Worker, and Waiter. 1988-1991.

References available upon request.

Classical Civilization Major

80 Orchard Avenue
Bristol, Rhode Island 02851
401/555-5962

July 7, 1993

Personnel Department
Kay-Bee Toy Stores
100 West Street
Pittsfield, Massachusetts 01201

To the Personnel Manager:

I am very interested in obtaining a position with your
organization. Please find enclosed my resume for your review.

As you can see, I am a recent graduate of Rhode Island College,
majoring in Classical Civilization. I was very active in school,
having earned good grades while participating in a number of
extracurricular activities, including the Photography Club and
intramural soccer. I also have a diverse background of work
experience, having been a student ambassador, a camp counselor, and an
assistant production manager.

During my summer at *The Queen City Times*, I managed all production
aspects of the newspaper. Not only did I enjoy this position very
much, but I was very successful at it and was given a good deal of
authority and decision-making power.

I feel that I am a good match for Kay-Bee because I am
hard-working, creative, and very much interested in the toy business.
I offer superior management and supervisory skills that would lend
themselves well to a career in retail management.

I would very much like to be part of your team. I am available to
meet with you at your convenience.

Sincerely,

Evelyn J. Depalma

Evelyn J. Depalma

enc.

Classical Civilization Major

EVELYN J. DEPALMA
80 Orchard Avenue
Bristol, Rhode Island 02851
401/555-5962

education
1990-1993 RHODE ISLAND COLLEGE   PROVIDENCE, RHODE ISLAND
Awarded the degree of Bachelor of Arts in May 1993, majoring
in Classical Civilization. Other courses include Creative
Writing, Modern Art, Photography, and Popular Culture. 3.5
grade point average in major. Dean's List.

Member of the Photography Club. Organized a photography ex-
hibit of students' works to help pay for a new campus dark
room and dark room supplies. Intramural soccer.

fall 1992 INTERCOLLEGIATE CENTER FOR CLASSICAL STUDIES   ROME, ITALY
Studies included Classical Archeology, Latin, and Art History. Joined Italian students' soccer team.

1989-1990 SALVE REGINA COLLEGE   NEWPORT, RHODE ISLAND
Studied Art History, Film/Photography, Dance, and Classical
Music for two semesters.

experience
summer 1992 THE QUEEN CITY TIMES   PROVIDENCE, RHODE ISLAND
Assistant Production Manager. Managed all production aspects of newspaper. Supervised three production staff
members. Developed and sized photos, pasted up pages. wrote
ad copy, produced color screens, and prepared pages for
printing.

summer 1991 GREAT PINES CAMP   ALTON, NEW HAMPSHIRE
Camp Counselor. Taught canoeing, boating, sailing, swimming
and basic water ecology courses to grade school campers.
Worked as lifeguard. Organized and led activities and supervised groups of campers.

part-time
1992-1993 RHODE ISLAND COLLEGE   PROVIDENCE, RHODE ISLAND
Student Ambassador. Promoted RIC to students and parents in
writing, over the phone, and in person. Guided campus tours,
hosted overnight guests, and answered questions about the
college. Represented the college on several visit days. Further developed skills in interpersonal relations.

interests Canoeing, sailing, outdoor sports, and creative writing.

references Available upon request.

Classics Major

445 Horrigan Street
Lawrenceville, NJ 07644
201/555-5454

June 5, 1993

Mr. J. Thomas
PO Box 4551
New Brunswick, NJ 07221

Dear Mr. Thomas:

In response to your advertisement in the Sunday, June 8 edition of The Newark Post, enclosed please find my resume for your review. I am very interested in securing the position of Publicity Assistant available within your organization.

I am interested in pursuing employment in the publicity/promotion field. I recently graduated from Rutgers University with a Bachelor of Arts degree in Classics. I also studied a number of different areas, including creative writing, communications and media, applications in computing, business administration, and marketing.

My previous work experience includes a paid marketing internship for the United Way of New Jersey, where I became familiar with various aspects of marketing and promotion. Through this and other undertakings, I have developed excellent writing, communication, and organizational skills, a flair for detail work, and a professional work ethic.

I offer proven writing ability and extensive computer skills which include Lotus 1-2-3, Microsoft Word, and GW Basic. I can type 55 words per minute, and am familiar with basic office procedures and operations.

I hope you will find my qualifications desirable, and will consider me as a future employee of your company. I may be reached at the above listed phone number and will be available to interview at your convenience.

Thank you for taking the time to review my credentials.

Sincerely,

Anthony Lambrose
Anthony Lambrose

enc.

Classics Major

ANTHONY LAMBROSE

445 Horrigan Street
Lawrenceville, NJ 07644
201/555-5454

Education

1989-1993 RUTGERS UNIVERSITY   NEWARK, NEW JERSEY
Awarded the degree of Bachelor of Arts in May 1993, majoring in Classics. Courses included Creative Writing, Communications & Media, Applications in Computing, Business Administration, and Marketing. 3.2 grade point average.

1995-1989 THAYER PREPARATORY ACADEMY   NEWPORT, RHODE ISLAND
Awarded High School Diploma in June 1989. Editor-in-Chief of school newspaper. Awarded the Lewis-Brackman Award for Outstanding Literary Achievement.

Experience

Summer 1992 UNITED WAY OF NEW JERSEY   NEW BRUNSWICK, NEW JERSEY
Marketing Intern. Assisted the Marketing Director in promoting a new program designed to increase corporate interest and participation in the United Way. Collected data and incorporated this information into public relations articles to be used in company newsletters and bulletins.

Summer 1991 LEEDS BROTHERS, INC.   NEWARK, NEW JERSEY
Assistant to the Warehouse Manager. Responsible for supervising warehouse operations. Trained new summer staff. Received incoming shipments and verified contents. Assisted home-owners, construction contractors, and building professionals with product selection.

Summer 1990 FOODMART SUPERMARKET   NEW BRUNSWICK, NEW JERSEY
Front End Clerk. Dealt with customers in a courteous, honest, and professional manner. Handled, changed, and kept large sums of money. Familiarized self with relevant company policies to enable myself to explain them to customers and new employees. Helped supervise new employees.

Skills Familiar with Lotus 1-2-3, Microsoft Word, and GW Basic. Typing: 55 WPM.

References Available upon request.

Communications Major

1221 Oak Garden Road
Brookline, MA 02351
(617) 555-8850

April 1, 1993

Mr. Shawn Belleau, Director
WGUR TV-Channel 46
133 Business Park Drive
Brighton, MA 02215

Dear Mr. Belleau:

Sharon Lafferty, director of the "A.M. Boston" program suggested that I contact you regarding an opening you may have for a Production Assistant.

I am presently studying Communications at Emerson College and will be graduating next month. My course work is concentrated in Broadcast Journalism and I have studied such topics as Ethics in Reporting, Broadcast Journalism I-IV, and Television Production. I was the top student in my Broadcast Journalism classes and was consistently recognized for academic excellence on the Dean's List.

I also have experience working in television, having worked as a Television Program Intern for "A.M. Boston". Here, I was responsible for acquiring and booking guests to debate controversial public interest topics with the host and fielding viewers' reaction calls provoked by on-air debates. Also, I gained valuable experience assembling and editing video clips of upcoming entertainment events and movies which were aired during the show.

My resume is enclosed. I would value the opportunity to meet with you to discuss a possible position with your station. I can be reached at the above address and telephone number.

I have included several writing samples and hope to get a chance to show you some of my other work soon. Thank you for your time.

Sincerely,

Jennifer Barnes

Jennifer Barnes

enclosure: resume

Communications Major

JENNIFER BARNES

409 Walters Hall
Emerson College
Boston, MA 02116

1221 Oak Garden Road
Brookline, MA 02351
617/555-8850

education
1989-present

EMERSON COLLEGE   **BOSTON, MA**
Candidate for the degree of Bachelor of Arts in May 1993, majoring in Communications. Concentration in Broadcast Journalism. Courses included Ethics in Reporting, Broadcast Journalism I-IV, and Television Production. Thesis topic: "The Future of Public Television in the United States." Dean's List.

Founding Member of the Delta Omega Sorority. Organized the first annual Emerson College Dance-a-thon to benefit the American Cancer Society.

internship
summer 1992

"A.M. BOSTON" - ABC Affiliate   **BOSTON, MA**
Television Program Intern. Responsible for acquiring and booking guests to debate controversial public interest topics with host. Assembled and edited video clips of upcoming entertainment events and movies which were aired during show. Fielded viewers' reaction telephone calls provoked by on-air debates.

experience
summer 1991

JACOB & LAFFERTY CONSULTING   **BOSTON, MA**
Research Assistant. Used a variety of media including public forum, radio, telephone, and mailings to alert constituents about political issues. Supervised the phone bank and ran the national political hotline.

summer 1990

BUFFORD & O'BRIAN ASSOCIATES   **CAMBRIDGE, MA**
Public Relations Assistant. Wrote press releases, designed and assembled product kits, typing, database management, and general clerical. Worked one-on-one with Vice-President on an account for LaJolie Cosmetics.

part-time
1988-present

Worked as an Office Assistant, Tutor, Waitperson, and Sales Clerk.

references   Available upon request.

Computer Science/Programming Major

2 Graham Street
Grove City, Pennsylvania 16126
412/555-5590

July 2, 1992

Sarah Cunningham
Opie Computer & Informational Systems
392 Richie Lane
Philadelphia, Pennsylvania 16002

Dear Ms. Cunningham:

I am enclosing my resume in response to your advertisement in *The Houston Times* for a computer programmer.

Briefly, I offer:

- B.S. in Computer Science and Programming from Gettysburg College
- Experience as an Applications Programmer with PC Systems, Inc.
- Experience as a Computer Lab Assistant and a Tutor for introductory computer science courses
- Thorough knowledge of and experience with many programming languages, including COBOL, Pascal, and Fortran
- Experience using a variety of hardware, including IBM, AT&T, and MacIntosh computers

I feel that I am well qualified for this position. If you would like to schedule an interview with me, I can be reached at the above listed number or at 555-8885 during daytime hours.

Thank you for considering me for this position!

Sincerely,

Leslie Pellham

Leslie Pellham

enc.

Computer Science/Programming Major

LESLIE PELLHAM

2 Graham Street
Grove City, Pennsylvania 16126
412/555-5590

EDUCATION

Gettysburg College   Gettysburg, Pennsylvania

Awarded a Bachelor of Sciences Degree in Computer Science with a Concentration in Programming. Key courses include Computer Organization & Architecture, Logic Design and Switching Theory, Discrete Mathematical Structures I-II, Data Structures and Algorithms, Operating Systems & Computer Networks, and Software Engineering. 3.65 grade point average. Graduated Summa Cum Laude in May 1992.

Member of Gettysburg Society of Computer Programmers. Tutor for introductory computer science courses. Member and competitor in Cycling Club.

WORK EXPERIENCE

PC Systems, Inc.   Philadelphia, Pennsylvania
Applications Programmer   Summer 1991

Wrote business-related software, including programs used for inventory control and order processing using COBOL. Tested finished programs for bugs and corrected them if they occurred.

Gettysburg College Computer Center   Gettysburg, Pennsylvania
Computer Lab Assistant   Part-time 1990-1992

Assisted students with software, hardware, and printing questions and problems. Trained students and faculty how to use word processing, database, spreadsheet, and desk-top publishing programs. Maintained and repaired equipment.

SOFTWARE

COBOL	dBase	Fortran	Lotus 1-2-3
Pascal	Unix Shell	Rexx	PageMaker
Assembly	Refal-5	WordPerfect	Microsoft Excel

HARDWARE

IBM 4341, 370VM/CMS, PC-XT, AT&T 3B2, AT, Mac SE, Mac 2E, Mac FX

REFERENCES

Available upon request

Earth Science/Forestry Major

32 North Shore Drive
Portland, Oregon 98651
503/555-4102

July 30, 1992

Mr. Jason R. Baxter, Director
Bureau of Land Management
U.S. Department of the Interior
Washington, D.C. 20240

Dear Mr. Baxter:

I am a recent college graduate with a degree in Earth Science and Forestry and am seeking a position in forestry in the Pacific states.

In June, I graduated from Oregon State University with a Bachelor's degree in Earth Science and Forestry. I have studied many relevant courses including Forest Economics, Range Management, Ecology, Soil Science, Hydrology, Wildlife, and Agronomy. In 1991, I was recognized for outstanding achievement in the natural sciences when I was awarded the prestigious Tepper Badge.

I also offer on-site work experience, having interned last summer for the Oregon State Soil Conservation Service. In this position, I was exposed to all aspects of applied soil science. I provided technical assistance primarily to farmers and ranchers to promote the conservation of soil, water, and related natural resources. Equally important, I helped to develop programs to combat soil erosion and maximize land productivity without damaging the environment.

I gained valuable experience in forestry when I attended Oregon State University's Field Camp in Klamath Falls. I planted and maintained trees and rare natural vegetation and recorded and charted their growth. In addition to testing soil and water samples, I tracked wildlife species and worked to preserve natural habitats for endangered species.

If you feel that I am suitable for a position with the Bureau of Land Management, I would greatly appreciate an interview. I may be reached at the above listed number during the morning hours. Thank you for your consideration!

Sincerely,

Douglas J. McNaugton

enc. resume

Earth Science/Forestry Major

DOUGLAS J. MCNAUGHTON

School Address:
121 Leper Street
Apartment 3A
Corvallis, Oregon 97335
Phone: 503/555-9546

Permanent Address:
32 North Shore Drive
Portland, Oregon 98651
Phone: 555/556-4102

education
1988-1992 OREGON STATE UNIVERSITY   CORVALLIS, OREGON
Awarded the degree of Bachelor of Arts in June 1992, majoring in Earth Science and minoring in Forestry. Courses of study include Forest Economics, Range Management, Ecology, Soil Science, Hydrology, Wildlife, and Agronomy. Independent Research topic: The Effect of Hydrolechicin Treatment on Blue Alpine Firs Infected with Pulloma Disease. 3.7 grade point average.

Member of the Oregon State Ecological Society. Awarded the Tepper Badge for outstanding achievement in the natural sciences.

internship
summer 1991 OREGON STATE SOIL CONSERVATION SERVICE   PORTLAND
Provided technical assistance to farmers, ranchers, and others concerned with the conservation of soil, water, and related natural resources. Aided in the development of programs designed to maximize land productivity without harm or damage. Developed programs to combat soil erosion.

experience
summer 1990 OREGON STATE UNIVERSITY FIELD CAMP   KLAMATH FALLS
Planted and maintained trees and rare natural vegetation, recorded and charted growth. Tracked wildlife species and worked to preserve natural habitats for endangered species. Tested soil and water samples.

part-time
1898-1992 Unrelated work positions include Bus Person, Cashier, and Service Station Attendant.

interests Playing acoustic guitar, hiking, camping, and competition swimming.

references Available upon request.

Economics Major

12 Island Road
Salinas, CA 21131

July 15, 1992

Mr. James R. Evans
Human Resources Department
B.G.R. Enterprises
192 East 47th Street, Ste. 708
New York, NY 10025

Dear Mr. Evans:

Having majored in Economics at Notre Dame College, where I also worked as a Telephone Salesperson for the Alumni contribution fund, I am confident that I would make a very successful International Sales Trainee in your International Sales Department.

In addition to my strong background in economics, I have studied International Relations, International Business Law, and Communications. I am sure that my fluency in German will also prove particularly useful in this position.

I am interested in pursuing a career in International Business because my extensive travelling has made me very much aware of and very curious about the business world outside of the United States.

I am attracted to B.G.R. Enterprises because of its solid reputation and its numerous strong connections in Germany. I am convinced that I can make valuable contributions to your company.

My preference is to live in Germany, but I'm far more interested in working for a fine company with strong international ties. Enclosed is my resume that summarizes my qualifications. I will be glad to furnish any additional information that you may require. I am best reached weekdays between 8 A.M. and 1 P.M. at 619/555-9902.

Sincerely,

Nancy Allen

Nancy Allen

Enc. Resume

Economics Major

NANCY ALLEN

---

12 Island Road
Salinas, CA 21131
(619) 555-9902

EDUCATION
1988-1992   **NOTRE DAME COLLEGE**   **BAY CITY, OREGON**
Bachelor of Arts degree awarded in June 1992, majoring in Economics. Minor in German language. Courses included: International Relations, International Business Law, and Communications. Ranked 4 in a class of 53.

Dean's List. Resident Assistant for Freshman Dormitory for two consecutive years. Organized student activities and field trips and managed $500/semester budget.

1984-1988   **BAY CITY HIGH SCHOOL**   **BAY CITY, OREGON**
Received High School Diploma in June 1988. High honors list. Took advanced college-level courses in English, Mathematics, and Physics. Cheerleader for the Bay City Cougars Basketball team.

EXPERIENCE
summers
1989-1991   **WATERSIDE BAR & GRILL**   **BAY CITY, OREGON**
Began work as busperson. Promoted to short-order cook.

part-time
1990-1992   **NOTRE DAME COLLEGE**   **BAY CITY, OREGON**
Telephone salesperson for the Parents and Alumni Contribution Fund. Consistently solicited the highest donation levels for my sales group.

LANGUAGES   Able to speak fluently and write in German.

PERSONAL   Willing to travel and relocate, particularly in Europe.

INTERESTS   Enjoy photography, karate, and collecting antique books, particularly 19th Century German novels. Have travelled extensively in Europe, Asia, and South America.

REFERENCES   Available upon request.

Education Major

14 Bradley Road
Boise, Idaho 49965
(451) 555-2222

April 8, 1992

Christine R. Davis
Human Resources Manager
Idaho School District 5
Boise, Idaho 49662

Dear Ms. Davis:

In response to last week's advertisement in the <u>Boise Chronicle</u> for an English teacher, I have enclosed my resume for your consideration.

I have recently graduated from the University of Idaho at Boise with a Bachelor's degree in Secondary Education. I am certified to teach both English and Special Education. In addition to fulfilling my practice teaching requirement in your district, I participated in a volunteer literacy program to tutor both youths and adults suffering with reading difficulties. I also organized and performed in a variety show at Boise Central High that benefited special needs students.

As I fulfilled my practice teaching requirement in District 5, I was continually impressed by its high educational standards and its long-standing record of producing students who achieve among the nation's highest SAT scores. I would consider it a great opportunity to teach in such an accomplished district.

I will be calling you on Monday, April 13 to confirm that you received my resume and answer any questions you may have. I look forward to speaking with you.

Sincerely,

Caleb J. Nash

enclosure

Education Major

CALEB J. NASH
14 Bradley Road
Boise, Idaho 49965
(451/555-2222)

CAREER
OBJECTIVE: A classroom position teaching high school English and/or Special Education.

EDUCATION:
1988-1992 UNIVERSITY OF IDAHO   BOISE, IDAHO
Awarded a Bachelor of Arts Degree in June 1992, majoring in Secondary Education. Concentration in English and Special Education. Thesis topic: "The Future of Special Education in Public Schools". 3.8 grade point average.

Member of Volunteers in Action. Tutored illiterate adults and youths with reading difficulties. Organized and performed in variety show to benefit special needs students. Member of varsity wrestling team.

CERTIFICATION:
May 1992 Idaho state certificate in English (Grades 9-12) and Special Education.

STUDENT
TEACHING:
1991-1992 CENTRAL HIGH   BOISE, IDAHO
Assistant Teacher for a twelfth-grade college-level English Composition class. Took attendance, corrected papers, helped students with writing skills, conducted workshop on preparing essays for college applications.

PROFESSIONAL
ASSOCIATIONS: National Council of Teachers of English.
Council for the Advancement and Support of Education.

INTERESTS: Enjoy reading, basketball, and wrestling competitions.

REFERENCES: Personal references available upon request.

Electrical Engineering Major

456 Duval Street
Fort Wayne, IN 60542
January 6, 1993

Recruiting Manager
Hewlett-Packard Company
4 Choke Cherry Road
Rockville, MD 20850

Dear Sir/Madam:

Having recently graduated from the University of Colorado at Boulder with a major in Electrical Engineering and a concentration in Computer Engineering, I am confident that I would make a very successful Computer Programmer at your prestigious company.

In addition to my strong educational background, I also offer significant on-hands experience, having worked as a Research Associate at the University of Colorado as well as having participated in the Scientific Supercomputing Workshop at UCB. In conjunction with my studies, I designed and built a short wave radio, developed a microprocessor-based system to measure heart rate and blood pressure and successfully coordinated a method of producing a circuit board coplanar waveguide prototype.

I am sure that my coursework in microprocessor applications, digital systems, and computer organization, as well as my extensive computer skills and valuable experience, would prove particularly useful in the position of Computer Programmer.

Enclosed is my resume. I may be reached at 213/555-9857. I will be glad to make myself available for an interview at your convenience to discuss how my qualifications would be consistent with your needs. Thank you for your time and consideration.

Sincerely,

Sun Quan Lin

Enc.

Electrical Engineering Major

SUN QUAN LIN
456 Duval Street
Fort Wayne, IN 60542
213/555-9857

JOB OBJECTIVE:

To find a position as a computer engineer that will use my skills in microprocessor applications, digital systems, logic design and computer programming.

EDUCATION:

University of Colorado at Boulder

B.S. in Electrical Engineering, Fall 1992. Area of concentration: Computer Engineering. GPA: 3.6/4.0.

Relevant Coursework:

- Microprocessor Applications and Organization
- Data Structures in C
- Digital Systems Engineering
- Computer Organization

Academic Honors:

- President's and Dean's List
- Trustees' Scholarship
- Member of Omega Honor Society

Extra-curricular Activities:

- Student member of the American Society of Computer Engineers
- Volunteer for Disabled Student Services at UCB

EXPERIENCE:

University of Colorado at Boulder

Research Associate: **January 1989 to present**

Participated in Scientific Supercomputing Workshop at UCB and familiar with using the supercomputers of Alliant FX-8 at Argonne National Laboratory, IBM 3090/600 series at University of California at Los Angeles, and Cray X-MP at Duke University.

Teaching Assistant: **January 1988 to present**

Taught college-level mathematics and basic computer skills.

COMPUTER SKILLS:

Languages:

- C++, Fortran, Pascal, and Basic

Operating Systems:

- UNIX, MS DOS, Alliant FX-8, IBM 370/3090, Cray X-MP, and VAX/VMS

Projects:

- Developed microprocessor-based system to measure heart rate and blood pressure.
- Designed and built a short wave radio.
- Successfully coordinated a method of producing a circuit board coplanar waveguide prototype.

INTERESTS:

- Enjoy photography, basketball, and softball.

References available upon request.

English Major

102 Stonegate Lane
Auburn, AL 36849

June 14, 1993

William T. Harrison
FNW - Los Angeles
460 West End Avenue
Los Angeles, CA 92265

Dear Mr. Harrison:

I am writing in response to your advertisement in the <u>Los Angeles Sun</u> for an Assistant Buyer. I am interested in pursuing a career as a buyer and believe that I could make a significant contribution to your organization.

I will be graduating in December from Huntingdon College in Alabama. My degree is in English, but I have also taken other courses to prepare me for the business world including Accounting, Finance, and Management. In addition, I offer solid work experience, having worked as an Assistant to the Financial Consultant and a Receptionist/Bookkeeper for busy, professional firms.

Enclosed is a copy of my resume. References will be forwarded upon request by the Student Resource Center at Huntingdon College.

I would greatly appreciate the opportunity to meet with you and discuss possible employment opportunities with your company. I may be reached at home at (205) 555-7771 or at school at (205) 555-3558.

Thank you for your time and consideration!

Sincerely,

Diane De Matto

Diane De Matto

Enclosure

English Major

DIANE DE MATTO

School Address:
36 Granite Street
Montgomery, AL 36103
(205) 555-3558

Permanent Address:
102 Stonegate Lane
Auburn, AL 36849
(205) 555-7771

Education
1989-present HUNTINGDON COLLEGE   MONTGOMERY, ALABAMA
Candidate for the degree of Bachelor of Arts in December
1993, majoring in English. Courses include Speech, Accounting, Finance, and Management. 3.1 GPA overall, 3.5 in major.
Dean's List honors.

Student Government representative. Volunteer tutor for underprivileged children.

Spring 1992 UNIVERSITY COLLEGE OF IRELAND   GALWAY, IRELAND
Studied courses in Irish literature, history, and culture.
3.2 GPA.

Experience
Summer 1992 LILLITH & McGRATH ASSOCIATES   MONTGOMERY, ALABAMA
Assistant to the Financial Consultant. Worked closely with
a vice-president researching various stocks, keeping detailed records, supervising and conducting business in her
absence, interacting with clients. Learned how to fundamentally analyze a company and to construct a balanced
portfolio.

Summer 1991 KENDALL & LAIRD, INC.   AUBURN, ALABAMA
Receptionist/Bookkeeper. Greeted clients, answered phone
inquiries and performed assorted office tasks in an architectural firm. Processed accounts payable and receivable,
and prepared deposits.

Summer 1990 SUNNYDAY CHILD CARE SERVICES   AUBURN, ALABAMA
Provided basic care, overnight, and weekly supervision for
groups of 10-20 preschool children. Instituted and taught
art classes; organized art show for parents and relatives
of children.

Interests Travel, skiing, painting, and photography.

References Available upon request: Student Resource Center, Huntingdon
College, Montgomery, AL 36106.

English Literature Major

1312 Liberty Street
Lowell, Massachusetts 02145

June 29, 1993

Ms. Deidra Lovering
President
Lovering Publications, Inc.
793 Desmoines Road
Quincy, Massachusetts 02158

Dear Ms. Lovering:

This letter is in response to your Boston Sunday Globe advertisement of June 27 for the position of administrative assistant.

I am a recent graduate of Brown University and am seeking an entry-level opportunity in the publishing industry. I believe that my skills and experience qualify me for the advertised position.

This past summer, I worked as an Editorial Assistant for The Bostonian Journal, a small monthly publication. While at The Bostonian, I not only gained excellent editorial experience, confirming my interest in the field, but performed all of the duties mentioned in your advertisement: writing business correspondence, filing, answering telephones, and word processing.

I also have significant writing and copy-editing experience, having worked for almost three years on The Brown U. Newspaper, where I originally started as a Copy Editor, was promoted to Associate Editor, and then was selected for the much-coveted position of Editor-in-Chief.

My resume is enclosed. I would value the opportunity to meet with you to further discuss my qualifications. If you wish to contact me to arrange an interview, I may be reached at (617) 555-5208 during business hours. I look forward to hearing from you soon.

Sincerely,

Janet Dubois

Janet Dubois

enc.

English Literature Major

Janet Dubois
1312 Liberty Street
Lowell, MA 01854
(617) 555-5208

EDUCATION Brown University, Providence, RI.
Bachelor of Arts degree received May 1993
Major: English Literature GPA: 3.10

<u>Internship</u>, Boston Literacy Program, Boston, MA.
Assisted in reading program, teaching illiterate children
and adults reading skills.

EXPERIENCE <u>Editorial Assistant</u>, The Bostonian Journal
June 1993-August 1993
Edited articles, features, and illustrations for monthly
publication.

<u>Editor-in-Chief</u>, Brown U. Newspaper
September 1992-May 1993
Selected submissions, edited and wrote headlines for submissions and columns, laid out page, dealt with public,
recruited columnists, trained associates.

<u>Associate Editor</u>, Brown U. Newspaper
January 1991-May 1992
Trained for Editor-in-Chief position; assisted in selecting
submissions, edited and wrote headlines for submissions and
columns, laid out pages, miscellaneous other tasks.

<u>Copy Editor</u>, Brown U. Newspaper
January 1990-December 1990
Edited news stories, wrote headlines, assisted with layout
of page, occasionally solicited advertising and helped with
distribution.

COMPUTER SKILLS <u>Word Processing</u> - Working knowledge of WordPerfect and Microsoft Word.
<u>Spreadsheets</u> - Familiar with all aspects of creating and
using a spreadsheet using Lotus 1-2-3.

ACTIVITIES Senior Class Secretary, Dean's List.

Finance Major

65 Cortland Avenue
Honolulu, HI 98604
(808) 555-3280

October 15, 1992

Stephanie Malone
Human Resources Director
Bank of Hawaii
32 Island Avenue
Honolulu, HI 96855

Dear Ms. Malone:

I would like to explore the possibility of joining your organization at the entry level, perhaps in your Financial Management Division. I believe that my Finance major and my recent work experience qualify me for such a position. I have enclosed my resume for your consideration.

I am seeking a position which will capitalize upon and further develop the skills I previously developed as a Sales Analyst for Tecchi Corporation, a Financial Accounting Assistant for Redden & Mitchell, an Investigator for First Hawaiian Bank, and a Statistical Analyst for Chaminade University. These jobs, particularly my position at the First Hawaiian Bank, confirmed my interest in the field of finance and in the banking industry. Also, I have extensive computer experience and knowledge of spreadsheet and statistical programs which I am confident will assist me throughout my banking career.

I am particularly interested in working for the Bank of Hawaii because of its long-standing reputation as a solid and trustworthy institution. I have been a customer of your bank all of my life and found your services to be excellent. I would consider it a great opportunity to contribute to the future success of such a fine institution.

I would like to interview with you at your convenience. I will be calling you the week of October 25 to make sure that you received my resume. Perhaps we could schedule an interview at this time? In the meantime, thank you for your consideration of my qualifications.

Sincerely,

Arthur H. Goldman

Arthur H. Goldman

enc.

Finance Major

ARTHUR H. GOLDMAN

65 Cortland Avenue
Honolulu, Hawaii 96804
(808) 555-3280

Education: **Chaminade University Of Honolulu** in Honolulu, Hawaii
Bachelor of Science degree in Finance.
Concentration: Investment Management
Date of graduation: May, 1992. GPA: 3.4
Dean's List, Who's Who Among College Students.

Relevant Courses

Business Law	Entrepreneurship
Ethics in Business	Financial Accounting
International Economics	Macro & Microeconomics
Managerial Accounting	Statistics
Money & Credit	Calculus

Activities: Chairman of Finance Club. Freshman Orientation Counselor. Treasurer of Phi Gammu Nu Fraternity.

Experience: **Sales Analyst.** *Tecci Corporation,* Honolulu, HI. Summer 1991.
Prepared sales budgets and controlled inventory using Lotus 1-2-3. Interacted with Sales staff.

Financial Accounting Assistant. *Redden & Mitchell,* Honolulu, HI. Summers 1989-1990.
Worked closely with a vice-president researching various stocks, keeping detailed records, supervising and conducting business in his absence, interacting with clients. Learned how to fundamentally analyze a company and to construct a balanced portfolio.

Investigator. *First Hawaiian Bank,* Honolulu, HI. Summer 1988.
Evaluated branch operations, appraised the performance of bank tellers and customer service representatives. Input and analyzed data using SASSE.

Statistical Analyst. Chaminade University, Honolulu, HI. Part-time from January 1989 to April 1992.
Assisted Biochemistry professor analyze data for large-scale research project on the cell-regeneration capabilities of Brine shrimp using SPSSX.

Skills and Abilities: Proficient in the use of Lotus 1-2-3, Microsoft Excel, SASSE, and SPSSX. Excellent communication and interpersonal skills.

Personal: Single, in good health. Willing to travel and/or relocate.

References: Personal references available upon request.

Food Science Major

605 Ellis Avenue
Lindsborg, Kansas 67488
(913) 555-6501

October 4, 1992

Mr. Bruce Jeffries
College Relations Representative
Sky Chefs
PO Box 9901
Dallas, Texas 75102

Dear Mr. Jeffries:

I am writing and enclosing my resume to apprise you of my interest in working for your airline catering service.

I will receive my B.S. degree in Food Science from Bethel College in January. In addition to studying such valuable courses as Chemical Science, Organic Chemistry, Nutrition, and Food Service Administration, I learned a great deal about the food industry as an active member of the Student Association for Agricultural Science students. Additionally, I offer solid experience in the food industry by working as an Assistant Manager for two summers at a local yogurt shop.

I would be very interested in securing an entry-level position with Sky Chefs. If you feel that my qualifications might meet your needs, please contact me at (913) 555-5664. Otherwise, a message may be left at my above listed phone number.

Thank you for your attention to this matter and I look forward to your response.

Sincerely,

Brandon J Hurley

Brandon J. Hurley

enc.

Food Science Major

BRANDON J. HURLEY

605 Ellis Avenue
Lindsborg, Kansas 67488
(913) 555-6501

education
1988-1992   BETHEL COLLEGE   NORTH NEWTON, KANSAS
Candidate for the degree of Bachelor of Sciences in January 1992, majoring in Food Science. Courses include Chemical Science, Organic Chemistry, Nutrition, and Food Service Administration. Thesis topic: "Advances in Refrigeration Techniques and their Applications to the Fresh Meats Industry".

Member of the Student Association for Agricultural Sciences Students. Exhibitor and prize-winner in local exhibitions of modern sculpture.

experience
summers
1991-1992   YOGURT NIRVANA   NORTH NEWTON, KANSAS
Assistant Manager of local shop. Increased sales by offering student discounts and launching a direct mail advertising campaign.

summer 1990   JAKE'S PLACE   BALDWIN CITY, KANSAS
Bartender in local restaurant and pub.

summer 1989   NADINE'S DEPARTMENT STORE   LINDSBORG, KANSAS
Retail Sales Associate. Identified customer needs and tracked sales. Hourly sales exceeded hourly quota. Sales 19% above department average.

part-time
1989-1992   BETHEL COLLEGE   NORTH NEWTON, KANSAS
Student Government Representative. Planned various events such as Student Senate Elections, Senate Leadership Retreat, and Student Budget Meetings; planned and ran three successful political campaigns. Moved from Student Senator to Student Senate Speaker.

interests   Modern sculpture, pottery, playing guitar.

references   Available upon request.

Geography Major

23 Lamar Street
Charlotte, NC 27601

February 21, 1993

Ms. Sandra Hall
Travel World, Inc.
23 Syracuse Street
Suite C
Charlotte, NC 27602

Dear Ms. Hall:

I was recently speaking with Dan Johnson of Tri-Travel Corporation about opportunities in the travel industry, and he recommended that I contact you. I am interested in pursuing a career in the tourism industry and would like to be considered for an entry-level position at your company.

Currently a senior at Duke University, I will be graduating this June with a Bachelor's degree in Geography and International Studies. Although my area of study will no doubt assist me in the tourism field, I have taken additional courses which may also prove useful, including Business Management, Introductory Accounting, Computer Science, and Spanish. My participation in the Raths Debate Club helped me to enhance my verbal skills and communicate more effectively, which I'm sure will also increase my effectiveness in the travel industry.

In addition to my strong educational background, I offer solid work experience. As an Administrative Assistant in a wholesale glass and framing supplies company, I gained experience in all aspects of customer service, including taking large numbers of phone orders and assisting customers with questions and problems. My duties also included data entry, typing business letters, filing, and other clerical tasks.

I can type 50 WPM and have experience using a number of word processing, spreadsheet, and database programs. I am fluent in Spanish.

I would be very grateful if you would consider me for any entry-level positions that you may have openings for. I am especially interested in working as a travel agent or promotional assistant. I may be reached at 704/555-8881 after 3:00 P.M. or a message can be left any time at 919/555-7891. Thank you.

Sincerely,

Margaret A. Reed.

Margaret A. Reed

enc.

Geography Major

MARGARET A. REED

School Address:
304 Wing Hall
Duke University
Durham, NC 27706
919/555-8881

Home Address:
23 Lamar Street
Charlotte, NC 27601
704/555-7891

Education:

1989-present DUKE UNIVERSITY   DURHAM, NORTH CAROLINA
Candidate for the degree of Bachelor of Arts in June 1993,
majoring in Geography and minoring in International Studies. Courses include Business Management, Introductory
Accounting, Computer Science and Spanish.

Member of Raths Debate Club. Play second chair flute for
the Duke University Band. Performed in annual Christmas con-
cert to benefit the homeless.

1988-1989 ATLANTIC CHRISTIAN COLLEGE   WILSON, NORTH CAROLINA
Studied Physical Therapy and related health sciences fields
for three semesters.

Experience:

summer 1992 MONARCH GLASS COMPANY   CHARLOTTE, NORTH CAROLINA
Administrative Assistant to the President. Took phone orders, assisted customers with questions and problems, data
entry, some written correspondence, filing, and general
clerical. Restructured and reorganized entire database system to increase efficiency.

summers
1989-1991 THE CAJUN QUEEN   CHARLOTTE, NORTH CAROLINA
Hostess for popular local restaurant. Was promoted from busperson.

part-time
1990-present BI-LO CORPORATION   DURHAM, NORTH CAROLINA
Cashier and Inventory clerk for busy supermarket. Won employee of the month award on two separate occasions.

Skills: Typing: 50 WPM. Familiar with Microsoft Word, MacWrite, Lotus, and rBase. Fluent in Spanish.

Interests: Enjoy playing the flute, writing music, jogging, and speed
walking for competition.

References: Available upon request.

German/Italian Language Major

455 Michigan Avenue
Apartment #308
New York, New York 10022

February 3, 1993

Mr. Howard Ulrich
Lerocher Imports, Inc.
4312 4th Street
Building C
New York, New York 10010

Dear Mr. Ulrich:

In response to your advertisement in the February 1 edition of The New York Times for an International Purchasing Agent, I would like to submit my resume for consideration.

As you can see, my qualifications match those you are looking for:

Your requirements:	I offer:
A college graduate	A Bachelor's degree from Long Island University
Fluency in Italian and French	Fluent in Italian, German, and French
Office experience	Experience as a receptionist at a busy accounting firm
Typing skills	Type 40 WPM
Willingness to travel	Willing to travel regularly, if necessary

I feel that I am well qualified for this position and can really make a difference at your company. My salary requirements are reasonable.

I would welcome the opportunity for a personal interview with you at your convenience. I may be reached at 212/555-1121 during regular business hours.

Sincerely,

Marcie Dejeuner

Marcie Dejeuner

enc.

German/Italian Language Major

Marcie Dejeuner

455 Michigan Avenue
Apartment #308
New York, NY 10022
212/555-1121

education
1988-1992 **LONG ISLAND UNIVERSITY**   **NEW YORK, NEW YORK**
Awarded a Bachelor of Arts degree in December of 1992, with a dual major in Italian and German. Courses included Marketing, Economics, Statistics, Business Administration, and Foreign Business Law.

President of the Foreign Language Committee. Responsible for $2,000/semester budget. Organized and directed club participation in LIU Career Day. Wrote copy for club brochures.

internship
summer 1991 **MILAN UNIVERSITY**   **MILAN, ITALY**
Studied Italian language and society. Thesis topic: The Role of Dialect in Italian Social Structure.

experience
1987-present **MANHATTAN FIGURE SKATING ASSOCIATION**   **NEW YORK**
Taught basic and advanced figure skating to children and adults. One of my students went on to compete in the Figure Skating Nationals. Summers 1987-1992 and part-time during every school year.

summer 1986 **RYAN & SMITH CORPORATION**   **NEW YORK, NEW YORK**
Receptionist for busy accounting firm. Duties included handling and appropriating telephone calls, sorting mail, and filing.

part-time
1989-1992 **LONG ISLAND UNIVERSITY BOOKSTORE**   **NEW YORK**
Sales clerk in clothing department. Also worked as inventory clerk and cashier when needed.

personal
background Enjoy reading, travelling, and competing in figure skating events. Won New York State Championships in 1987 and 1988.

skills and abilities Fluent in German, Italian, and French; typing 40 WPM; some computer experience.

references Personal references available upon request.

Government Major

107 Allston Way
Prairie View, Texas 77644
409/555-4401

February 4, 1993

Mr. Robert J. Strauss
Program Director
Big Brother Program
42 Fulton Street
Houston, Texas 76051

Dear Mr. Strauss:

Thank you for taking the time to speak with me on Wednesday. As I told you on the phone, I am interested in the position of Assistant Director which, you mentioned, should be opening up some time next month.

I graduated in December from Rice University with a Bachelor's degree in Government and a dual concentration in Psychology and Sociology. I was consistently on the Dean's list and my final grade point average was 3.54.

I have also had a good deal of work experience in human services, having worked as a Management Intern for the United Way. Here, I learned the many different aspects and responsibilities associated with management, including improving departmental efficiency, evaluating different charitable organizations, organizing fundraisers, and budgeting funds.

At the Boy's Club of Prairie View, I worked as a Youth Counselor for two consecutive summers. I was responsible for orienting youngsters and new supervisors to the program, placing youths in various programs based on their abilities and interests, organizing fun and educational events for the boys, and assisting in the preparation of a weekly newsletter.

It was during my time at the Boy's Club that I decided that I would like to pursue human service as a career. I especially find working with children very rewarding and would love the opportunity to contribute to the Big Brother program.

Could we schedule an interview? I can be reached at 409/555-7764 during late afternoon and evening hours. Thank you for your consideration!

Sincerely,

Michael Burke

Michael Burke

enclosure

Government Major

MICHAEL BURKE

107 Allston Way
Prairie View, Texas 77644
409/555-4401

Objective   An entry-level position in human/social services.

Education   Rice University, College of Arts and Sciences, Houston, Texas. Bachelor of Arts degree awarded with honors in December 1992. Major: Government; Concentrations: Psychology/- Sociology.
Dean's List; 3.54 grade point average.

Relevant Courses

U.S. Government	International Policy
Business Law	Sociology of Poverty
Ethics & Ethics in Public Life	Comparative Politics
The Politics of Economics	Public Speaking

Experience   **Management Intern** *United Way of Texas*, Houston, Texas.
Analyzed efficiency of various departments, recommended areas for improvement, visited and evaluated different charitiable organizations, organized fundraisers, assisted in preparing budgets for the new fiscal year. Collected, organized and evaluated data. Summer-Winter 1992.

Youth Counselor *Boy's Club of Prairie View*, Texas.
Responsible for orienting youngsters and supervisors in terms of the purpose and rules of the various programs, placing youths in various programs based on their abilities and interests, organizing fun and educational events for the youngsters, and assisting in the preparation of a weekly newsletter. Summers 1990-1991.

Paralegal Intern *Johnson & Wright*, Dallas, Texas.
Organized files, gathered information, met and received information from clients, researched case and client histories in a general practice law firm. Hired and trained other interns. Part-time 1990-1991.

Other Positions   Worked as a Lifeguard, Summer Camp Counselor, Machine Operator, Cashier, and Waiter. 1989-present.

Activities   Volunteer for VOTE AMERICA! campaign. Chairman for the Committee on Student Life, Intramural Athletic Chairman, and Member of Society for Distinguished Collegiate Americans.

References   Available upon request.

International Relations Major

156 Newton Heights
Salisbury, Maryland
301/555-9874

July 5, 1992

Ms. Marie Manette
Director
French-American Foreign Council
1127 Avenue of the Americas
New York, New York 10029

Dear Ms. Manette:

I am writing in hopes that you will consider me for the position of Translator as advertised in the today's Sunday New York Times.

I graduated last month with a B.A. in International Relations and French Language from George Washington University. Consistently on the Dean's List and graduating one year early with honors and Advanced Standing, I was recognized throughout my academic career for excellent scholarship.

I was very active in college, having participated in many extracurricular events and organizations, including a residential honors program studying Ethics and Politics. By my junior year, I had become a Model United Nations Advisor, an Alumni Ambassador, and President of the International Affairs Society. Last summer, I participated in a valuable and exciting summer program at the College of International Relations in Paris, called the International Studies Session.

I also have some work experience in the field of international affairs, having worked as an interpreter and translator for a Parisian film corporation. In this position, I interpreted for negotiations over film co-productions and translated agreements, film scripts, scenarios, and foreign correspondence. I also worked as the Assistant to the Parisian Correspondent for Deshabilles Associates, a prestigious import/export company. Here, my duties included translation of documents, interpretation of telephone and live communications, and general office duties.

I feel confident that an interview would demonstrate that my expertise in international affairs and French language and culture makes me well-qualified for this position. I am not limited by location and would enjoy the opportunity to live and work in New York City for the Foreign Council.

I look forward to meeting you, Ms. Manette, and will give you a call to follow up on this letter towards the end of next week.

Sincerely,

Lynne Ann Jordan

Lynne Ann Jordan

enc.

International Relations Major

LYNNE ANN JORDAN

156 Newton Heights
Salisbury, Maryland
301/555-9874

education
1989-1992 **GEORGE WASHINGTON UNIVERSITY** **WASHINGTON, D.C.**
Awarded the degree of Bachelor of Arts in June 1992, majoring in International Relations. Minor in French Language. Thesis concentration in International Law. Completed 4-year requirements in 3 years. Honors with Advanced Standing and Dean's List.

Participant in Ethics and Politics residential honors program. Model United Nations Adviser. President of International Affairs Society. Alumni Ambassador and Student Admissions Representative.

summer 1991 **COLLEGE OF INTERNATIONAL RELATIONS** **PARIS, FRANCE**
Participant in summer International Studies Session. Studied French, International Politics, Comparative Government, and History of the United Nations. Received Bilingual Proficiency Certification.

experience
summer 1990 **FRENCH FILM PRODUCTION CORPORATION** **PARIS, FRANCE**
Interpreted for negotiations over film co-productions, translated agreements, film scripts, scenarios, and foreign correspondence.

part-time 1992 **DESHABILLES ASSOCIATES** **WASHINGTON, D.C.**
Worked as an Assistant to Parisian Correspondent. Duties included translation of documents, interpretation for telephone and live communications, and general clerical.

part-time
1990-1991 Worked in unrelated jobs to pay for college tuition. Positions included: Sales Clerk, Bank Teller, Temporary Worker, Teaching Aide, and Research Assistant.

personal
interests Enjoy modern French literature and film, photography, and racquetball.

references Available upon request.

Linguistics Major

8 Oakland Drive
Bluffton, Ohio 45817
419/555-4990

August 27, 1993

Mr. Howard J. Hizer
Tropical Travels, Inc.
332 Franklin Avenue
Cleveland, Ohio 44115

Dear Mr. Hizer:

I am very interested in obtaining a position with your travel organization. Please find enclosed my resume for your review.

You will find most of the necessary information about my educational and employment background in my resume. However, I would like to point out that I am eager to begin a career in the tourism field and am willing to relocate, if necessary.

I graduated in May from Bowling Green State University with a Bachelor of Arts degree in Linguistics. In addition to studying such subjects as Effective Communication and Speech and Debate, I was exposed to a variety of liberal arts courses such as English Composition, Geography, History, and Computer Science, all of which I am confident will help me in my professional career. I have customer service and telephone sales experience, which has given me better insight into and appreciation of service industries.

I would like to schedule a personal interview wherein we can discuss my qualifications for a position with your organization. I may be reached at the address and telephone number listed above.

Thank you for your time; I look forward to hearing from you.

Regards,

Joseph C. Brady

Joseph C. Brady

enc.

Linguistics Major

Joseph Christopher Brady

8 Oakland Drive
Bluffton, Ohio 45817
419/555-4990

OBJECTIVE   A challenging position in the field of tourism.

EDUCATION
1989-1993   **BOWLING GREEN STATE UNIVERSITY   BOWLING GREEN, OHIO**
Bachelor of Arts Degree in Linguistics awarded in May 1993. Courses include Effective Communication, Speech and Debate, English Composition, Geography, History, and Computer Science. 3.8 grade point average.

Member of the Drama Club. Acted and sang in on-campus productions. Member in a creative writer's group. One short story published in The Oracle, a campus literary publication. Member of the Burnt Coffee Comedy Club.

EXPERIENCE
summers
1991-1992   **SEARS CORPORATION   HURON, OHIO**
Customer Service Representative. Responsibilities included taking catalog orders, processing charge card payments, issuing refunds, and general problem solving. Awarded "Employee of the Month" award.

summer 1990   **FUTURE PRODUCTS COMPANY   BLUFFTON, OHIO**
Telephone Sales Representative. Made an average of 200 calls per work day, promoting product lines and taking orders. Also sent out mailings and other general clerical. Represented company at various trade shows.

part-time
1990-1992   **BLISS ICE CREAM PARLOR   BOWLING GREEN, OHIO**
Ice Cream Scooper and Cashier. Created idea for "Around the World Ice Cream Flavors" campaign, which inspired a local contest and generated significant media attention.

1990-1991   **BEST BARGAINS DISTRIBUTORS, INC.   HURON, OHIO**
Jewelry Salesclerk and Cash Depositor. Assisted manager in jewelry department by selling and repairing jewelry. Collected daily cash intake from all departments and made appropriate cash deposits for the store. Updated computer inventory system.

INTERESTS   Volleyball, skiing, photography, and travel.

PERSONAL AND PROFESSIONAL REFERENCES AVAILABLE UPON REQUEST

Management Major

1334 23rd Street, #104
New York, New York 10022
212/555-5512

September 23, 1992

Ms. Christine Leroux
Personnel Director
Leger Enterprises
122 Fourth Street, Suite 3
New York, NY 10003

Dear Ms. Leroux:

Are you currently seeking an entry-level management trainee for your company? If so, I would like to apply for the position. I am interested in pursuing a career at Leger Enterprises, where I feel I can make a valuable contribution.

I recently graduated from New York University, where I majored in Management and studied related subjects including Statistics and Economics. As a student member of the American Management Association, I gained additional practical knowledge of the field.

I also offer a great deal of work experience, having worked as an Executive Assistant for the President and Senior Vice President of a large business consulting firm. I have additional administrative experience, as I spent two summers working as an Administrative Assistant for a New York management corporation and a fast-paced investment firm. These jobs have given me valuable insight into the corporate world and have strengthened my interest in the management field.

I have enclosed my resume for your perusal. Please feel free to call me to discuss any questions that you may have. I look forward to our meeting.

Sincerely,

Frank Hamilburg

Frank Hamilburg

enc.

Management Major

Frank Hamilburg
1334 23rd St., #104
New York, NY 10022
212/555-5512

EDUCATION

New York University, Manhattan
Bachelor of Science degree awarded in June 1992, majoring in Management. Courses include Physics, Biochemistry, Economics and Statistics. 3.4 grade point average in major. Honors: Dean's List.

Student member of the American Management Association. Props assistant for College Theatre. Co-captain of Intramural Volleyball Team. Actively involved in Students Against Drunk Driving.

EXPERIENCE

Executive Assistant - John D. MacDougall, Inc., 55 East 10th St., New York NY (Summer 1991)
- Responsible for providing extensive and highly confidential administrative assistance and support to the President and Senior Vice President
- Heavy involvement with the Young Executive Program; reviewed personnel reports for content, personal and professional objectives, kept records of job performance over time, and made recommendations of salary adjustments based on overall rating
- Acted as the on-site computer resource with respect to the explanation and solving of all company computing problems
- Coordinated company social functions and very large semi-annual company meetings

Administrative Assistant/Coordinator - Tecchi Management Corporation, 833 Fifth Avenue, New York NY (Summer 1990)
- Assistant to the President and the Accounting Manager
- Responsible for the orientation of new employees on all company benefits policies, and procedures
- Extensive communication with high level staff and outside agencies
- Performed customer service functions, including the resolving of all consumer and agency complaints and problems

Administrative Assistant - Avenue Investments, 1323 Avenue of the Americas, New York NY (Summer 1989)
- Extensive typing and filing
- Generated charts and data
- Operated switchboard
- Responsible for the travel arrangements of 10 company executives, including scheduling, coordination, and budgeting

COMPUTER SKILLS

- Working knowledge of WordPerfect and dBase programs

Management Information Systems (MIS) Major

12 Shady Lane
Brattleboro, Vermont 05211

July 17, 1993

Mr. Wayne Peterson
President
HBR Systems, Inc.
Science Park Road
Los Angeles, California 90045

Dear Mr. Peterson:

Recently I completed the requirements for my BS degree in Management Information Systems at Adams State College. I am writing to you now because I am interested in a career at HBR Systems, Inc.

I believe that my intensive study of MIS during the past four years and my vast knowledge of computers and computer software, along with my previous professional experience in MIS and other business areas would make me a valuable Systems Analyst at HBR Systems.

I have enclosed my resume and would welcome the opportunity to speak with the appropriate person about current or anticipated openings at your company.

Thank you for your attention to this matter.

Sincerely,

Gigi D. Russell

Gigi D. Russell
802/555-8315

enc.

Management Information Systems (MIS) Major

GIGI D. RUSSELL
12 Shady Lane
Brattleboro, Vermont 05211
802/555-8315

Education
1989-1993   ADAMS STATE COLLEGE   ALAMOSA, COLORADO
Awarded the degree of Bachelor of Science in May 1993, ma-
joring in Management Information Systems. Courses include
Programming in Pascal, Programming in COBOL, Programming in
FORTRAN, and Computer Engineering. 3.2 grade point average.

Member of the Beta Kappa Gamma Honor Society. Member of Tri
Delta sorority. Helped to organize the First Annual Adams
State Computer Symposium.

Experience
Summer 1992   D. MCGILL & ASSOCIATES   ALAMOSA, COLORADO
Data Entry Clerk for busy accounting firm. Also maintained
correspondence with key accounts. Found major accounting
error that saved one account over $50,000.

Summer 1991   INCO SYSTEMS, INC.   DENVER, COLORADO
Intern, Management Information Systems (MIS). Audited PC
software with an emphasis for viruses. Troubleshooted and
logged customer problems and dispatched appropriate technical support. Maintained tape library (for IBM 9370 and
System/36) by initializing scratch tapes, rotating
tapes/cassettes, and running various tape management utilities (CA-DYNAM/T).

Summer 1990   UNITED DELL CORPORATION   LAKEWOOD, COLORADO
Assistant to the Finance Officer. Responsible for the
monthly analyses of cash disbursements, accounts payable,
petty cash, bank reconciliations, and expense reports.
Aided in the preparation of the monthly budget report using
Symphony. Entered journal entries into the general ledger
and produced financial statements using Platinum software
package.

Skills   Working knowledge of BASIC, Microsoft Windows, dBase III
Plus, dBase IV, WordPerfect, Lotus 1-2-3, Microsoft Excel,
MS-DOS, Nastec DesignAid Case 2000, RAMIS II MARVEL.
Experience with UNIX/C, Turbo Pascal, COBOL, Intel 8086 As-
sembly Language, INTELESYS.
Exposure to VSE/SP, VSE/POWER, CICS/VS, JCL, CA-TOP SECRET.

References   Transcript and references available upon request.

Marketing Major

81 Sandypine Road
Joppa, Maryland 20707
(301) 555-1551

March 22, 1993

Mr. Henry Stanhope
Personnel Manager
Lisa Fleischman Associates
2125 Wisconsin Avenue NW
Suite 202
Washington, DC 25507

Dear Mr. Stanhope:

I am writing in response to your advertisement in the *Washington Press* for the position of Advertising Assistant. Enclosed is my resume for your review and consideration.

I am a recent graduate of Colgate University with a Bachelor of Science degree in Marketing. Throughout my education, I have developed excellent research, communication, editing, and interpersonal skills. I have gained experience in various marketing capacities (e.g., advertising, direct marketing and market research) by completing a student-team project for Bagel Bakery, Inc. I have also had exposure to international marketing through a summer program in Moscow which concentrated on Russian culture and the Soviet political and economic system.

Two summers of experience working in sales have given me the opportunity to employ my marketing knowledge while displaying initiative and responsibility. My ambitious attitude helped me win several employee incentive contests at The Limited. In both positions, I utilized my marketing background to make recommendations that improved employee efficiency and increased sales.

I believe that my skills and experience would be an asset to your advertising firm and I would appreciate the opportunity to discuss the Advertising Assistant position with you. I may be reached at the above listed phone number between 9 AM and 5 PM for an interview at your convenience. Thank you for your consideration.

Sincerely,

Rosemary L. Brandenburg

Rosemary L. Brandenburg

Enc.

Marketing Major

Rosemary L. Brandenburg

81 Sandypine Road
Joppa, MD 20707
(301) 555-1551

OBJECTIVE An entry-level position in the advertising industry.

EDUCATION Colgate University, Hamilton, New York. Bachelor of Science degree in Marketing to be completed in May 1993. Courses include International Marketing, Marketing Research, Business Communications, and Statistics and Computer Programming. 3.2/4.0 grade point average.

Secretary of the Marketing Club. Member of Beta Gamma Sigma Honor Society for Business Administration Students. Member Women's Rugby Team.

RELATED EXPERIENCE *Direct Marketing Association's Collegiate ECHO Competition*, Hamilton, NY
Fall Semester 1992.
Participated on student team project to create direct marketing campaign for Bagel Bakery, Inc. Gained practical experience in developing marketing report.

Colgate in Moscow
Summer 1992.
Comprehensive study of Russian culture and thorough analysis of the Soviet political and economic system.

WORK EXPERIENCE *The Limited*, Laurel, MD
Summer 1991.
Sales associate. Acquired retail sales experience and developed personal selling skills through excellent customer relations. Two-time winner of employee sales contests.

Janice's Boutique, Joppa, MD
Summer 1990.
Sales associate. Assisted in layout of store merchandise, stocking and quality control of inventory and operated cash register. Evaluated and presented recommendations for changes in store displays

SPECIAL SKILLS *Typing:* 50 WPM.
Word Processing: 65 WPM.
Computer: Wordperfect 5.1, dBase III, Lotus 1-2-3, and Harvard Graphics.

PERSONAL BACKGROUND Enjoy rugby, horseback riding, reading fiction, and playing chess

REFERENCES Available upon request.

Mathematics Major

1015 Commonwealth Avenue
Apartment 16
Boston, MA 02145

February 15, 1993

Mr. Clark T. Johnson
Vice-President/Human Resources
Boston City Bank Corporation
110 Milk Street
Boston, MA 02114

Dear Mr. Johnson:

Having majored in Mathematics at Boston University, where I also worked as a Research Assistant, I am confident that I would make a very successful Research Trainee in your Economics Research Department.

In addition to my strong background in mathematics, I also offer significant business experience, having worked in a data processing firm, a bookstore, and a restaurant. I am sure that my courses in statistics and computer programming would prove particularly useful in the position of Research Trainee.

I am attracted to City Bank by your recent rapid growth and the superior reputation of your Economic Research Department. After studying different commercial banks, I have concluded that City Bank will be in a strong competitive position to benefit from upcoming changes in the industry, such as the phasing out of Regulation Q.

I would like to interview with you at your earliest convenience. I am best reached between 3 and 5 p.m. at 555-1483.

Sincerely yours,

Steven M. Phillips

Steven M. Phillips

Enc. Resume

Mathematics Major

STEVEN M. PHILLIPS

School Address: Permanent Address:
1015 Commonwealth Avenue   507 North 6th Street
Apartment 16   Houston, TX 77024
Boston, Massachusetts 02145   Phone: 713/555-2341
Phone: 617/555-1483

education
1989-1993   **BOSTON UNIVERSITY**   **BOSTON, MASSACHUSETTS**
Candidate for the degree of Bachelor of Arts in June 1993, majoring in Mathematics.
Courses include Statistics and Computer Programming. Thesis topic: "New Applications
of Co-Linear Coordinates." 3.4 grade point average. Awarded the Elliot Smith Scholarship
in 1991.

Treasurer of the Mathematics Club. Responsible for 7,000.00 annual budget. Co-chair-
person of Boston University's semi-annual symposium on The Future of Mathematics.
Exhibitor and prize-winner at local photography shows. Helped to establish university
darkroom.

1985-1989   **HOUSTON PUBLIC HIGH SCHOOL**   **HOUSTON, TEXAS**
Received High School Diploma in June 1989. Achieved Advance Placement Standing
in Calculus and Physics. Academic Honors all terms. Assistant Editor of Year-Book.

experience
summer 1992   **DATA PUNCH ASSOCIATES, INC.**   **NEW YORK, NEW YORK**
Mail Clerk and Courier for the Accounting Department. Reorganized mail distribution and
sorting system in the department. Delivered sensitive documents to the executive branch.

summers 1990,
1991   **HARVEY'S BEEFBURGERS, INC.**   **HOUSTON, TEXAS**
Began work as a dishwasher. Was promoted to short-order cook.

part-time   **BOSTON UNIVERSITY**   **BOSTON, MASSACHUSETTS**
One of six students invited to tutor for The Department of Mathematics. Also graded
student papers and worked as a Research Assistant in Theoretical Calculus.

part-time
1989-1990   **BOSTON UNIVERSITY BOOKSTORE**   **BOSTON, MASSACHUSETTS**
Floor and Stockroom Clerk. Responsibilities included arranging merchandise displays,
customer service and checking invoices against shipments.

personal
background   Enjoy photography, reading science fiction, and playing bridge. Published two articles
in mathematics journals.

references   Personal references available upon request.

Mechanical Engineering Major

4 Squirrel Drive
Sarasota, FL 34234

November 2, 1992

Ms. Loretta Wexler
Recruiting and Placement
Ford Motor Company
2000 Rotunda Drive
Dearborn, MI 48121

Dear Ms. Wexler:

Thank you for taking time out of your schedule to speak with me on the telephone today. As we discussed, I am interested in an entry-level position in your Powertrain Engineering division.

I graduated in June from the University of North Carolina with an Associates degree in Engineering. Although my studies concentrated on Mechanical Power Engineering, I also took related courses in electrical and ergonomics engineering, as well as advanced classes in mathematics, physics, and chemistry. In May of this year, I was honored with the Newton Award for Engineers for my research on magnetic fields.

In addition to my degree, I also offer solid work experience in the engineering field. Last summer, I interned for the Power Generation Service Division of a local electric plant where I assisted in the overhaul, maintenance and repair of large generators and auxiliary equipment. In the summer of 1990, I interned for the Production Division of J.R. Coleman Company, where I assisted in the redesign of conveyors and elevators. Here, I conducted a study for which the results were used to increase manufacturing efficiency by 33%, without sacrificing product quality. Additionally, I have worked part-time over the past two years for a nuclear service company, where I not only designed and tested tools used in nuclear power plants, but developed processes for using the tools that were designed.

I have a working knowledge of VERSACAD and can program in Basic, Pascal, and Fortran. I possess an inquisitive, analytical mind and love a challenge. Ford Car Product Development interests me because of its innovative and exciting working atmosphere. I believe that I can contribute to its future success.

Enclosed is a copy of my resume. Please consider me for any appropriate job opportunities that may arise. Thank you.

Sincerely,

Daniel R. Pappas

Daniel R. Pappas

enc.

Mechanical Engineering Major

DANIEL R. PAPPAS

School Address: Permanent Address:
121 University Terrace, Room 402   4 Squirrel Drive
University of North Carolina   Sarasota, FL 34234
Chapel Hill, NC 27510   Phone: 813/555-2955
Phone: 919/555-5581

education

1990-1992 UNIVERSITY OF NORTH CAROLINA   CHAPEL HILL, NORTH CAROLINA
Awarded an Associates degree of Engineering in June 1992, concentrating in Mechanical Power Engineering Technology. Winner of the Newton Award for Engineers for research in magnetic fields in 1992.

Member of University Engineering Association. Member of cross-country track team.

1986-1990 MEMORIAL HIGH SCHOOL   SARASOTA, FLORIDA
Awarded High School Diploma in 1990. Achieved Advance Placement Standing in Calculus and Physics. High Honor roll. Varsity member of spring, winter, and cross-country track.

experience

summer 1991 QUEEN CITY ELECTRIC   SARASOTA, FLORIDA
Intern for the Power Generation Service Division. Assisted in the overhaul, maintenance and repair of large generators and auxiliary equipment. Analyzed energy conservation projects for the maximization of energy management system and for interior lighting reduction.

summer 1990 J.R. COLEMAN COMPANY   MEMPHIS, TENNESSEE
Intern for Production Division. Assisted in redesign of conveyors and elevators. Conducted study to reduce manufacturing labor while maintaining product quality. Modified and improved existing system using resulting data; increased group efficiency as measured by time and quantity parameters by 33%.

part-time

1990-1992 R & W NUCLEAR SERVICE COMPANY   CONCORD, NORTH CAROLINA
Designed and tested tools used in nuclear power plants. Developed processes for using tools designed. Conducted computer training sessions for engineers using Computer Aided Design.

skills and
abilities Working knowledge of Computer Aided Design (VERSACAD). Programming in GW Basic, Pascal, and Fortran.

references Personal references available upon request.

Philosophy/World History Major

42 North Main Street
Cleveland, OH 44211
(916) 555-1484
April 7, 1993

Ms. Julie Stevenport
Human Resource Manager
Liberty Life Insurance of Maryland
1144 Independence Street
Washington, DC 11243

Dear Julie:

Having spoken to you earlier this week regarding your current opening for an underwriter, I am submitting my resume for your perusal. I am very interested in securing this position within your organization.

I will be graduating this May from Georgetown University with a dual major in Philosophy and World History. I have also studied Calculus and Advanced Mathematics, Statistics, Business Management, and Computer Science, which I am sure will be very useful to me as an underwriter. I also have experience in the insurance industry, having spent last summer working as a Customer Service Representative for Allstate Insurance Company, where I won the Employee of the Month Award.

Recently I read about the expansion of your company in the Baltimore Sun. As the insurance industry is of great interest to me, I was excited to learn of the new developments within Liberty Life. I would consider it to be a great career opportunity to be associated with your dynamic organization.

I look forward to hearing from you in the near future to schedule an interview at your convenience, during which I hope to learn more about the underwriting position and how I might contribute to the success of your operations.

Sincerely,

James A. Murray

James A. Murray

enc.

Philosophy/World History Major

JAMES A. MURRAY

Current Address
P.O. Box 24
Georgetown University
Washington, D.C. 20005
(202) 555-8879

Permanent Address
42 North Main Street
Cleveland, OH 44211
(916) 555-1484

Objective   An entry-level position in the insurance industry.

Education   **Georgetown University**, College of Arts and Sciences.
Expected date of graduation: May 1993.
Dual major in Philosophy and World History.
Relevant courses: Calculus and Advanced Mathematics, Statistics, Business Management and Computer Science.

President of the Philosophy club. Member of the Debate Team. Vice-President of the Senior Class Council.

Experience   **Customer Service Representative** - Allstate Insurance Co.
Cleveland, Ohio. Summer 1992.
- Involved in all aspects of customer-service including answering questions, problem solving, interfacing with sales force.
- Won Employee of the Month Award

Cashier/Floor Clerk - JR's Wholesale Club
Cleveland, Ohio. Summers 1990 and 1991.
- Responsible for replenishing floor stock, rearranging floor displays, and operating cash register.
- Offered position in Management Training Program.

Sales Clerk - Athlete's Foot Shoestore
Washington D.C. Part-time 1991-1993.
- Responsible for tabulating inventory and merchandise lists.
- Trained new employees.
- Maintained excellent record of quality customer service.

Skills and Abilities   Working knowledge of MacWrite II, MacPaint, WordPerfect, and Lotus 1-2-3. Programming in GW Basic.

Interests   Enjoy jogging, cross-country skiing, and gardening. Participate regularly in charitable events such as Washington Walk for Hunger, Run for Life, etc.

References   Available upon request.

Physics Major

332 Oakland Drive
Lake Charles, LA 70610
(318) 555-5557

March 16, 1993

Ms. Lisa Stanhope
Professional Recruiter
Eastman Kodak Company
121 Technology Drive
Rochester, NY 14650

Dear Ms. Stanhope:

Perhaps you are seeking an addition to your excellent team of physicists. A new person can provide innovative approaches and ideas to the challenges of research and development.

As you can see from my resume, I will be graduating in June from Loyola University with a Bachelor's degree in Physics. I also studied such related fields as chemical engineering, mathematics, and systems applications, all of which I am sure will help me in as a physicist with Eastman Kodak. I offer solid experience, having worked for two summers for the Physics Department at Loyola both as an intern and as a laboratory technician.

Additionally, I have a personal interest in photography, having been an avid amateur photographer for many years. I built my own dark room and have won several awards for my photographs. Because of this, I feel that Eastman Kodak is an especially good match for my skills and interests.

Please advise me of any positions that may become available. Your consideration of my credentials is greatly appreciated.

Sincerely,

Donald R. Sutherland

Donald R. Sutherland

DS
enclosure

Physics Major

DONALD R. SUTHERLAND

Loyola University   332 Oakland Drive
Stone Hall   Lake Charles, LA 70610
New Orleans, LA 70114   (318) 555-5557
(504) 555-9951

EDUCATION

1989 - Present LOYOLA UNIVERSITY   New Orleans, Louisiana
Candidate for the degree of Bachelor of Science in June
1993, majoring in Physics. Additional areas of study include
Chemical Engineering, Mathematics, and Systems Applications. 3.42 grade point average.

Golden Key Honor Society. Cycling Team. Varsity Wrestling.
Helped establish Council on Racial Relations for New Orleans
campus.

WORK EXPERIENCE

Summer 1992 LABORATORY TECHNICIAN   New Orleans, Louisiana
PHYSICS DEPARTMENT, LOYOLA UNIVERSITY
Designed and constructed signal filters and power amplifi-
ers for research on bird behavioral patterns. Tested and
modified equipment after preliminary use.

Summer 1991 PHYSICS INTERN   New Orleans, Louisiana
PHYSICS DEPARTMENT, LOYOLA UNIVERSITY
Assistant to the department head. Helped to design and exe-
cute experiments testing electromagnetic waves and fields.
Compiled and analyzed data.

Summer 1990 ASSISTANT TO THE MANAGER   Ruston, Louisiana
FOLLEN'S VIDEO STORE
Maintained daily bookkeeping. Organized inventory and repair of video equipment. Rented videos and electronic
equipment. Customer service and some sales.

Part-time 1992 CIRCULATION ASSISTANT   New Orleans, Louisiana
KING MEMORIAL LIBRARY/LOYOLA UNIVERSITY
Processed borrowed books, assisted students and faculty
with questions, managed and updated enormous library database.

SKILLS Familiar with WordPerfect, Lotus 1-2-3, dBase, and Fortran.

REFERENCES Available upon request.

Psychology Major

233 Vetnor Avenue
Oklahoma City, OK 93304
November 13, 1992

Ms. Stephanie Long
Personnel Manger
Evans Corporation
1799 Business Park Drive
Sumter, SC 20034

Dear Ms. Long:

Can you utilize the talents of a competent, motivated, and well-organized Personnel Assistant who is interested in pursuing a career in the Human Resources field?

I am a college student at Furman University who is graduating this June with a Bachelor's degree in Psychology and Sociology. I offer a strong talent for dealing with many different kinds of people, excellent communication skills, and a strong desire to learn and grow within your company.

I believe that Human Resources is the backbone of any company because each company is only as good as the people working for it. If staffed poorly, a company will suffer and perhaps even fail. However, if Human Resources does a great job with staffing, then the company becomes strong and is likely to not only succeed but thrive.

I am particularly interested in Evans Corporation because it is a very strong, dynamic firm. I was very impressed to discover that your company was among the fastest growing in the state. I would like to become a part of such a fine company and the Personnel Department that no doubt contributed to its success.

I would like to interview with you at your earliest convenience. I am best reached at (701) 555-9421 during business hours. Thank you for your consideration.

Sincerely,

Louis T. Barnes

enc.

Psychology Major

LOUIS T. BARNES

233 Vetnor Avenue
Oklahoma City, OK 93304
(701) 555-9421

education
1989-1993 FURMAN UNIVERSITY   GREENVILLE, SOUTH CAROLINA
Candidate for the degree of Bachelor of Arts in June 1993,
majoring in Psychology and minoring in Sociology. Courses
included: Public Speaking, Mathematics, and Computer Science. Independent Study topic: The Psychological Impact of
Commercial Advertising on Teenage Eating Disorders. Won the
Alfred Pinder Award for Outstanding Students of Psychology
in 1992.

Teaching Assistant for Introductory Psychology class. Member of Furman Cycling Club. Volunteer for local food
shelter. Helped organize on-campus food donation drive for
the needy; collected over one-half ton of food that was distributed to over 75 different families.

summer 1992 OXFORD UNIVERSITY   OXFORD, ENGLAND
Participated in summer abroad program, studying English
popular culture. Thesis topic: The Role of Music in the English Punk Sub-Culture.

experience
summer 1991 THE COCA-COLA COMPANY   GREENVILLE, SOUTH CAROLINA
Public Relations Assistant. Wrote promotional material,
sent out mass mailings, and supervised company sponsorship
in various charitable events.

summer 1990 ANNIE'S CANDIES   GREENVILLE, SOUTH CAROLINA
Assistant candy-maker and counter person for local sweets
shop.

part-time
1989-1992 Part-time positions include Mail Clerk for college dormitory, Bus-Person at local restaurant, and Pizza Delivery
Person.

interests Enjoy hiking, cycling, and building model cars. Compete in
state-wide cycling races.

references Personal references available upon request.

Quantitative Analysis Major

133 Kasper Lane, #3A
Brooklyn, NY 10025

March 3, 1993

Ms. Danielle Smith
Manager, Actuarial
Lyons & Sons Insurance Agency
324 6th Avenue, 8th Floor
New York, NY 10009

Dear Ms. Smith:

Suzanne Davis of Shearson Lehman Brothers suggested that I contact you regarding a potential entry-level opening at your firm.

I am a recent graduate of New York University with a Bachelor of Sciences degree in Quantitative Analysis. In addition to my required coursework, I took advanced classes such as Economics of International Business, Analysis for Corporate Financing Policies, Advanced Statistics, Calculus I-IV, and Statistical Analysis Through Computer-Based Systems. In 1991, I was awarded the Actuarial Society Scholarship. I was consistently included on the Academic Dean's List and took part in the Stern School Honor Program.

As for work experience, I worked as a Prospector for Merrill Lynch & Company part-time over a period of three years, where I organized a seminar which resulted in $125,000 in new accounts. At Shearson Lehman Brothers, I acted as a Broker's Assistant and organized and created a database of client listings using dBase III Plus. For the past two summers, I have been working at Lawless Insurance Company as an Actuarial Intern. Here, I assisted two Senior Analysts in compiling data, analyzing trends, and setting rates.

Through my contacts at these and other insurance firms, I have learned of Lyons & Sons excellent reputation as a dependable yet innovative company. Its smaller size also attracts me, as I feel that I could learn and grow more at a smaller firm than at a large one.

I would be very grateful for the opportunity to meet with you to discuss the possibility of my working for your firm. I may be reached at 718/555-1508 during daytime hours. Thank you for your consideration!

Sincerely,

Jason Codier

Jason Codier

enc.

Quantitative Analysis Major

JASON CODIER
133 Kasper Lane, #3A
Brooklyn, NY 10025
(718) 555-1508

EDUCATION	**NEW YORK UNIVERSITY, NEW YORK** **The Stern School of Business** Bachelor of Science Degree, January 1993 Major: Quantitative Analysis. GPA: 3.32
HONORS	Recipient of Actuarial Society Scholarship Academic Dean's List Stern School Honor Program
RELEVANT COURSEWORK	Economics of International Business Analysis for Corporate Financing Policies Advanced Statistics Calculus I-IV Statistical Analysis Through Computer-Based Systems
ACTIVITIES	Member of NYU Swim Team Contributing Writer for *The Stern School Bulletin*
EMPLOYMENT Summers 1991, 1992	**LAWLESS INSURANCE COMPANY, New York** Actuarial Intern Assisted two Senior Analysts in compiling data, analyzing trends, and setting rates. Performed extensive research and data manipulation. Taught Lotus 1-2-3 to three analysts in the department.
Summer 1990	**SHEARSON LEHMAN BROTHERS, New York** Broker's Assistant Organized and created a database of client listings using dBase III Plus. Duties included extensive client contact through correspondence and over the telephone. Resolved problems with clients and vendors
Part-time 1989-1991	**MERRILL LYNCH & COMPANY, New York** Prospector Made cold calls for a Financial Consultant. Organized a seminar which resulted in $125,000 in new accounts. Experience with Quotron.
COMPUTER SKILLS	Proficient in Lotus 1-2-3, dBase III Plus, SPSSX, WordStar, and Microsoft Windows.
REFERENCES	Available upon request.

Sociology Major

76 Roanoak Avenue
Hartford, CT 06519
203/555-8877

June 23, 1992

Ms. Eileen Drexel, Director
State of Connecticut Agency on Aging
1222 Vermont Street
Hartford, CT 06522

Dear Ms. Drexel:

Thank you for taking the time to speak with me today. As I mentioned on the phone, I am interested in beginning a career in the field of gerontology.

I am currently a senior at Yale University, majoring in Sociology. I have studied a variety of subjects including Gerontology, where I first became interested in this field. Other related courses I've taken include Poverty and Crisis, The Political Economy of Health Care in the United States, Race Relations, and Women in Society. My current grade point average is 3.64 and I am a member of the Phi Beta Kappa honor society.

In addition to my school work, I am an active member of the student-run Volunteers for a Better World Program. Some of the experiences I've gained through this organization include serving Thanksgiving dinner to homeless people at a local soup kitchen, tutoring underprivileged junior high students in math and English, and co-directing a very successful annual campus food drive. As a contributing writer for *The Vanguard Press*, I wrote many articles and editorials concerning various social issues, including the plight of the elderly.

As a result of my classroom studies and my volunteer experience, I feel that I have an excellent grasp on the social and political issues that affect the elderly in the United States. I feel that at your agency, I could make a real difference in the lives of elderly people.

I've enclosed my resume and a sample article for your perusal. Thank you for your attention to this matter and I look forward to your response.

Sincerely,

Herbert Rosenwriter
Herbert Rosenwriter

enc.

Sociology Major

HERBERT ROSENWRITER
76 Roanoak Avenue
Hartford, CT 06519
203/555-8877

Objective:
A challenging position in the field of gerontology which would enable me to utilize my writing and analytical skills.

Education:

YALE UNIVERSITY
New Haven, Connecticut
Candidate for the Degree of Bachelor of Arts in Sociology. Concentration in Economic Stratification and Social Hierarchies. Courses include Poverty and Crisis, The Political Economy of Health Care in the United States, Gerontology, Race Relations, and Women in Society. Independent Study topic: The Feminization of Poverty in the United States". 3.64 grade point average. Member of the Phi Beta Kappa honor society. Expected date of graduation: May 1993.

Member of student-run Volunteers for a Better World program. Served Thanksgiving dinner to homeless people at local soup kitchen, tutored four underprivileged junior high students in math and English, co-directed campus food drive. Contributing writer for *The Vanguard Press*.

Experience:

CUSTOMER SERVICE REPRESENTATIVE
ONTEGA SAVINGS BANK; Stamford, Connecticut.
Duties included facilitating new account referrals, processing deposits, withdrawals, check cashing, balancing daily cash blotters and utilizing the CRT. Summers 1991, 1992.

ASSISTANT TO EXECUTIVE ASSISTANT U.S. ATTORNEY
U.S. ATTORNEY'S OFFICE, CRIMINAL DIVISION; Boston, Massachusetts.
Gathered and organized evidence for trial and filed complaints. Acted as a liaison between attorney and press. Summer 1990.

CREDIT CARD PAYMENTS CLERK
ONTEGA SAVINGS BANK; Stamford, Connecticut.
Responsibilities included data entry of new customer credit card accounts; sorting, balancing and posting credit card/home equity/cash advance payments to the CRT and general ledger; customer service. Part-time 1992-present.

References:
Available upon request.

Speech Major

39 Rocky Ridge Road
Johnson City, Tennessee 37655
615/555-9654

June 2, 1993

Mr. Carter Burke
Director of Personnel
International Paper
2557 Liberty Street
Memphis, Tennessee 37850

Dear Mr. Burke:

I am writing in reference to your opening for a Salesperson, which I learned of through the Career Services Department at Fisk University. I am a May graduate of Fisk, where I obtained a Bachelor of Arts degree in Speech. I feel that I am an ideal candidate for this position due to my strong sales background and my excellent written and oral communication skills.

I am very interested in pursuing employment in sales. As you can see, I have held a number of sales-related positions which I greatly enjoyed, such as sales clerk, phone sales representative, public relations intern, and cashier. In addition, I am a true "people person", and a hard worker who loves a good challenge.

Enclosed is my resume, detailing my qualifications. I would greatly appreciate the chance to speak with you further, regarding this or other entry-level opportunities for employment at your company.

Thank you for your time!

Sincerely,

Carl P. Anderson

Carl P. Anderson

enc.

Speech Major

CARL P. ANDERSON

39 Rocky Ridge Road, Johnson City, Tennessee 37655 615/555-9654

EDUCATION

Fisk University: Nashville, Tennessee, 1989-1993. Awarded the degree of Bachelor of Arts in May 1993, majoring in Speech. Courses include Marketing, Business Administration, and Computer Applications. 3.6 grade point average. Dean's List.

Member of the Debate Club. Won Fisk University Debate Championship three consecutive times. Represented Fisk at State Championships. Karate Association.

Tennessee Wesleyan College: Athens, Tennessee, 1988-1989. Studied English and Communications. Karate Club.

WORK EXPERIENCE

Sales Clerk: Anderson Small Clothiers, Nashville, Tennessee, February 1992 through present. Won annual employee contest for the greatest sales.

Phone Sales Representative: Fisk University, Summer 1991. Helped raise money for the university by soliciting alumni and parents of students for donations. Won award for the greatest amount of donations solicited during a three-month time period.

Public Relations Intern: Schneider & Associates, Summer 1990. Wrote press releases and pitch letters for release to the media. Prepared media lists, answered phone inquiries, data entry, and general clerical.

Cashier: Hamilton News & Books Bookstore, Summer 1989. Worked as cashier, assisted customers with questions, took inventory, handled special orders.

Server: Amesbury Cafe, Athens, Tennessee, part-time 1988-1989. Promoted from busperson.

INTERESTS

Enjoy basketball, softball, tennis, and chess.

REFERENCES

Available upon request.

Statistics Major

460 Brook Road
Santa Fe, New Mexico 87541
505/555-5561

August 5, 1993

Joseph C. Barber
Director of Human Resources
Kendall Pharmaceuticals
11241 Sundown Drive
Albuquerque, New Mexico 87154

Dear Mr. Barber:

Please accept this letter as application for the Statistician position currently available with your company, as advertised in Sunday's *Albuquerque Sun*. My resume is enclosed for your consideration, and I believe that you will find me well-qualified.

I have a Bachelor's degree in Statistics from New Mexico State University. I offer a solid background in computers, in addition to having studied mathematics, economics, and business administration. To further my studies, I interned for a summer at the California Institute of Technology, where I took courses in Applied Mathematics and Advanced Macro Economics.

As an Assistant to a top Economist in the U.S. Department of Labor, I devised and interpreted the numerical results of surveys concerning the decline of manufacturing in the country. In this position, I gained in-depth knowledge into the use of a variety of statistical software programs, including SPSSX and SASS.

I'm organized and detail-oriented, work well under pressure, and have a great attitude. I'm looking for a challenging, growth-oriented position and would like the opportunity to learn more about your company and this position. I look forward to hearing from you to schedule a personal interview at your convenience.

Sincerely,

Alison A Granville
Alison Ann Granville

enclosure

Statistics Major

ALISON ANN GRANVILLE
460 Brook Road
Santa Fe, New Mexico 87541
505/555-5561

education

1988-1993 NEW MEXICO STATE UNIVERSITY   LAS CRUCES, NEW MEXICO
Awarded the degree of Bachelor of Sciences in May 1993, majoring in Statistics. Also concentrated studies in Mathematics, Economics, Business Administration, and Computer Applications. Thesis topic: New Applications of the Probability Theory Using Differential Equations. 3.1 grade point average.

Member of the Math Club. Recipient of the Connor Foundation Scholarship in 1991. Varsity basketball.

1984-1988 SANTA FE WEST HIGH SCHOOL   SANTA FE, NEW MEXICO
Received High School Diploma in 1988. Achieved Advance Placement Standing in Calculus. Scored highest math SAT score in history of high school. Junior varsity and varsity basketball. State Championships two years in a row.

internship

summer 1992 CALIFORNIA INSTITUTE OF TECHNOLOGY   PASADENA
Studied Applied Mathematics and Advanced Macro Economics. Attended week-long seminar on "Future Applications of Mathematics and Statistics in Space-Age Technology".

summers

1991-1990 UNITED STATES DEPARTMENT OF LABOR   WASHINGTON, DC
Assistant to a top Economist. Devised and interpreted the numerical results of surveys concerning the decline of manufacturing in the United States. Used a variety of statistical programs, including SPSSX and SASS.

summer-winter

1989 BOHEM INDUSTRIES   SANTA FE, NEW MEXICO
Data Entry Clerk. Promoted to Computer Operator within two months.

personal

background Enjoy chess, music, playing keyboard in a blues band, and basketball.

references Available upon request.

Theatre Major

12 Shady Acres, #34
Fort Wayne, IN 46808
(812) 555-5589

August 14, 1993

Mr. Oliver Browne
Stage Director
Sarris Productions
433 27th Street
New York, NY 10001

Dear Mr. Browne:

Amy Sullivan recently indicated to me that you may have an opening for a Set Designer and suggested that I contact you. I seek a creative position involving stage design in television.

I graduated in December from Purdue University with a B.A. in Theatre Arts and a concentration in Studio Art. In addition to Modern Drama, and Music and Sound in Theatre, I studied Set Creation and Design, Intermediate Painting, and Woodworking. As a member of the Drama Club, I designed and helped create props for numerous campus productions including "A Midsummer Night's Dream" and "Vinegar Tom".

As for work experience, I co-designed and co-created the props and decorations for a new miniature golf course with a tropical island theme, which turned out to be a big hit. I also gained valuable skills working as an apprentice to a busy carpenter and painting houses for a large company.

Enclosed is my resume as well as some photographs of my work. I have some great ideas for the sets for "Wheel of Trivia" and "Late Night Videos" which I would like to discuss with you in a personal interview. I may be reached at the above-listed number before 1:00 p.m. weekdays. Thank you for your consideration of my application.

Sincerely,

Jacquelyn R. Brady

Jacquelyn R. Brady

enc.

Theatre Major

JACQUELYN R. BRADY

School Address:
Wilks Hall, Room 314
Purdue University
West Lafayette, IN 47907
317/555-8858

Permanent Address:
12 Shady Acres, #34
Fort Wayne, IN 46808
812/555-5589

OBJECTIVE   To obtain a position in the theatre or a related area which enables me to utilize my creative talent and experience.

EDUCATION   **PURDUE UNIVERSITY**, West Lafayette, IN
B.A. in Theatre Arts awarded in December, 1992. Concentration in Studio Art. Courses included: Modern Drama, Music and Sound in Theatre, The History of Theatre in America, Intermediate Painting, Set Creation and Design, and Woodworking.

ACTIVITIES   Member of the Drama Club. Designed and helped to create props for numerous campus productions, including "A Midsummer Night's Dream", "The Crucible", "Vinegar Tom", and "One Act Plays". Played minor role in "The Crucible" as one of the townspeople.

RELEVANT EXPERIENCE   **MINI-GOLF ISLAND**, Fort Wayne, IN. Spring-Fall 1992.
Co-designed and co-created different props and decorations for new mini-golf course with a tropical island theme. Props included palm trees, exotic birds, a pink rhinoceros, lions, zebras, a dozen pythons, and a friendly panther that purrs when ball drops into the hole. Most elaborate creation was a working ten-foot waterfall in the center of the course.

GRADY'S CARPENTRY AND WOODWORKING, Fort Wayne, IN. Summer 1991.
Acted as general assistant to busy carpenter. Helped to build small structures and construct shelves, cabinets, and other custom orders.

COLLEGE-PRO PAINTING, Fort Wayne, IN. Summer 1989-90.
Member of a college-age house-painting team. Painted over twenty local houses.

OTHER WORK EXPERIENCE   Worked as a hostess, switchboard operator, bank teller, and grocery store clerk.

REFERENCES   Available upon request

Western Civilization Major

21 Royall Drive
Detroit, MI 48209
(313) 555-8982

February 3, 1993

Mr. Jason Breckman
Music Shack, Inc.
10887 Hamilton Avenue
Torrance, CA 90544-4541

Dear Mr. Breckman:

I am interested in applying for the position of Associate Product Manager, as advertised in the January 31 edition of The Golden Gazette.

I have recently completed my undergraduate degree from Central Michigan University with a BA in Western Civilization and a minor in Political Science. I also have work experience in a professional setting, having worked as a Customer Service Representative at a large Detroit bank and as a Receptionist/Administrative Assistant for a local development company.

Being enthusiastic and dependable with a strong desire to learn and excel, I am confident that I will make a significant contribution to your company now, and an increasingly important one in years to come.

Enclosed is my resume which provides additional information about my education and experience. I will be glad to make myself available for an interview at your convenience to discuss how my qualifications would be consistent with your needs.

Thank you for your time and consideration.

Sincerely,

Alina Hooper

Alina Hooper

Enclosure: Resume

Western Civilization Major

ALINA HOOPER

School Address: Permanent Address:
1305 Pleasant Way   21 Royall Drive
Mount Pleasant, MI 48859   Detroit, MI 48209
Phone: 517/555-8955   Phone: 313/555-8982

education

1989-present CENTRAL MICHIGAN UNIVERSITY   MOUNT PLEASANT, MICHIGAN
Awarded the degree of Bachelor of Arts in May 1993, majoring in Western Civilization. Minor in Political Science. Courses also included Mathematics, Statistics, Economics, and Business Administration.

Secretary of Alpha Chi Epsilon sorority. Member of Ski Team. Regular competitor in downhill ski races; including three annual state-wide ski races.

1986-1989 WESTSIDE HIGH SCHOOL   DETROIT, MICHIGAN
Received High School Diploma in May 1989. High honors all terms. Completed high school requirements in three years. Member of Rhine Literary Group. Co-captain of the ski team.

experience

summer 1992 BANK OF DETROIT   DETROIT, MICHIGAN
Customer Service Representative. Duties included facilitating new account referrals, processing deposits, withdrawals, check cashing, balancing daily cash blotters, and utilizing the CRT.

summer 1991 CLARK DEVELOPMENT COMPANY   DETROIT, MICHIGAN
Receptionist/Administrative Assistant. Responsible for managing the organization of proposed projects and appointments for prospective sales. Extensive use of Word-Perfect and Lotus 1-2-3.

summer 1990 ALLEGRO'S SUPERMARKET   DETROIT, MICHIGAN
Cashier. Recognized for accurate work and outstanding customer service with "Employee of the Week" award.

interests Mount Pleasant Youth Center Big Sister Program. Tennis, skiing, and basketball.

references Available upon request.

Women's Studies Major

756 Maple Street
Manchester, NH 03104

October 15, 1992

Mr. Jason Stevenson
Office Manager
Dougherty, Clay, and Howe
Attorneys-at-Law
1519 Elm Street
Manchester, NH 03105

Dear Mr. Stevenson:

In response to your advertisement in the October 12 edition of <u>The Union Leader</u>, I am making application for the position of Legal Assistant.

I am a recent graduate of the University of Vermont, where I earned my Bachelor's degree in Women's Studies. I studied a variety of subjects outside of my major, including Political Science and Public Speaking, which I'm sure will benefit me a great deal as a Legal Assistant. Because of my outstanding academic record and notable extra-curricular activities, I was awarded the prestigious Bailey-Howe Scholarship in 1990.

I have always been interested in the law, and I decided to pursue it as a career after I worked as a summer intern for the Public Defender's Office in Burlington. I worked for five different attorneys, performing extensive research, attending court sessions, and corresponding with the District Attorney's Office. Playing a role in the justice system and actually affecting the lives of others was the most exciting and worthwhile thing I have ever done.

As for practical skills, I can file, write business correspondence, type 55 WPM, and am proficient with computers and word processors. I have an excellent phone manner and am very organized and detail- oriented. I am eager to begin a career in the legal profession and would consider it a great opportunity to work for your firm.

I would like to interview with you at your earliest convenience. I may be reached at 555-0856 during afternoon hours.

Sincerely,

Linda McFarlane

Linda McFarlane

Enc.

Women's Studies Major

LINDA McFARLANE

School Address:
167 South Union Street
Burlington, VT 05401
Phone: 802/555-3354

Permanent Address:
756 Maple Street
Manchester, NH 03104
Phone: 603/555-0856

education
1988-1992 **UNIVERSITY OF VERMONT**   **BURLINGTON, VERMONT**
Awarded Bachelor of Arts degree in May 1992, majoring in Women's Studies, minoring in Art. Courses include Economics, Statistics, Political Science and Public Speaking. Thesis topic: The Political Economy of Our Domestic Health Care System. 3.5 grade point average. Awarded the Bailey-Howe Scholarship in 1990.

Contributing editor for campus newspaper, The Cynic. Member of the Outing Club. Member of Varsity Crew Team. Designed and painted university-sponsored mural with the theme of cultural diversity.

experience
summer 1991 **OFFICE OF THE PUBLIC DEFENDER**   **BURLINGTON, VERMONT**
Summer Intern working with five attorneys. Performed extensive research to support court cases and attended court sessions. Handled confidential documents and paperwork. Liaison with District Attorney's Office.

summers
1989-1990 **SWEETWATER'S RESTAURANT**   **BURLINGTON, VERMONT**
Began work as hostess, promoted to waitstaff. Also relief bartender.

part-time
1989-1992 **ACADEMIC COMPUTING SERVICES**   **UNIVERSITY OF VERMONT**
Computer counselor for campus computer lab. Maintained hardware and worked on network and mainframe. Performed extensive troubleshooting for students and faculty regarding software, hardware, and printing problems. Instituted "Freshman Orientation Session" for new lab users.

part-time
1988-1989 **UNIVERSITY BOOKSTORE**   **UNIVERSITY OF VERMONT**
Cashier/Clerk. Acted as cashier, stocked shelves, and miscellaneous other duties.

personal
background Enjoy painting, sculpture, aerobics, and camping. Member of the National Organization of Women.

references Personal references available upon request.

CHAPTER SIXTEEN

Before the Job Interview

IN A TYPICAL job search you will have very few interviews relative to the number of companies you contact. Don't pass up any realistic opportunities for job interviews. Even if it appears to you at first that you are not really interested in the company or the position, remember that you want as much experience as possible. Why waste a single opportunity to improve your skills? Prepare yourself thoroughly and you will eventually approach each interview with confidence and excitement!

JOB SEARCH FOCUS

Interview preparation should begin long before you start lining up interviews. If you've followed my advice, you've already taken the first step by deciding which industry and job function to pursue. By limiting your job search in this way, you are showing a corporate recruiter that you are serious about a long-term professional career.

One favorite interview question employers ask to eliminate candidates from consideration is, "What other firms are you interviewing at and for what positions?" Often, the candidate tries to impress the employer by naming some large firms in unrelated industries with completely different types of jobs. This is a big mistake! What employers want to hear is that you are interviewing for *similar* jobs in the same industry at *similar* firms (such as their competitors).

COMPANY RESEARCH

You should do a little bit of research about a company in order to sound knowledgeable while you're networking and contacting companies directly. It is best to concentrate your research efforts on the relatively small number of firms that you will actually interview with.

Once you have an interview scheduled, however, you must find out everything you possibly can about that company! Your efforts could make all the difference in distinguishing you from the competition from the very first interview onward.

At the very least, determine the following about the firm at which you are interviewing:

- ☐ The principal products or services
- ☐ Their types of customers
- ☐ Their subsidiaries
- ☐ Their parent companies
- ☐ Their type of ownership

☐ Their approximate industry rank
☐ Their sales and profit trends
☐ Their announced future plans

To find this information and more, you will need to dig into every resource you can find. You can locate some information in business directories available at libraries. For larger companies you can call the investor relations department and request an annual report and search at the library for recent articles written about the company. Of course, if you are following my advice to focus your job search in one industry, you are probably already familiar with the industry's trade magazines—go through the back issues and look for relevant articles.

Your research may lead you to conclude that you don't want to work for the firm after all. If this happens, by all means, *interview anyway*. You might come across something that changes your mind. You will definitely get more practice and improve your interview skills.

DRESSING FOR SUCCESS

How important is proper dress for a job interview? Well, the final selection of a job candidate will rarely be determined by dress. However, first-round candidates for an opening *are* often quickly eliminated by inappropriate dress. I am not suggesting that you rush out to buy a whole new wardrobe, but that you must be able to put together an adequate interview outfit.

For a man, a clean, conservative two-piece suit, white dress shirt and simple tie is the basic corporate wardrobe. However, standards will vary, and fashion for men is swinging towards more casual attire. For some industries and some companies, a quality jacket, pants, shirt and tie is fine. If you're not sure what dress is appropriate at a certain firm, play it safe and opt for a two-piece suit. Remember even at a company that encourages fairly casual dress around the office, job-seekers may be expected to dress somewhat more formally. Note that a man should always wear a jacket and tie to an interview—even if everyone else in the office is in shirtsleeves. Dressing in this way shows that you are taking your interview seriously and treating the company with respect. As for shoes, basic black is preferable, but you won't need to buy a new pair if you already have a pair of quality, conservative brown shoes.

Rules are more difficult to apply to women's dress. Women should either wear a relatively conservative dress or a suit. In traditionally more conservative industries, such as investment banking, a suit is a safer bet than a dress. For most other industries, however, a professional-looking dress may be preferable; it makes a stronger statement without being out of place. Still, either approach is generally acceptable for a professional interview.

Top personal grooming is more important than finding the perfect outfit. Careful grooming indicates both thoroughness and self-confidence. Be sure that your clothes fit well and that they are immaculate, that your hair is neat and freshly washed, and that your shoes are clean and attractive. Women need to avoid excessive jewelry, makeup, or perfume. Men should be freshly shaven, even if the interview is late in the day.

You will also need a watch, a pen, and pad of paper for taking notes. Finally, a briefcase or folder will help complete the look of professionalism. Women should avoid carrying both a briefcase and a purse—it will subtract from your professional image. Instead, transfer any essential items into a small bag you can store in the briefcase. And don't forget to take a few extra copies of your resume!

HAVE THE OBVIOUS ANSWERS READY

You can never be sure exactly what you will be asked at a job interview, but certain questions are more likely to arise than others, and you should be prepared for them. By developing solid answers to questions that are likely to be asked, you will probably be in a better position to answer questions that you hadn't anticipated.

Take a look at your resume, pretending for a moment that you are a corporate recruiter looking at it for the first time. What questions would you ask? You should bear in mind that questions you are asked in one interview are likely to be repeated in another. Immediately after each interview, take a moment to write down each new question that you are asked; prepare a solid response in case you are asked the question again.

Some common questions will be relatively easy to prepare for. A recruiter is very likely to ask you for more information about your work history and academic achievements. Be prepared to talk about any one of them for about three minutes. You may also be asked about the personal interests listed on your resume. If a distant home address is listed, the recruiter might ask why you decided to attend college far away from home. As you prepare responses to recruiter's inquiries, try to structure them in a way that conveys that you are someone the recruiter would want to hire. In other words, project yourself as someone who is likely to stay with the company for a number of years, who is achievement oriented, who will fit in well with the other people, who is mature and likeable. Of course, you should try to project yourself as someone who is capable of doing the job extremely well.

Commonly asked interview questions are examined in detail in Chapter Eighteen.

BE PREPARED TO ASK QUESTIONS

Toward the end of the interview the recruiter will usually ask if you have any questions. You should be prepared to ask about something; if you don't you may be perceived as being uninterested in the company. *Do not* under any circumstances inquire about salary or fringe benefits until after you have been offered the job. (During the first interview you are unlikely to receive a job offer—this usually happens only after one or more follow-up interviews.) During the first interview, you will have three reasons to ask questions: to show your knowledge of the firm, to underscore your deep interest in the firm and the position, and to add to your chances of being invited to the second interview. Save the questions about salary, benefits, and related issues for later, after you receive an offer. You will still be free to negotiate—or to decline the position—at that point.

What questions should you ask? One good question is: "What is the next position or positions that typically follow the entry level job?" This question implies that you are looking for a company where you can build a career and are less likely to change jobs often.

Ask questions that will subtly show the recruiter your knowledge of the industry and of the firm. For example, "I noticed in the business press that your company is the market leader in industrial drill bits in North America. I am curious to know how much of the product line is sold overseas—and whether there are many career opportunities in marketing abroad."

PRACTICE INTERVIEWING

Once you have developed solid responses to likely interview questions, you should write the questions on index cards. Shuffle the cards and practice answering them into a tape recorder, moving from one question to the next. Play it back. How did you do? What can you improve? Practice with some friends; ask them for feedback. Then be sure to have your friends ask you many questions you *haven't* prepared answers to. Are you able to formulate answers quickly? If not, keep practicing.

OVERCOMING NERVOUSNESS

As if formulating solid answers to interview questions weren't tough enough, you will have the added difficulty of overcoming your own nervousness, at least for the first few interviews. Virtually everyone is just as nervous as you are in this situation. In fact, next to speaking in public, job interviews are the most dreaded event in the average person's entire life!

You should expect to be somewhat nervous during a job interview, but excessive nervousness is certainly a disadvantage. The best way to overcome nervousness is to practice interviewing as much as you can—especially with real companies.

If you happen to have a terrible interview, don't let this shake your confidence! *Everyone* has a terrible interview sooner or later, and almost everyone who interviews is nervous. If you have a bad experience, don't dwell on it. Learn from it, work on your interview performance, and sooner or later you'll find another opportunity.

INTERVIEW STRATEGY

For your first few interviews, or at least until you are feeling very confident, focus your efforts on remaining calm and collected, focusing carefully on what the recruiter is saying and on responding promptly and thoroughly to the recruiter's questions. Don't try too hard. If you have been practicing your responses, you should be able to offer appropriate answers without too much difficulty.

Once you begin to feel more confident about interviewing you may wish to think strategically about each interview. One effective tactic is to adjust your speed of speech to match that of the interviewer. People tend to talk at the speed at which they like to be spoken to. If you can adjust your speech rate to that of the recruiter without sounding unnatural, the recruiter will probably feel more comfortable (after all, interviewing others isn't much fun, either) and have a more favorable impression of you.

Another strategy is to adapt your answers to match the type of company for which you are interviewing. For example, if you are interviewing for a job at a large product marketing company that emphasizes group decision-making and spends much of its energy focused on battles for market share with its competitors, you might want to talk about how much you enjoy team sports—especially being part of a team and competing to win.

When filling professional career positions, few companies will make a job offer after only one interview. Usually, the first interview is meant to narrow down the field of applicants to a small number of very promising candidates. During the first interview, then, the ideal strategy is to stand out from a large field of competitors, in a positive way. The best way to do this is to subtly emphasize one of your key, distinctive strengths as much as possible throughout the interview. (At the same time, you must be sure not to make awkward responses or become overbearing.)

During later interviews, the competition for the position will be dropping off and recruiters will tend to look not for strengths, but for weaknesses. At this point you should focus on presenting yourself as a well-balanced choice for the position.

You will want to listen carefully to the interviewer's questions so you can unearth underlying concerns and try to dispel them.

TALK WITH PREVIOUS INTERVIEWEES

Particularly if you are interviewing with an on-campus recruiter, you might have an opportunity to talk with people who have already been interviewed by the recruiter. Find out who else is on the interview schedule; perhaps there is someone you know. If there is, and if you are scheduled for a later interview, try to find out what questions were asked during the interview.

ARRIVE ON TIME

As I noted earlier, graduating college students often arrive late for interviews. There are two major reasons for this: First, inexperienced candidates are likely to forget something or to take a little unplanned extra time to prepare. Second, they often underestimate how long it will take to get to the interview location.

Clearly, then, you must allow yourself plenty of time to get ready and travel to your job interview. You should not arrive at the interviewer's office more than ten minutes in advance. However, if you are driving across town, planning ten minutes of extra time is probably not enough. Plan to *get to the location* at least thirty minutes early; you can then spend twenty minutes in a nearby coffee shop or take a walk around the building. Interviews are important enough to build in a little extra time. Here's another tip: If you have never been to the interview location before, visit it the day before so you know exactly where you are going.

CHAPTER SEVENTEEN

At the Interview

YOU'VE SCHEDULED an interview.

By this time, you will have spent a great deal of time preparing for job interviews in general and this job interview in particular. However, you must not let your preparation become a disadvantage. Once the interview begins, your focus must be on interacting well with the interviewer—as opposed to trying to recall the exact responses you prepared earlier. If you prepared for the interview well, your conduct and responses will convey to the interviewer the image that you want to project without effort. (If you did not prepare thoroughly, it will be too late to focus on making the ideal presentation. Instead you should simply try to present yourself as a likeable, mature person who will fit in well with the company.)

The recruiter's decision about whether or not you will be invited back for an additional interview will probably be influenced more by your conduct during the interview than by what you say. This is especially true if you are applying for your first professional position. Remember that the recruiter's biggest concerns in hiring entry professionals are threefold: Is the candidate mature? Will the candidate fit in well in our organization? Will the candidate be enjoyable to work with? Answers to all of these questions will not be determined by what you say when you answer specific interview questions as much as by the general impression you make. So while preparing for the interview is important, how you conduct yourself during the interview can make even more of a difference.

Beware of appearing artificial; don't concentrate too much on trying to project the perfect image. Visualize yourself as smooth, confident, mature, and likeable, and you will project those qualities.

THE CRUCIAL FIRST FEW MOMENTS

The first minutes of the interview are the most important. A recruiter begins sizing up your potential the instant you walk in the room. If you make a bad impression initially, the recruiter may rule you out immediately and not pay close attention to your performance during the rest of the interview. An excellent initial impression, on the other hand, will put a favorable glow on everything else you say during the rest of the interview—and could well encourage the recruiter to ask less demanding questions.

How can you ensure that you make a terrific first impression? The easiest answer is to be sure you are dressed well. When the recruiter meets you, your clothes and grooming will be noticed first. As mentioned earlier, nothing less than impeccable grooming is acceptable. Your attire must be professional, well-fitted and squeaky clean.

In virtually the same instant the recruiter notices your clothes and grooming, even before either of you speaks, your body language will begin to affect the way you are perceived. Even an inexperienced recruiter who is not consciously seeking to make a "first read" will notice and react to your body language. Are you smiling before greeting? (Smiling sincerely is a universally attractive trait.) Do you walk straight up to the recruiter with a confident (but not overly aggressive) gait? Do you extend your right hand naturally to begin a firm (but not vise-like) handshake? Is your briefcase, note pad, and coat in your left hand or do you have to juggle them around in order to shake hands? Do you make just enough eye contact without staring at the recruiter? Do your eyes travel naturally to and from the recruiter's face as you begin to talk? Do you remember the recruiter's name and pronounce it with confidence?

Do you wait for the recruiter to invite you to sit down before doing so? Alternatively, if the recruiter forgets to invite you to take a seat, do you awkwardly ask if you may be seated as though to remind the recruiter of a lapse in etiquette? Or do you gracefully help yourself to a seat? Do you make small talk easily, or do you act formal and reserved, as though under attack? As you can see, much of the first impression you make at an interview will be dramatically affected by how relaxed and confident you feel. This is why it is so important to practice for each interview—so you can truly give your best impression.

GREETING AND SMALL TALK

The following is an example of proper greeting and initial small talk between a recruiter (Ms. Jane Smith) and a job candidate (Pauline Harris):

Assuming the door is wide open, Pauline should walk into the threshold of the doorway and wait to make eye contact with the recruiter. (If the door is fully or even partially closed, the candidate should knock and wait for a response before entering the interview room.) Immediately, as eye contact is made, Pauline should smile at the recruiter and say in an inquiring and pleasant tone:

Pauline: Ms. Smith, I assume?
Ms. Smith: (*Rising from her chair.*) Yes. Pauline Harris?
Pauline: Yes, I am.
Ms. Smith: Come in, please.

Pauline now walks up to about three feet from Ms. Smith. Presumably Ms Smith has already extended her hand. If she has, Pauline should now shake her hand. If not and if Ms. Smith is not otherwise occupied, Pauline should extend her hand anyway. (In the unlikely event that Ms. Smith has neither extended her hand or accepted Pauline's within a second or two, Pauline should withdraw her hand.)

Pauline: "It's a pleasure to meet you."
Ms. Smith: "It's nice to meet you too, Pauline. Please have a seat."

Pauline sits down and respectfully waits for a few moments to give Ms Smith a chance to initiate conversation. (If Ms. Smith does not initiate conversation after five seconds or so, Pauline may initiate conversation with an innocuous comment such as "It's really a beautiful day today, isn't it?"

Ms. Smith: How are you today, Pauline?

> *Pauline:* Fine, thank you. (Slight pause.) And yourself?
> *Ms. Smith:* Fine, thank you.

If Ms. Smith does not continue the conversation within a second or two, Pauline might now wish to add one short comment in hopes of further encouraging some small talk, which generally creates a more relaxed and amiable atmosphere for both people at a job interview.

> *Pauline:* "Tuesdays are always a good day for me, because I have two of my favorite classes today."

Pauline has made an excellent conversational opener. She has given Ms. Smith the opportunity to ask what her favorite classes are. But she is not aggressively forcing the conversation by asking a direct question. She is also making a statement that she really enjoys at least two of her classes, thereby implying that she enjoys school. She allows the recruiter to infer that she would probably enjoy work and is a pleasant person to be around. Pauline is also discreetly guiding the interview towards a strength of hers that she wishes to highlight: academics. If her strengths were elsewhere, she might have made a different comment, such as: "Today's really been a great day for me—in fact, I just got back from a terrific track practice."

STRUCTURED OR UNSTRUCTURED?

Interviewing styles fall into one of two categories, structured and unstructured. In a structured interview, the recruiter asks a prescribed set of questions seeking relatively brief answers. In the unstructured interview, the recruiter asks more open-ended questions to prod you to give longer responses and reveal as much as possible about yourself, your background and your aspirations. Some recruiters will mix both styles, typically beginning with more objective questions and asking more open-ended questions as the interview progresses.

Be very careful to answer questions in the manner the recruiter desires. Try to determine as soon as possible if the recruiter is conducting a structured or unstructured interview; respond to the questions accordingly. As you answer the questions, watch for signals from the recruiter as to whether to your responses are too short or too long. For example, if the recruiter is nodding or looking away, wrap up your answer as quickly as possible.

It is very important that you follow the style the recruiter establishes during the interview. This will make the interview easier and more enjoyable for both of you and leave the recruiter with a more favorable impression of you.

BEING SO POSITIVE THAT IT HURTS

Many inexperienced job candidates kill their chances for a job by making negative comments during an interview. A college student or recent grad should never make a negative statement about a former boss or teacher—even if it is completely true and fully justified. If the recruiter asks why you had an unsatisfactory grade in a particular course, *do not* say "the professor graded me unfairly" or "I didn't get along with the professor."

A recruiter would rather hire someone who gets and deserves an unsatisfactory grade in a course than someone who either doesn't get along with people or shifts blame to others. On the other hand, you can greatly increase your chances of getting any job by projecting a positive, upbeat attitude during your job interview. This is one of the very best ways you can stand out from the competition. You can project this image by smiling from time to time during the interview; by responding to interview questions with enthusiasm; by demonstrating excitement about your past accomplishments; and by showing optimism about the prospect of starting your career.

HANDLING IMPOSSIBLE QUESTIONS

One of the biggest fears that job candidates harbor about job interviews is the unknown question for which they have no answer. To make matters worse, some recruiters may ask a question knowing full well that you can't possibly answer it!

Sometimes recruiters do ask seemingly impossible questions, just to see how you will respond. They usually don't ask such questions because they enjoy seeing you squirm in your seat; rather, they want to judge how you might respond to pressure or tension on the job. If you are asked a tough question that you simply can't answer, think about it for a few seconds. Then with a confident smile and without apology, simply say, "I don't know" or "I can't answer that question."

ANSWERING QUESTIONS THAT REQUIRE COMMITMENT

You may, even in some first interviews, be asked questions that seem to elicit a tremendous commitment on your behalf. For example, the recruiter might ask "Would you be willing to travel overseas for four-week stretches?" Or, "Would you be willing to move to our overseas technical training center for two years?" Or, "Would you be willing to work twelve-hour shifts on Saturdays and Sundays?" While it may be true that such questions are extremely unfair to ask during an initial job interview, you probably have nothing to gain and everything to lose by saying "No"—or even "I need to think about it." A negative answer could cost you a second interview. I suggest that if you are asked such a question unexpectedly during an initial job interview that you simply answer in the affirmative. If you are offered a job, you can find out what specific work conditions apply and then decide if you wish to accept the position. Could this approach jeopardize your candidacy for any other, perhaps better job the recruiter might have? Probably not. You might explain to the recruiter that now that you have had time to think about it, you cannot accept a position that involves (for instance) travel, but that you would like to be considered for other positions that come up.

ASKING YOUR OWN QUESTIONS

As the interview is winding down, the recruiter will probably say something like, "Are there any questions that you would like to ask?" As mentioned earlier, it is essential that you have a few questions to ask at this point, otherwise you will not seem serious about pursuing a career at this company. Some of your planned questions may already have been covered by the time your reach this stage of the interview; you should have some extra questions ready just in case.

Use the questions that you ask your interviewer to subtly demonstrate your knowledge of the firm and the industry, and to underscore your interest in seeking a long-term career position at the firm. But do not allow your questions to become an interrogation—pose only two or three thoughtful questions. Do not ask any questions that will be difficult or awkward for the recruiter to answer. This is not the time to ask, for example, "Does your company use recycled paper for all of its advertising brochures?"

It bears repeating that you should never ask about salary or fringe benefits until after you have definitely been offered the position. If the recruiter brings up the subject by stating what the salary and benefits are, your best course is not to comment on them. If the recruiter specifically asks for your opinion, you should indicate that the terms are acceptable, even if this is not necessarily true. Later, when and if you are offered the job, you can say that you have given the matter more thought and would like to negotiate the terms. (Please note, however, that this advice is different than advice I would give to a professional with years of solid work experience.)

The following are good sample questions to ask, assuming the issues have not already been covered:

Assuming I was hired and performed well as a (the position you are applying for) for a number of years, what possible opportunities might this lead to?

This question implies you are looking to build a long-term career.

I have noticed in the trade press that your firm has a terrific reputation in marketing. What are the major insights into the marketing process that I might gain from this position?

This question implies that you are very interested in a long-term career in this industry, that you might lean towards taking a career with this firm because of positive reports you have read about them, and that you have a real interest in building your job skills.

What skills are considered most useful for success in the job I am applying for?

This question implies you are really care about your success at your first job and also provides important information for further interviews — or your follow-up after this interview.

I would really like to work for your firm. I think it's a great company and I am confident I could do this job well. What is the next step of the selection process?

More than a question, this is a powerful statement that will quickly set you apart from other job hunters. However, you should only make this statement if you mean it. If you are offered the position but then say you need two weeks to think it over, you will lose your credibility. However, even after making this statement, it is reasonable to ask for 24 or 48 hours to "digest the details."

CHAPTER EIGHTEEN

Commonly Asked Interview Questions—and Their Answers

THE FOLLOWING RESPONSES to interview questions are listed as examples to show you how questions should be handled. They should not be used as the basis of "canned" or scripted answers. Adapt these responses for your own circumstances, but remember that, especially for college students or recent grads, how an answer is given can be more important than what is said. Be positive, project confidence, smile and make eye contact with the interviewer, listen carefully, and go with the flow!

QUESTIONS ABOUT SCHOOL GRADES

Question: Why didn't you get better grades in school?

Answer: I really enjoy school and learning, I study consistently, and I'm attentive in class. But I never cram before the night of an exam just to get a higher grade or stay up all night finishing a term paper. I really believe I have learned just as much as many students who "went for the grades."

Question: Why are your grades so erratic?

Answer: I never hesitated to sign up for a course just because it had a reputation for being difficult. In fact, my American History professor, whose course I enjoyed tremendously, is notorious for only giving out one "A" grade for each class. You may have noticed that, while my major is English, I did take four courses in physics which I thought these courses were important to round out my education and I enjoyed the challenge that they presented. Almost everyone else in these courses was a physics major.

QUESTIONS ABOUT ACADEMICS

Question: What was your favorite class?

Answer: Outside of my major, one of the classes I particularly enjoyed was an introductory course in economics that I took last semester. It was a completely new subject area to me and I enjoy new challenges! I was particularly fascinated with macroeconomic theory where complex mathematical equations can be combined with psychology to explain past economic events and predict future trends.

Question: What course did you find most challenging?

Answer: Initially, I was completely overwhelmed by the introductory chemistry course that I took last year. No matter how hard I studied, I seemed to be getting nowhere. I failed the first three quizzes. So I tried a new approach. Instead of just studying by myself, I had a friend — a chemistry major — help me with my studies. I also began to seek help after class from the professor from time to time. And I found that more time spent in the lab was critical. I ended up with a B+ in the course and felt I achieved a solid understanding of the material. More than that, I learned that tackling a new field of study sometimes requires a new approach, not just hard work, and that the help of others can be crucial!

Question: How do you organize yourself for a large project such as writing a term paper?

Answer: My first step is to read a book that presents a survey of the time period involved and work up a tentative one-page outline. Then I gather all of the appropriate books for reference and begin compiling notes onto index cards. I organize the index cards as logically as possible and tentatively form my thesis statement in my mind. After that, I compose a revised and much more detailed outline. Finally I put my thoughts on paper, following both my outline and index cards.

Question: How do you prepare for a major examination?

Answer: Well, let's take a recent exam I had in 20th Century Art as an example. First I skimmed the material from two lessons that I felt particularly weak in. Then I went through all my class notes again, marking with a highlighting pen the most important points from each class. I went back through the chapter summaries in the basic textbook for every lesson except for those I had just read this last week. Then I reviewed the key points from each class that I had marked with a highlighting pen.

Question: Why did you decide to major in history?

Answer: It was a difficult choice because I was also attracted to government, international relations and economics. But the study of history allowed me to combine all three, especially since I focused on economic history. What's more, I found several of the professors in the department to be exceptionally knowledgeable and stimulating.

Question: I see the title of your senior thesis is "A Comparative Study of Causal Analyses of the Great Depression." Tell me about your thesis and the conclusions of your study.

Answer: It's fascinating to me that even today, there is tremendous disagreement among scholars about the relative importance of various factors leading to the Great Depression. I examined the methodologies used in some of the most prominent works and critically compared their ability to explain this phenomenon. I concluded that the most meaningful analysis gave essentially equal weight to psychological and economic factors.

QUESTIONS ABOUT EXTRACURRICULAR ACTIVITIES

Question: Why did you participate so little in extracurricular activities?

Answer: I wanted to give as much effort as possible to my studies. I came from a high school in a very small town where I received mostly "A's," but this did not prepare me very well for college. So I have studied very hard. I have, however, found time to make a lot of friends in the area and I do enjoy informal socializing on the weekends.

Question: You seem to have participated a little bit in a lot of different extracurricular activities. Didn't any of them really hold your interest?

Answer: I've always felt it was important to have a well-rounded education, and I looked at extracurricular activities as an important part of that education. That's why I participated in many different activities—to broaden my experience and to meet new people. I did particularly enjoy the drama club and the cycling team but I made a conscious effort not to spend too much time on them and try new and different activities.

Question: You are certainly a talented athlete: you won a school-wide singles ping-pong championship, you have a low handicap at golf, and you participate in horse riding competitions. But I'm surprised that you don't list any team sports on your resume.

Answer: I am the kind of person who enjoys staying with an activity for a long period of time and becoming extremely proficient at it. While I do play team sports on a "pickup" basis, I have chosen to focus on sports that I can play for years to come, long after I have left college.

Question: I see you made the football team as a sophomore. Why didn't you play varsity football your junior or senior years?

Answer: While I enjoyed the comradeship and being "part of the team," I did find practices and drills to be tedious and unchallenging. I always was assigned to play guard, and how many different ways can you block a rusher? Instead I joined the Drama Club and was able to give some more time to my studies. While I didn't become a great actor, it was an enriching experience.

Question: I see that you were vice president of your class for three years. Did you run for president?

Answer: Yes, I ran for president every year and lost every year. If I wasn't graduating this year, I would run for president next year too—I never quit! I campaigned hard each year, but never to the detriment of my studies.

Question: Where would you like to be in five years?

Answer: I plan to remain in the banking industry for the foreseeable future after my graduation. I hope that within five years I will have developed a successful track record as a lending loan officer, first perhaps with consumer loans, but then switching to business loans. Ideally, I would hope that within five years I will also have advanced to servicing middle-market-size companies.

QUESTIONS ABOUT TOUGH ACADEMIC SITUATIONS

Question: Your transcript reads "incomplete" for your second semester sophomore year courses. Why?

Answer: I was suspended from school for the second half of the semester for being at a party where there was excessive drinking and damage to school property. While I did not cause any damage to school property myself, I accept responsibility for the incident; I paid the penalty; and I learned my lesson. I was grateful for the opportunity to return to school. I applied myself with vigor to my studies and have never been involved in any other incident.

Question: I see that you failed two courses your last semester freshman year and then took a year off before returning to school. I assume there is a connection?

Answer: Four years ago, as a freshman, I did not know what I wanted to study, what career I wanted to pursue or what direction I was headed in. The year off from school was one of the most constructive experiences of my life. After working as a dishwasher in a restaurant for much of the year, I developed a lot of respect for the value of a college education. I came to school completely refreshed, embarked on a major in English and committed myself to pursuing a career where I could use my mind a little more and my hands a little less.

QUESTIONS ABOUT PAST WORK EXPERIENCE

Question: What were your responsibilities as a clerk during your summer job at Reliable Insurance Brokers?

Answer: The company was in the process of computerizing its files. The primary task for which I was hired was to check the computerized files for accuracy vis-a-vis the manual files. I recorded premium payments, prepared bank deposits, and sorted payables during the two weeks the bookkeeper was on vacation.

Question: Did you enjoy your summer job as a dishwasher at Washington Street Grill?

Answer: I wouldn't want to do it for the rest of my life, but it was fine for a summer job. The work was more interesting than you might think, I enjoyed my co-workers, and I had a great rapport with my boss!

Question: I see you worked as lifeguard one summer, mowed lawns another summer, and did babysitting the two other summers. Which job did you find most interesting?

Answer: Actually, by far the most interesting job I held wasn't a summer job, but a part-time job I had at school performing research for my political science professor's just-published book entitled "The Disaffected Electorate." The book is based on extensive surveys showing that most people feel that state and federal politicians are not responsive to their constituents. I personally conducted hundreds of door-to-door interviews to compile the information and helped tabulate the results. It was fascinating to be a part of this study almost from start to finish and at the same time it was dismaying to see, from the results, how disenfranchised people feel today.

Question: I see that you've been working as a waitperson at Sam's Bar & Grill since graduation. How much notice would you have to give them if I offered you this position?

Answer: I would feel obliged to offer my current employer two weeks notice. But if my boss does not object, I may be able to leave earlier.

QUESTIONS ABOUT EVALUATING YOUR FORMER EMPLOYERS

Question: Who was the toughest boss you ever had and why?

Answer: That would be Mr. Henson at Henson's Car Wash. He would push people to their limits when it got busy, and he was a stickler for detail. But he was always fair, and he went out of his way to be flexible with our work schedule and generous in advancing salaries when one of the kids was in a pinch. I would call him a tough boss, but a good boss.

Question: Tell me about a time last summer when your employer was not happy with your job performance.

Answer: In the first week on the job there were two letters that had typos in them. Frankly, I had been a little sloppy with them. But that's all that comes to mind. Ms. Heilman did tell me on at least two occasions that she was very happy with my work.

QUESTIONS ABOUT LACK OF WORK EXPERIENCE

Question: What did you do during the summer between your freshman and sophomore years at college? Your resume doesn't indicate anything about this period of time.

Answer: I tried to get a job, but the town I live in was hit very hard by a major automobile plant closing and several smaller industrial manufacturer closings. I personally visited at least 100 businesses searching for work, but to no avail. That took much of June. In July, I reviewed much of my calculus course, which was one of the toughest classes I ever took. Then in August, I moved in with a friend who had a small apartment near campus, sleeping on his living room couch. I did this so I could work temporary labor jobs in the city.

Question: I see that while you returned to your hometown each summer you worked at a different company. Why didn't you work the same job two summers in a row?

Answer: My career goal is to get a job in business after graduation. Because

I attend a liberal arts college, I can't take any courses in business. So even though I was invited back to each summer job I held, I thought I could develop more experience by working in different positions. Although I didn't list high school jobs on my resume, I did work for almost three years at the same grocery store chain.

Question: I see that you traveled each of the last two summers rather than taking a summer job. Do you expect to be traveling a lot after you graduate from college?

Answer: I figured that once I graduate from college I'll spend the next forty years of my life working, so I might as well get in some extended travel while I have a chance. I hope to begin a career position immediately upon graduating and I plan to stay with that company for some time to come.

QUESTIONS ABOUT PROBLEMS AT PREVIOUS JOBS

Question: Were you ever fired from a summer or part-time job?

Answer: Yes. I had a part-time courier job during my freshman year. I became violently ill with a stomach bug after lunch one day and had to call in sick thirty minutes before my shift began. I was immediately told that I was fired. I knew it was difficult for my boss to get a substitute courier on such short notice. But I was very dizzy and thought there would be too much risk of an accident if I reported to work.

QUESTIONS ABOUT FUTURE PLANS

Question: Do you plan to attend graduate school?

Answer: Definitely not on a full-time basis. At some point, though, I might like to take some courses at night that could contribute to my work performance.

Question: I see that you grew up in Hawaii. That's a long way away. Do you plan on going back there to live sometime in the future?

Answer: No. I would prefer to be based in a large mainland city, such as where your company is located, but I would be perfectly happy to go wherever my career might take me.

QUESTIONS ABOUT YOUR WORK PREFERENCES

Question: Why do you want to work in retailing?

Answer: I have been fascinated by the retail trade for as long as I can remember. To me each store is a stage or theater for its merchandise; there is an infinite variety of ways in which the exact same merchandise can be sold. I know it's a very challenging field, too. Merchants need to think about the current fashion trends, the needs of local consumers, building a niche in the market, and all the other aspects of running a business. Also, retail is a field that is changing very quickly today, and I want to see firsthand in what direction retailing is going in the future.

Question: What other types of positions are you interested in, and what other companies have you recently applied to for work?

Answer: Actually, I have definitely decided to pursue a career as a restaurant manager, so I am only applying for restaurant management training programs. I have recently had interviews with several other large national fast-food chains such as Super Burger and Clackey's Chicken.

Question: Have you thought about why you might prefer to work with our firm as opposed to one of the other firms to which you've applied?

Answer: Yes. I like your policy of promotion from within. I think the company's growth record is impressive and I am sure it will continue. Your firm's reputation for superior marketing is particularly important to me because I want to pursue a career in marketing. Most important of all, it seems that your firm would offer me a lot of opportunities—not just for possible advancement but also to learn about many different product lines—all within one company.

QUESTIONS ABOUT YOU AS A PERSON

Question: Tell me about yourself.

Answer: It takes me about thirty minutes in the morning to wake up but after that I'm all revved up and ready to go. I have a tremendous amount of energy and love challenges at school, at work, and at home. This is true even when I'm performing mundane tasks, such as when I worked at the direct mail house last summer stuffing brochures into envelopes. I set up a challenge for myself to have the highest pace of anyone in the office; and I succeeded on every day but four during the entire summer. I also enjoy being around other people and working with them and doing anything I can to help the other people around me. For example, I really enjoyed tutoring freshmen in math. So while I push myself to high levels of performance and to achieve constantly more challenging goals, I try to remain sensitive to the concerns of people around me.

Question: How would you like other people to think of you?

Answer: I like people to think that I am always there when my friends need me. But even more than that, I want to be thought of as always fair, considerate and even-handed with anyone I meet. I want everyone I come into contact with to be able to say afterwards that it was a positive experience.

CHAPTER NINETEEN

After the Interview

NOW THAT YOU'VE made it through the toughest part, what should you do? First, breathe a sigh of relief! Then, as soon as you've left the interview site, write down your thoughts about the interview while they're still fresh in your mind. Ask yourself key questions. What does the position entail? What do you like and dislike about the position and the company? Did you make any mistakes or have trouble answering any of the questions? Did you feel you were well prepared? If not, what could you do to improve your performance in the future? Carefully consider all of these questions; if you find that your performance was lacking, work to improve it.

Be sure to record the name and title of the person you interviewed with, as well as the names and titles of anyone else you may have met. Don't forget to write down what the next agreed-upon step would be. Will they contact you? How soon?

WRITING YOUR FOLLOW-UP LETTER

Next, write a brief follow-up letter thanking the interviewer. You should do this immediately—within one or two days of the interview in order to make sure that you stay in the forefront of the recruiter's mind. The letter should be typewritten and no longer than one page. Express your appreciation for the opportunity to interview with the recruiter and your continued enthusiasm about the position and the company. Above all, make sure that the letter is personalized—don't send out a form letter!

An example of a follow-up letter to send to an employer after a job interview is included at the end of this chapter.

WHEN TO CALL

Allow the employer a week to ten days to contact you after receiving your letter. If you still haven't heard anything after this time, you should follow up with a phone call. Express your continued interest in the firm and in the position; inquire as to whether or not any decisions have been made or when you will be notified.

WHAT'S NEXT?

Don't be discouraged if you do not get an immediate response from an employer—most companies interview many applicants before making a final decision. The key is to remain fresh in the recruiter's mind. Beyond that, it's a waiting game.

But don't just sit by the phone! Take advantage of this time: contact other firms and schedule more interviews so that if rejection does come, then you have other options open. This is a good idea even if you end up receiving a job offer because you'll have a number of options to choose from and you'll be in a better position to make an informed decision. If you place too much importance on a single interview, you will not only waste time and energy—you will also increase the chances of a drop in your morale if the offer doesn't come through. So keep plugging!

HANDLING REJECTION

Rejection is inevitable, and it will happen to you as it happens to all other job-hunters. The key is to not take it personally.

One way you can turn rejection around is by contacting each person who sends you a rejection letter. Thank your contact for considering you for the position and ask for feedback so that you can improve your resume or your interview performance. Ask for suggestions that will help you improve your chances for getting a job in the industry. Ask for the names of people who might require your skills—or just be willing to talk with you about the industry. Ask, "What would you do in my situation? Who would you call?"

Two cautions are in order. First, do not ask employers to tell you why they didn't hire you. Not only will this put the employer in an awkward position, you will probably get a very negative reaction. And second, realize that even if you contact employers solely for impartial feedback, not everyone will be willing to talk with you.

But above everything else, don't give up. Stay positive and motivated, and learn from the process. Success might be right around the corner.

Sample Follow-up Letter

460 Brook Road
Santa Fe, New Mexico 87541
505/555-5561

September 22, 1993

Joseph C. Barber
Director of Human Resources
Kendall Pharmaceuticals
11241 Sundown Drive
Albuquerque, New Mexico 87154

Dear Mr. Barber:

Thank you for the opportunity to discuss your opening for a statistician. I enjoyed meeting with you and Ms. Tate, Director, and learning more about Kendall Pharmaceuticals.

I believe that my experience at the Department of Labor and my educational background in statistics, economics, and business administration qualify me for the position. My extensive knowledge of computers and statistical software would also be especially valuable to me as a statistician with your firm.

I was particularly impressed with Kendall's strong commitment to innovation and growth, as well as its plans to expand into the overseas market. I feel that this type of environment would challenge me to do my best work.

I look forward to hearing from you within the next two weeks. In the meantime, please call me if I can provide more information or answer any questions to assist in your decision.

Sincerely,

Alison A. Granville

Alison Ann Granville

CHAPTER TWENTY

The Job Offer

CONGRATULATIONS! You've won a job offer—or maybe even a few. What do you do now?

Let's start with some basic considerations. What is the minimum salary you can live on? What is the going rate in the current market for that particular position? Don't wait until you get to the offer stage to determine these figures, though—do it long before entering into negotiations with potential employers.

To consider the offer seriously, you should feel confident that this is a job you really want, that the field is one you'd like to pursue a career in and that you are willing to live and work in the area in question. Ask yourself: is the lifestyle and work schedule associated with your potential new occupation one you would enjoy? Presumably you've had time to think about these issues and about whether or not this particular position satisfies your basic financial requirements.

IMPORTANT FACTORS TO CONSIDER

Once you've received the offer, of course, you should have all the information about the position necessary for you in order to make a sound decision. This includes:

- □ start date
- □ job title and associated responsibilities
- □ potential for career progression
- □ salary, overtime and compensation
- □ bonus structure
- □ tuition reimbursement or possible graduate students
- □ vacation and parental leave policy
- □ life, medical, and dental insurance coverage
- □ pension plan
- □ job location
- □ travel

If you're unsure of any of this information, don't assume that it will be to your satisfaction. Contact the personnel representative or recruiting contact and confirm all important details.

MONEY

Money may seem like the biggest criterion in accepting a job, but it can often cloud the decision-making process. Don't accept a job that you are not enthusiastic about simply because the starting salary is a few thousand dollars higher. (After taxes, the few thousand dollars may be virtually meaningless.) Concern yourself with finding a job that lets you do something you enjoy. Ask yourself whether the job presents a career path with upward movement and experience, and whether it will enable you to establish yourself and have greater career mobility in your future. Don't make the mistake of convincing yourself that you "want" a job solely because of a few extra dollars.

BENEFITS

Benefits can make a big difference in your compensation package—don't overlook them! Perhaps the most important benefit to consider is health insurance. With health insurance costs skyrocketing, you should be sure to find out if the company covers these costs in full. If the company, like many others, only pays a percentage of these costs, make certain that you can afford to pay the difference out of your own pocket.

What about life and dental insurance? Does the company have a bonus structure? This can contribute significantly to your salary. Is there a pension plan? What is the organization's policy on vacation and sick time? You should consider all of these factors carefully.

If graduate school is in your future plans, it is important for you to find out if the organization will pay for your education and if the employer will give you the time to attend classes. Some organizations offer tuition incentives but require so much overtime that it is almost impossible to take advantage of the benefit.

CAREER PROGRESSION

Career progression is another important factor in evaluating an offer. Some organizations may bring you on board at a relatively high level and then curtail your movement. Be clear about future opportunities for advancement. Find out how often performance reviews are conducted—this could have a considerable impact on your salary in the long run. Don't let a low initial salary discourage you too much; understand the long-range income potential, as well.

WORK ENVIRONMENT

Another important factor to consider is the kind of environment you will be working in. Is the company's atmosphere comfortable, challenging, and exciting? Consider specifics, including office or work station setting, privacy, proximity to other staff, amount of space, noise level and lighting. What is the level of interaction among co-workers? Some organizations strongly encourage teamwork and dialogue among staff, while others prefer to emphasize individual accomplishment and discourage a great deal of interaction among employees. Which approach do you prefer? It's important to consider all of these factors carefully; if you don't like the work environment before you accept the job, you probably won't like it as an employee.

DO YOUR HOMEWORK

Supplement the information provided by the organization by searching journals and newspapers for articles about the company and, if possible, by talking to current employees. Try to get objective comments—not (for instance) information from someone who was recently fired by the company. Alumni of your college or university in similar positions or employed by the same organization may be an excellent source of information.

THE ART OF NEGOTIATION

If you are disappointed or dissatisfied with any of the conditions, find out what's negotiable. Some organizations offer flexible benefits packages or "menu" benefit plans where an employee gets to choose from a variety of options.

Now is the best time to ask about such plans. If you're unable to negotiate an arrangement you feel comfortable with, this may be an indication that you should consider other offers or continue looking for a more suitable position. Don't make the mistake of accepting a position that you are unhappy with. Trust your instincts—if you are dissatisfied with the employer before your start date, this feeling will probably have a negative impact on your work and your success.

At the same time, however, you must keep in mind that competition for jobs is fierce in today's tough economy. Employers don't have to look very far to find somebody else to fill a position you turned down. Keep your expectations realistic and don't ask for the stars right now. Once you've been working for that employer for a while and have proven yourself to be a valuable commodity, you can attempt further negotiations.

MAKING YOUR FINAL DECISION

Probably the most important thing to consider in evaluating an offer is whether you will be happy with the job and accomplish what is important to you. Don't accept a job because your friend works there or because a relative thinks it sounds great. Talk the offer over with other people but trust your own reasoning ability. If you are confused, discuss your concerns with a career counselor and then make an informed decision based on what is right for you.

CHAPTER TWENTY-ONE

Any Questions?

FOLLOWING ARE ANSWERS to some of the most common questions college students and recent grads have about job searching.

How many companies should I expect to contact before I can find a job?

This varies from person to person, but you can be sure that you'll have to contact many companies before you find an acceptable job. The typical graduating student might contact between 300 and 700 companies before getting a job. For some it could be less. There might be an occasional lucky student who finds a job soon after beginning the search, but cases such as these are few and far between.

Remember, if you put all of your effort into your job search and contact many companies each week, it is much more likely that you'll get a job sooner than someone who is only searching casually and sending out only one or two resumes a week. It bears repeating: making only a half-hearted job search effort is a major error. Students who make this mistake typically find themselves discouraged after making little or no progress even after several months, and often settle for the first job offer they are presented with—even if it isn't a job they want.

How do I decide which job to seek?

Consider the good part-time jobs you've had, the classes you enjoyed most, or your extracurricular interests. Identify the activities or skills you'd like to develop further. Do you prefer to work alone or with a team? You may enjoy a work environment where there is a lot of teamwork and socializing, or where problem solving alone is the norm. What kinds of people do you like to work with? You may shine among imaginative people who like to brainstorm solutions, or you may do better with highly-organized friends and co-workers who like to make data-driven decisions quickly.

Do you prefer to work on many projects at once, or to concentrate on one assignment at a time? What about your social and lifestyle preferences? Some jobs require certain behaviors and dress. Can you see yourself on the phone a lot, in meetings making presentations, in front of a computer terminal, or even outdoors most of the time? You may decide that the values and goals of the organization you work for may mean more to you than the tasks you perform or the physical environment you work in.

Companies vary greatly in work environments—and in what they expect from employees. It is up to you to determine what you like most and what you want to develop in yourself, and to decide whether a given job represents a good match.

Another way to gain insight is to meet with people already employed in the field. Contact your career services office and/or your alumni office to see if they have a mentor program or if they can refer you to alumni or other contacts who can help you meet with established professionals in a certain field. This is one of the best ways to get inside information about a job. Ask questions: what does the individual like (and dislike) about the job? How did your contact get started in the field? If you decide to pursue a job in this area, you'll have not only information, but a potential contact as well.

Above all, keep in mind that first jobs do not necessarily reflect a person's career. A career is a long-term process that can take years to develop; rather than asking yourself, "What is the job that's right for me?" ask yourself, "What would I like to try first?"

Will it hurt my chances of getting a good job if I take time off the summer after graduation?

Unfortunately, it will. Companies like to hire students who want to work. You have a much stronger chance of getting a great job while you are still a student just before you graduate than you do after graduation. Of course, you can still get a good job after graduation, especially if you are aggressive about it. But you shouldn't wait, if you can avoid it, until after graduation to start looking for a job. Your best bet is to begin your job search early in your senior year so that you have an advantage over other students who do procrastinate.

I'm having a hard time getting informational interviews. what should I do?

Many people, when they are contacted by job-seekers, assume that they will be asked to give that person a job. In order to avoid this problem, tell your contact right away that all you would like is to learn more about the industry or company in question, and that you'll be the one asking all the questions. Also, unless it's specifically requested, you should not send your resume to someone you'd like to meet for an informational interview. This will almost always give the wrong impression.

What benefits should I expect?

That depends on the size of the company. A very small company with less than a dozen or so employees might not offer any benefits at all. But a large company with hundreds or thousands of employees will probably offer very good benefits. The most commonly offered benefit (besides vacation time and sick days) is a health plan. Typically companies offer health insurance or a Health Maintenance Organization (HMO) plan. Today, however, very few companies pay for 100% of your health insurance or HMO costs. You might be expected to pay 50% or more of these costs. This is certainly an important factor to take into consideration when weighing job offers.

Other benefits that might be offered to you are life insurance, disability insurance, tuition reimbursement, pension plans, and profit sharing plans. When you are evaluating job offers, you will certainly want to find out what the fringe benefits are because they can make a significant difference. However, it bears repeating that you shouldn't ask about fringe benefits until after you are offered the position.

Can I expect to find a job if there is a high unemployment rate in my city or town?

No matter how high the unemployment rate is in a particular area, there will still be jobs available. You should realize, though, that these jobs will be hard to find, and that the competition for these positions will be intense. You might be better off trying to find a job in another city where the unemployment rate isn't so high. On the other hand, the movement within the workforce itself—the regular transition of people entering and leaving the workforce, those changing jobs, and new jobs being created—is going on despite the rate of unemployment at any given time. This creates opportunities even when the unemployment rate is high across the country.

Don't let statistics scare you. Remember, you are only looking for one job; you have a considerable amount of control over what kind of job you get and how long it takes because you control how much effort you put into your job search campaign.

I'm a full scholarship student. Won't employers understand if I don't buy a professional outfit for interviews?

No! Employers fully expect that you will be dressed professionally. You don't need to be on the leading edge of fashion, but your interview attire must fit well, be meticulously clean, and be somewhat more conservative than what you'd expect to wear in that position on a daily basis.

I'm sending out lots of letters—but I'm not getting interviews. What should I do?

Perhaps you are sending out enough letters—but are you making enough phone calls? Many students try to avoid making phone calls, assuming that employers will contact them. Following up your resume and cover letter with a phone call is very important and will dramatically increase your chances of getting an interview.

But what if you are sending out lots of letters *and* making lots of phone calls, and you still aren't getting interviews? If this is the case, then you really need to reconsider all of the different aspects of your job search campaign. Ask yourself:

- ☐ Is this a realistic position for you to be striving for?
- ☐ Does your resume look sharp?
- ☐ Is your cover letter personalized, or does it resemble a form letter?
- ☐ Are you sending out a large number of letters each month or just a few dozen?
- ☐ Are you contacting companies that are smaller and less known? Are you using all the different job-search methods outlined in Chapter Four?
- ☐ Are you networking as much as you should be?

If you are getting a number of interviews but no job offers, chances are you need to work on your interview performance. Remember, you should consider not only what you say during job interviews but how you are saying it. Do you present yourself as mature and confident or are you nervous and unsure of your answers? If you need to improve your interview skills, you might want to read *Knock 'Em Dead: The Ultimate Job-Seeker's Handbook* by Martin Yate. The most popular and best-written job hunting book ever written, *Knock 'Em Dead* should help you to improve your interview skills dramatically and increase your chances of winning job offers.

Whatever you do, *practice*: practice interviewing with different relatives and friends—and even in the mirror! There is no substitute for practice. The more you do it, the more confident you'll feel and the better you'll present yourself during your actual interviews.

Is the phone book a good place to find companies to contact?

The phone book, like other directories, can be a useful source of company listings for job-hunters. However, I suggest that you use other resources (such as the *JobBank* series) which give information about the company itself, typical positions within the company, and the names of contact persons.

I really want to work for a certain large company. How can I get a job there?

As a general rule, it is a bad idea to target one large company. One of the keys of job searching is applying at many different companies. By this I don't mean five or six or even twenty, but hundreds of companies. Don't make the mistake of waiting for one company to call you. If you do, your chances of getting a good job are extremely slim, and you will cut yourself off from other great opportunities that might be available.

If, despite these warnings, you still insist on working for a certain large company, there are some things you can do to improve your chances. First, find out everything there is to know about this company. Research it in trade literature, find articles written about it, read books about it (if you can find them), and read books about the industry in general. Apply to every job opening the company advertises in the newspaper, and write to the personnel office as well as the head of the department you want to work in.

But the most important thing you should do is network. If the firm is a very large company, someone from your high school or college may work there. If this doesn't yield any leads, you should request an interview with someone from the company to find out more about the industry and the company itself. If you can't find people in your alumni journal or through networking, find networking leads on your own. Look in articles and your other sources of information to find names of people you can contact at that company.

Large companies will often have an inside newsletter that is distributed within the organization that lists job openings. Universities and hospitals, for example, often have such newsletters. Try to get a copy from the human resources department—it could be a valuable resource for job leads.

Don't most companies hire almost exclusively through college recruiting, and mostly in the spring?

No! Most companies, even companies that recruit, will tell you that about half of their hires are from unsolicited resumes and walk-in candidates. Most companies hire throughout the year. The fall is actually a good time to look for a job, because production cycles are beginning in many industries.

If I have to travel a long distance for an interview, can I expect the company to pay for my expenses?

More and more, companies are cutting back on recruitment expenses. This means that some companies will rely more heavily on telephone screening and on career fairs, which enable them to review hundreds of applicants per day. Furthermore, if you're looking for a job in a distant city, transportation and hotel fees may have to come out of your own pocket. However, you should know that companies that are willing to pay for the travel costs of out-of-state applicants often cut costs by accomplishing more in fewer visits. You may be asked to complete all of your interviews, physical exams, and the like during your first visit.

I'm very shy and the thought of going on job interviews petrifies me. What should I do?

For most employers, shyness is not a major problem unless it interferes with your work. In fact, employees are often valued for their shyness because they tend to get along well with other workers and don't participate in office politics. However, shyness can hurt your chances of landing a job if you resist contacting new people and communicating that you're qualified for the position.

There are several steps you can take to overcome shyness. First, when networking, contact only people you feel comfortable with and ask them to introduce you to others. This way, you don't have to call any strangers and you know that all of your inquiries will be welcomed. Begin with friends, relatives, and neighbors and you will soon be well on your way to making important contacts.

Another idea is to seek out volunteer work or an internship in the field you would like to enter. Volunteering and interning allow you the opportunity to show an employer your skills and abilities rather than having to discuss them in an pressure-filled interview. Many employers prefer to hire volunteers and interns because they are known quantities.

You probably won't be able to avoid job interviews altogether, though. Your best bet is to manage your shyness as best you can. For the first few minutes of your interview, just listen to the interviewer talk, interject a few questions or comments here and there, and let yourself relax. When you're asked about your accomplishments, simply relate what occurred rather than telling the recruiter that you were brilliant or that you did a great job. Let recruiters come to their own conclusions; they'll not only see the positive qualities that led to your accomplishments, but they'll appreciate your modesty as well.

If it makes you feel more comfortable, tell the recruiter right away that you tend to be shy and you're feeling a little nervous. This often breaks the ice and will keep the employer from assuming that you're trying to hide something or that your shyness is a sign of something else.

Who are the best people to use as references?

The best references are always people you've worked for. Recruiters are always more interested in what previous employers thought of your work on the job than a professor in school, even if it's a relatively simple job. The best time to get a reference is while you're still working, but don't be shy about asking a previous employer to act as a reference.

You should have letters of recommendation sent directly to you and not to an employer. Promptly send a thank-you note after someone has written you a letter of recommendation. You should do this even if the letter isn't an enthusiastic one because that person could be called by an employer for a verbal reference. (However, if the letter of recommendation isn't glowing, you should not use it.)

How many letters of recommendation do I need?

You don't really need any letters of recommendation to get hired. It's more important to know a couple of people you can use as references if the employer asks. It's a good idea, however, to have two or three letters available to present at the interview. (Letters of recommendation can substitute for references if the employer has a hard time reaching them.)

Should I apply to ads in the newspapers that don't identify the employer?

Yes. As you now know, you're less likely to get a job through newspaper ads than through other methods such as networking or direct contact. Nonetheless, there are many legitimate job opportunities advertised through "blind" ads, and there are many good reasons companies choose to run blind advertisements. The firm may not wish to be deluged with phone calls or it may be trying to replace someone who hasn't been terminated yet.

Be aware that on rare occasions, blind ads have been used for deceitful purposes. For example, there have been instances where blind ads have been used as a means of selling employment marketing services or for obtaining sexual favors from the applicant.

When newspaper ads ask for salary requirements, should I give them?

State your salary requirements — but as a range. For example, your cover letter may read, "I seek a starting salary between $18,000 and $22,000."

Should I join a professional organization?

Generally you want to make as many contacts as you can in situations that you feel comfortable in. However, if you don't feel comfortable attending meetings of professional associations and you don't feel comfortable asking people for jobs or advice in these situations, don't join. If you're not sure how you'll feel, attend a meeting and find out.

What should I do if I'm asked an illegal interview question?

Many people who conduct job interviews simply don't know what is legal and illegal for interview questions. Questions about age, race, religion, and marital status are among those that are illegal. For more information on this issue, see *Knock 'Em Dead: The Ultimate Job-Seeker's Handbook* by Martin Yate.

If you are asked an illegal interview question, you should either answer the question or gracefully point out that the question is illegal and decline to answer it. Avoid reacting in a hostile fashion—remember that you can always decide later that this is a not a company you want to work for.

Shouldn't I find a job that justifies the investment in my education?

Your salary is important to the extent that it enables you to meet your financial obligations after college. If you choose a job primarily because of the financial rewards, you need to be aware that you may be putting money ahead of personal satisfaction.

Conclusion

"No person who is enthusiastic about his work has anything to fear from life."

— *Samuel Goldwyn*

"Nothing happens until you make it happen."

— *Anonymous*

BY THE TIME you read this, you should be well into your job search. Hopefully, you're turning up more contacts and job leads every day—and if not, you're reevaluating and revising your plan. Perhaps you're even interviewing and receiving job offers!

But whatever stage you happen to be at in your job search, realize that you're going to experience some setbacks. You may feel anxious and frustrated, and some days you simply won't want to send out any resumes or make networking calls. This is normal! But the key, at these times, is to make sure you don't let your job search come to a standstill. If you feel that you need a break, don't stop searching altogether—just slow down the pace for a day or two. Even if you're sending out only one letter or making one phone call, at least you're still making progress.

Job-searching is tough for everyone—but if you work hard and focus on your goals, the possibilities are endless! Your first job can be a source of great personal satisfaction and is well worth the effort it takes to find it.

Keep trying and keep learning. The rest will fall into place.

Great Jobs for College Grads of the 90's

THE FOLLOWING CHAPTER includes descriptions of some great jobs for college graduates, with an emphasis on those occupations that have especially strong growth outlooks for the 1990's. For each position, there is a brief description of what the job entails, the background or qualifications you would need for entering and advancing in that occupation, and an indication of working conditions. The occupations listed are as follows:

Accountant/Auditor
Actuary
Advertising Worker
Bank Officer/Manager
Biochemist
Buyer/Merchandise Manager
Chemist
Claims Representative
Commercial Artist
Dietician/Nutritionist
Economist
Engineer
Executive Assistant
Financial Analyst
Forester
Geographer
Geologist/Geophysicist
Hotel Manager/Assistant Manager
Industrial Designer

Insurance Agent/Broker
Manager
Mathematician
Personnel and Labor Relations Specialist
Physicist
Psychologist
Public Relations Worker
Purchasing Agent
Quality Control Supervisor
Reporter/Editor
Sales Representative for Manufacturers/Wholesalers
Securities and Financial Services Sales Representative
Sociologist
Statistician
Systems Analyst
Technical Writer/Editor
Underwriter

ACCOUNTANT/AUDITOR

Accountants prepare and analyze financial reports that furnish important financial information. Four major fields are public, management, and government accounting, and internal auditing. Public accountants have their own businesses or work for accounting firms. Management accountants, also called industrial or private accountants, handle the financial records of their company. Government accountants examine the records of government agencies and audit private businesses and individuals whose dealings are subject to government regulation.

Accountants often concentrate on one phase of accounting. For example, many public accountants specialize in auditing, tax, or estate planning. Others specialize in management consulting and give advice on a variety of topics. Management accountants provide the financial information executives need to make sound business decisions. They may work in areas such as taxation, budgeting, costs, or investments. Internal auditors examine and ensure efficient and economical operation. Government accountants are often Internal Revenue Service agents or are involved in financial management and budget administration.

About 60 percent of all accountants do management accounting. An additional 25 percent are engaged in public accounting through independent firms. Other accountants work for government, and some teach in colleges and universities. Accountants and auditors are found in all business, industrial, and governmental organizations.

Although the best way to enter the accounting field is with a four-year accounting degree, liberal arts grads should not overlook this field—especially when jobs are scarce. One disadvantage is that a non-accounting major would probably have to start in a clerical position and learn on the job in order to make career advances.

A typical entry-level position might be general accounting clerk, payroll clerk, accounts receivable clerk, or accounts payable clerk. In applying for these clerical positions, any background in computers or data-entry experience is desirable. Previous experience in accounting can help an applicant get a job; many colleges offer students an opportunity to gain experience through summer or part-time internship programs conducted by public accounting firms. Such training is invaluable in gaining permanent employment in the field.

Perhaps one of the best entry-level accounting positions for a person without an accounting degree is a collections clerk. A collections clerk telephones customers (and in some instances writes to customers) in order to speed payment of overdue bills. There is often a high turnover in this position because the work requires a great deal of energy and persistence. Nonetheless, for a mature, articulate college grad, this could be the first step in a rewarding career in accounting.

ACTUARY

Actuaries design insurance and pension plans that can be maintained on a sound financial basis. They assemble and analyze statistics to calculate probabilities of death, sickness, injury, disability, unemployment, retirement, and property loss from accident, theft, fire, and other hazards. Actuaries use this information to determine the expected insured loss. The actuary calculates premium rates and determines policy contract provisions for each type of insurance offered. Most actuaries specialize in either life and health insurance, or property and liability (casualty) insurance; a growing number specialize in pension plans. About two-thirds of all actuaries work for private insurance companies, the majority in life insurance. Consulting firms and rating bureaus employ about one-fifth of all actuaries. Other actuaries work for private organizations administering independent pension and welfare plans.

A good educational background for a beginning job in a large life or casualty insurance company is a bachelor's degree in mathematics or statistics; a degree in actuarial science is preferred. Courses in accounting, computer science, economics, and insurance also are useful. Of equal importance, however, is the need to pass one or more of the exams offered by professional actuarial societies. Three societies sponsor programs leading to full professional status in the specialty. The Society of Actuaries gives nine actuarial exams for the life and health insurance, and pension fields; The Casualty Actuarial Society gives ten exams for the property and liability fields; and the American Society of Pension Actuaries gives nine exams covering the pension field. Actuaries are encouraged to complete the entire series of exams as soon as possible; completion generally takes from five to ten years. Actuaries who complete five exams in either the life insurance segment of the pension series, or seven exams in the casualty series are awarded "associate" membership in their society. Those who have passed an entire series receive full membership and the title "Fellow".

Beginning actuaries often rotate among different jobs to learn various actuarial operations and to become familiar with different phases of insurance work. At first, their work may be routine, such as preparing tabulations for actuarial tables or reports. As they gain experience, they may supervise clerks, prepare correspondence and reports, and do research. Advancement to more responsible positions such as assistant, associate, or chief actuary depends largely on job performance and the number of actuarial exams passed. Many actuaries, because of their broad knowledge of insurance and related fields, are selected for administrative positions in other company activities, particularly in underwriting, accounting, or data processing. Many advance to top executive positions.

ADVERTISING WORKER

There are several different occupations commonly associated with the field of advertising. Advertising managers direct the advertising program of the business for which they work. They determine the size of the advertising budget, the type of ad and the medium to use, and what advertising agency, if any, to employ. Managers who decide to employ an agency work closely with the advertising agencies to develop advertising programs for client firms and individuals. Copywriters develop the text and headlines to be used in the ads. Media directors negotiate contracts for advertising for advertising space or air time. Production managers and their assistants arrange to have the ad printed for publication, filmed for television, or recorded for radio.

Most advertising companies prefer college graduates for entry-level positions. Some employers seek persons with degrees in advertising with heavy emphasis on marketing, business, and journalism; others prefer graduates with a liberal arts background; some employers place little emphasis on the type of degree. Opportunities for advancement in this field generally are excellent for creative, talented, and hard-working people. For example, copywriters and account executives may advance within their specialties, or to managerial jobs if they demonstrate ability in dealing with clients. Some especially capable employees may become partners in an existing agency, or they may establish their own agency.

BANK OFFICER/MANAGER

Because banks offer a broad range of services, a wide choice of careers is available. Loan officers may handle installment, commercial, real estate, or agricultural loans. To evaluate loan applications properly, officers need to be familiar with economics, production, distribution, merchandising, and commercial law, as well as have a knowledge of business operations and financial analysis. Bank officers in trust management must have knowledge of financial planning and investment research for estate and trust administration.

Operations officers plan, coordinate, and control the work flow, update systems, and strive for administrative efficiency. Careers in bank operations include electronic data processing manager and other positions involving internal and customer services. A correspondent bank officer is responsible for relations with other banks; a branch manager, for all functions of a branch office; and an international officer, for advising customers with financial dealings abroad. A working knowledge of a foreign country's financial system, trade relations, and economic conditions is beneficial to those interested in international banking. Other career fields for bank officers are auditing, economics, personnel administration, public relations, and operations research.

Bank officers and management positions generally are filled by management trainees, and occasionally by promoting outstanding bank clerks and tellers. A business administration degree with concentrations in finance or a liberal arts curriculum, including accounting, economics, commercial law, political science, or statistics, serves as excellent preparation for officer trainee positions. In large banks that have special training programs, promotions may occur more quickly. For a senior officer position, however, an employee usually needs many years of experience. Although experience, ability, and leadership are emphasized for promotion, advancement may be accelerated by special study. The American Bankers Association (ABA) offers courses, publications, and other training aids to officers in every phase of banking. The American Institute of Banking, an arm of the ABA, has long filled the same educational need among bank support personnel.

BIOCHEMIST

Biochemists study the chemical composition and behavior of living things. They often study the effects of food, hormones, or drugs on various organisms. The methods and techniques of biochemists are applied in areas such as medicine and agriculture. More than three out of four biochemists work in basic and applied research activities. Some biochemists combine research with teaching in colleges and universities. A few work in industrial production and testing activities. About one-half of all biochemists work for colleges or universities, and about one-fourth for private industry, primarily in companies manufacturing drugs, insecticides, and cosmetics. Some biochemists work for non-profit research institutes and foundations; others for federal, state, and local government agencies. A few self-employed biochemists are consultants to industry and government.

For the most part, the minimum educational requirement for many beginning jobs as a biochemist, especially in research and teaching, is an advanced degree. A PhD is a virtual necessity for persons who hope to contribute significantly to biochemical research and advance to many management or administrative jobs. But a BS in biochemistry, biology, or chemistry may qualify some persons for entry jobs as research assistants or technicians. Graduates with advanced degrees may begin their careers as teachers or researchers in colleges or universities. In private industry, most begin in research jobs, and with experience may advance to positions in which they plan and supervise research.

BUYER/MERCHANDISE MANAGER

All merchandise sold in a retail store appears in that store on the decision of a buyer. Although all buyers seek to satisfy their stores' customers and sell at a profit, the type and variety of goods they purchase depends on the store where they work. A buyer for a small clothing store, for example, may purchase its complete stock of merchandise. Buyers who work for larger retail businesses often handle a few related lines of goods, such as men's wear, ladies' sportswear, or children's toys, among many others. Some, known as foreign buyers, purchase merchandise outside the United States.

Buyers must be familiar with the manufacturers and distributors who handle the merchandise they need. They also must keep informed about changes in existing products and the development of new ones. Merchandise Managers plan and coordinate buying and selling activities for large and medium-sized stores. They divide the budget among buyers, decide how much merchandise to stock, and assign each buyer to purchase certain goods. Merchandise Managers may review buying decisions to ensure that needed categories of goods are in stock, and help buyers to set general pricing guidelines.

Some buyers represent large stores or chains in cities where many manufacturers are located. The duties of these "market representatives" vary by employer; some purchase goods, while others supply information and arrange for store buyers to meet with manufacturer's representatives when they are in the area. New technology has altered the buyers' role in retail chain stores. Cash registers connected to a computer, known as point-of-sale terminals, allow retail chains to maintain centralized, up-to-the-minute inventory records. With these records, a single garden furniture buyer, for example, can purchase lawn chairs and picnic tables for the entire chain.

Because familiarity with the merchandise and with the retailing business itself is such a central element in the buyer's job, prior retailing experience sometimes provides sufficient preparation. More and more, however, employers prefer applicants who have a college degree. Most employers accept college grads in any field of study and train them on the job. In many stores, beginners who are candidates for buying jobs start out in executive training programs. These programs last from six to eight months, and combine classroom instruction in merchandising and purchasing with short rotations in various store jobs. This training introduces the new worker to store operations and policies, and provides the fundamentals of merchandising and management.

The trainee's first job is likely to be that of assistant buyer. The duties include supervising sales workers, checking invoices on material received, and keeping account of stock on hand. Assistant buyers gradually assume purchasing responsibilities, depending upon their individual abilities and the size of the department where they work. Training as an assistant buyer usually lasts at least one year. After years of working as a buyer, those who show exceptional ability may advance to merchandise manager. A few find promotion to top executive jobs such as general merchandise manager for a retail store or chain.

CHEMIST

Chemists search for and put into practical use new knowledge about substances. Their research has resulted in the development of a tremendous variety of synthetic materials, such as nylon and polyester fabrics. Nearly one-half of all chemists work in research and development. In basic research, chemists investigate the properties and composition of matter and the laws that govern the combination of elements. Basic research often has practical uses. In research and development, new products are created or improved. Nearly one-eighth of all chemists work in production and inspection. In production, chemists prepare instructions (batch sheets) for plant workers that specify the kind and amount of ingredients to use and the exact mixing time for each stage in the process. At each step, samples are tested for quality control to meet industry and government standards.

Other chemists work as marketing or sales representative because of their technical knowledge of the products sold. A number of chemists teach in colleges and universities. Some chemists are consultants to private industry and government agencies. Chemists often specialize in one of several fields: analytical chemists determine the structure, composition, and nature of substances, and develop new techniques; organic chemists at one time studied only the chemistry of living things, but their area has been broadened to include all carbon compounds; inorganic chemists study non-carbon compounds; and physical chemists study energy transformations to find new and better energy sources.

A BS with a major in chemistry or a related discipline is sufficient for many entry-level jobs as a chemist. However, graduate training is required for many research jobs, and most college teaching jobs require a PhD. Beginning chemists with a master's degree can usually go into applied research. The PhD is generally required for basic research for teaching in colleges and universities, and for advancement to many administrative positions.

CLAIMS REPRESENTATIVE

The people who investigate insurance claims, negotiate settlements with policy holders, and authorize payments are known as claim representatives—a group that includes claim adjusters and claim examiners. When a casualty insurance company receives a claim, the claim adjuster determines whether the policy covers it and the amount of the loss. Adjusters use reports, physical evidence, and testimony of witnesses in investigating a claim. When their company is liable, they negotiate with the claimant and settle the case. Some adjusters work with all lines of insurance. Others specialize in claims from fire, marine loss, automobile damage, workers' compensation loss, or product liability.

A growing number of casualty companies employ special adjusters to settle small claims. These workers, generally called inside adjusters or telephone adjusters, contact claimants by telephone or mail and have the policy holder send repair costs, medical bills, and other statements to the company. In life insurance companies, the counterpart of the claim adjuster is the claim examiner, who investigates questionable claims or those exceeding a specified amount. They may check claim applications for completeness and accuracy, interview medical specialists, consult policy files to verify information on a claim, or calculate benefit payments. Generally, examiners are authorized to investigate and approve payment on all claims up to a certain limit; larger claims are referred to a senior examiner.

No specific field of college study is recommended. Although courses in insurance, economics, or other business subjects are helpful, a major in most college fields is adequate preparation. Most large insurance companies provide beginning claim adjusters and examiners with on-the-job training and home study courses. Claim representatives are encouraged to take courses designed to enhance their professional skills. For example, the Insurance Institute of America offers a six semester study program leading to an associate's degree in Claims Adjusting, upon successful completion of six exams. A professional Certificate in Insurance Adjusting also is available from the College of Insurance in New York City.

The Life Office Management Association (LOMA), in cooperation with the International Claim Association, offers a claims education program for life and health examiners. The program is part of the LOMA Institute Insurance Education Program leading to the professional designation FLMI (Fellow Life Management Institute) upon successful completion of eight written exams. Beginning adjusters and examiners work on small claims under the supervision of an experienced employee. As they learn more about claim investigation and settlement, they are assigned claims that are either higher in loss value or more complex. Trainees are promoted as they demonstrate competence in handling assignments and as they progress in their course work. Employees who show unusual competence in claims work or outstanding administrative skills may be promoted to department supervisor in a field office, or to a managerial position in the home office. Qualified adjusters and examiners sometimes transfer to other departments, such as underwriting or sales.

COMMERCIAL ARTIST

Commercial artists create concepts and artwork for a wide variety of items, including direct mail advertising, brochures, catalogs, counter displays, slides, and filmstrips. They also design or lay out newspapers, magazines, and advertising circulars. Some commercial artists specialize in producing fashion illustrations, greeting cards, or book illustrations, or in making technical drawings for industry.

Typically, a team of commercial artists is supervised by an art director, whose main function is to develop a theme, idea, or design for print media. After the art director has determined the main elements of a design, the project is turned over to specialists for further refinement. The sketch artist, also called a renderer, does a rough drawing of any artwork required. The layout artist, who is concerned with graphics rather than artwork, constructs or arranges the illustrations or photographs, plans the typography, and picks colors for the project.

Other commercial artists, usually with less experience, are needed to turn out the finished products. Typographers put together headlines and other words on the ad. Mechanical artists paste up mechanicals for making printing negatives. Paste-up artists and other less experienced employees do more routine work, such as cutting mats, assembling booklets, or running errands.

In addition to having a very strong background in art, today's commercial artists need to be computer experts. The commercial artist who can step right in and start using a company's computer and software is very desirable.

Computers are becoming such an integral part of design, layout, and production that most, if not all, aspects of the design process can be done by computer alone. For instance, once a design is finalized and saved on the computer, a print file can be sent to the printer, photographer, or film director for output into negatives, slides, film, or reflective artwork—all without paper, glue, layout boards, etc. Everything is in the memory of the computer for recall in seconds. With modems, artwork can be sent around the world in minutes without ever touching human hands!

Beginning a career in this field typically requires a degree in commercial art from a two- or four-year trade school, community college, college, or university offering a program in commercial art. As discussed, a background in computers and/or graphics arts software, as well as a great deal of natural artistic talent, is essential for anyone entering this field.

DIETITIAN/NUTRITIONIST

Dietitians, sometimes called nutritionists, are professionals trained in applying the principles of nutrition to food selection and meal preparation. They counsel individuals and groups; set up and supervise food service systems for institutions such as hospitals, prisons, and schools; and promote sound eating habits through education and administration. Dietitians also work on education and research. Clinical dietitians, sometimes called therapeutic dietitians, provide nutritional services for patients in hospitals, nursing homes, clinics, or doctors' offices. They assess patients' nutritional needs, develop and implement nutrition programs, and evaluate and report the results. Clinical dietitians confer with doctors and nurses about each patient in order to coordinate nutritional intake with other treatments-medications in particular.

Community dietitians counsel individuals and groups on sound nutrition practices to prevent disease and to promote good health. Employed in such places as home health agencies, health maintenance organizations, and human service agencies that provide group and home-delivered meals, their job is to establish nutritional care plans, and communicate the principles of good nutrition in a way individuals and their families can understand. Research dietitians are usually employed in academic medical centers or educational institutions, although some work in common programs. Using established research methods and analytical techniques, they conduct studies in areas that range from basic science to practical applications. Research dietitians may examine changes in the way the body uses food over the course of a lifetime, for example, or study the interaction of drugs and diet. They may investigate the nutritional needs of persons with particular diseases, behavior modification, as it relates to diet and nutrition, or applied topics such as food service systems and equipment.

The basic educational requirement for this field is a bachelor's degree with a major in foods and nutrition or institution management. To qualify for professional credentials as a registered dietitian, the American Dietetic Association (ADA) recommends one of the following educational paths: completion of a two-year coordinated undergraduate program which includes 900 to 1,000 hours of clinical experience; completion of a bachelor's degree from an approved program plus an accredited dietetic internship; completion of a bachelor's or master's degree from an approved program and six month's approved work experience.

ECONOMIST

Economists study the way a society uses scarce resources such as land, labor, raw materials, and machinery to produce goods and services. They analyze the costs and benefits of distributing and using resources in a particular way. Their research might focus on such topics as energy costs, inflation, business cycles, unemployment, tax policy, farm prices, and many other areas. Being able to present economic and statistical concepts in a meaningful way is particularly important for economists whose research is policy directed. Economists who work for business firms may be asked to provide management with information on which decisions such as the marketing or pricing of company products are made; to look at the advisability of adding new lines of merchandise, opening new branches, or diversifying the company's operations; to analyze the effects of changes in the tax laws; or to prepare economic or business forecasts. Business economists working for firms that carry on operations abroad may be asked to prepare forecasts of foreign economic conditions. Over one half of all economists work in private industry, including manufacturing firms, banks, insurance companies, securities and investment companies, economic research firms and management consulting firms. Some run their own consulting businesses. A number of economists combine a full-time job in government, business or an academic institution with part-time or consulting work in another setting.

A bachelor's degree in economics is sufficient for many beginning research, administrative, management trainee, and business sales jobs. However, graduate training is increasingly necessary for advancement to more responsible positions as economists. In government research organizations and consulting firms, economists who have master's degrees can usually qualify for more responsible research and administrative positions. A PhD may be necessary for top positions in some organizations. Experienced business economists may advance to managerial or executive positions in banks, industrial concerns, trade associations, and other organizations where they formulate practical business and administrative policy.

ENGINEER

Engineers apply the theories and principles of science and mathematics to tactical technical problems. Often, their work is the link between a scientific discovery and its useful application. Engineers design machinery, products, systems, and processes for efficient and economical performance. Engineering is a highly specialized field; the work of an engineer varies greatly by industry.

Aerospace engineers design, develop, test, and help produce commercial and military aircraft, missiles, spacecraft, and related systems. They play an important role in advancing the state of technology in commercial aviation, defense and space exploration. Aerospace engineers often specialize in an area of work such as structural design, navigational guidance and control, instrumentation and communication, or production methods. They also may specialize in one type of aerospace product, such as passenger planes, helicopters, satellites, or rockets.

Chemical engineers are involved in many phases of the production of chemicals and chemical products. They design equipment and chemical plants as well as determine methods of manufacturing these products. Often, they design and develop chemical processes such as those used to remove chemical contaminants from waste materials. Because the duties of the chemical engineer cut across many fields, these professionals must have knowledge of chemistry, physics, and mechanical and electrical engineering. This branch of engineering is so diversified and complex that chemical engineers frequently specialize in a particular operation such as oxidation or polymerization. Others specialize in pollution control or the production of a specific product, such as plastics or rubber.

Civil engineers, who work in the oldest branch of the engineering profession, design and supervise the construction of roads, harbors, airports, tunnels, bridges, water supply and sewage systems, and buildings. Major specialties within civil engineering are structural, hydraulic, environmental/sanitary, transportation, urban planning, and soil mechanics. Many civil engineers are in supervisory or administrative positions ranging from construction site supervisor, to city engineer, to top level executive. Others teach in colleges or universities, or work as consultants.

Electrical engineers design, develop, test, and supervise the manufacture of electrical and electronic equipment. Electrical equipment includes power-generating and transmission equipment used by electrical utilities, electric motors, machinery controls, and lighting and wiring in buildings, automobiles, and aircraft. Electronic equipment includes radar, computers, communications equipment, and consumer goods such as television sets and stereos. Electrical engineers also design and operate facilities for generating and distributing electrical power.

Electrical engineers generally specialize in a single major area, such as integrated circuits, computers, electrical equipment manufacturing, communications, or power distributing equipment, or in a subdivision of these areas, such as microwave communication or aviation electronic systems. Electrical engineers design new products, specify their uses, and write performance requirements and maintenance schedules.

Industrial engineers determine the most effective ways for an organization to use the basic factors of production—people, machines and materials. They are more concerned with people and methods of business organization than are engineers in other specialties, who generally are concerned more with particular products or processes, such as metals, power or mechanics. To solve organizational, production, and related problems most efficiently, industrial engineers design data processing systems and apply mathematical concepts. They also develop management control systems to aid in financial planning and cost analysis, design production planning and control systems to coordinate activities and control product quality, and design or improve systems for the physical distribution of goods and services. Industrial engineers also conduct plant location surveys, where they look for the best combination of sources of raw materials, transportation, and tax obligations, and develop wage and salary administration positions and job evaluation programs. Many industrial engineers move into managerial positions because the work is so closely related to management.

Metallurgical engineers develop new types of metals with characteristics tailored for specific requirements, such as heat resistance, lightweight strength, or high malleability. They also develop methods to process and convert metals into useful products. Most of these engineers work in one of three major branches of metallurgy: extractive or chemical, physical, or mechanical. Extractive metallurgists are concerned with extracting metals from ores, and refining and alloying them to obtain useful materials. Physical metallurgists deal with the nature, structure, and physical properties of metals and their alloys, and with the methods of converting refined metals into final products. Mechanical metallurgists develop methods to work and shape materials, such as casting, forging, rolling, and drawing.

Mining engineers find, extract, and prepare minerals for manufacturing industries to use. They design open pit and underground mines, supervise the construction of mine shafts and tunnels in underground operations, and devise methods for transporting minerals to processing plants. Mining engineers are responsible for the economical and efficient operation of mines and mine safety, including ventilation, water supply, power, communications, and equipment maintenance. Some mining engineers work with geologists and metallurgical engineers to locate and appraise new ore deposits. Others develop new mining equipment or direct mineral processing operations, which involve separating minerals from the dirt, rock, and other materials they are mixed with. Mining engineers frequently specialize in the mining of one specific mineral such as coal or copper. With today's increased emphasis on protecting the environment, many mining engineers have been working to solve problems related to mined land reclamation and water and air pollution.

Petroleum engineers are mainly involved in exploring and drilling for oil and gas. They work to achieve the maximum profitable recovery of oil and gas from a petroleum reservoir by determining and developing the best and most efficient methods. Since only a small proportion of the oil and gas in a reservoir will flow out under natural forces, petroleum engineers develop and use various artificial recovery methods, such as flooding the oil field with water to force the oil to the surface. Even when using the best recovery methods, about half of the oil is still left in the ground. Petroleum engineers' research and development efforts to increase the proportion of oil recovered in each reservoir can make a significant contribution to increasing available energy resources.

A bachelor's degree in engineering from an accredited engineering program is generally acceptable for beginning engineering jobs. College graduates trained in one of the natural sciences or mathematics also may qualify for some beginning jobs. Most engineering degrees may be obtained in branches such as electrical, mechanical, or civil engineering. College graduates with a degree in science or mathematics and experienced engineering technicians may also qualify for some engineering jobs, especially in engineering specialties in high demand. Graduate training is essential for engineering faculty positions but is not required for the majority of entry level engineering jobs. All 50 states require licensing for engineers whose work may affect life, health or property, or who offer their services to the public.

Beginning engineering graduates usually work under the supervision of experienced engineers, and, in larger companies, may receive seminar or classroom training. As engineers advance in knowledge, they may become technical specialists, supervisors, or (as noted earlier) managers or administrators within the field of engineering. Some engineers obtain advanced degrees in business administration to improve their growth opportunities, while others obtain law degrees and become patent attorneys.

EXECUTIVE ASSISTANT

Not to be confused with a strictly secretarial position, a true executive assistant's position involves a good deal of self-directed work and provides for a good opportunity to gain a quick understanding of how a particular company operates.

The duties and responsibilities of an executive assistant will vary from company to company and even from one manager to the next. Some managers might use this title to refer to a position that is only secretarial in nature—one in which, for example, all of the work would be highly directed towards clerical duties such as taking dictation and filing. A true executive assistant, however, will spend a good portion of time performing fairly autonomous duties that require some degree of decision-making. More commonly, however, an executive assistant will perform a mixture of highly-directed clerical tasks and more interesting self-directed work.

Perhaps the biggest advantage of this position is that an executive assistant is highly visible to the senior manager and, given a good performance record, has an excellent opportunity for advancement. It is quite possible for a recent college graduate to move into a management position via this channel.

This position requires strong office skills, such as fast and accurate typing and the ability to prepare business correspondence. Summer or part-time office experience, in addition to experience with computers or word processors, will greatly help a college graduate secure a job of this nature. Although a bachelor's degree is not always required for this position, it is becoming an increasingly valuable asset and will greatly improve an applicant's employability and chances for promotion.

FINANCIAL ANALYST

A financial analyst prepares the financial reports required by the firm to conduct its operations and satisfy tax and regulatory requirements. They also oversee the flow of cash and financial instruments and develop information to assess the present and future financial status of the firm.

A bachelor's degree in business, economics, accounting or finance is suitable academic preparation for a financial manager. An MBA degree in addition to a bachelor's degree in any field is also desirable, though not often required. Strong analytical, quantitative, and communication skills are also needed to succeed in this field.

FORESTER

Foresters plan and supervise the growing, protection and harvesting of trees. They plot forest areas, approximate the amount of standing timber and future growth, and manage timber sales. Some foresters also protect the trees from fire, harmful insects, and disease. Some foresters also protect wildlife and manage watersheds; develop and supervise campgrounds, parks, and grazing lands; and do research. Foresters in extension work provide information to forest owners and to the general public.

A bachelor's degree in forestry is the minimum educational requirement for professional careers in forestry. In 1986, 55 colleges and universities offered bachelor's or higher degrees in forestry, 47 of these were accredited by the Society of American Foresters.

GEOGRAPHER

Geographers study the interrelationship of humans and the environment. Economic geographers deal with the geographic distribution of an area's economic activities. Political geographers are concerned with the relationship of geography to political phenomena. Physical geographers study physical processes in the earth and its atmosphere. Urban geographers study cities and metropolitan areas, while regional geographers specialize in the physical, climatic, economic, political and cultural characteristics of a particular region or area. Medical geographers study the effect of the environment on health.

The minimum educational requirement for entry-level positions is a BA or BS degree in geography. However, a masters degree is increasingly required for many entry level positions. Applicants for entry level jobs would find it helpful to have training in a specialty such as cartography, photogrammerty, remote sensing data interpretation, statistical analysis including computer science, or environmental analysis. To advance to a senior research position in private industry and perhaps gain a spot in management, a geographer would probably be required to have an advanced degree.

GEOLOGISTS AND GEOPHYSICISTS

Geologists study the structure, composition and history of the earth's crust. By examining surface rocks and drilling to recover rock cores, they determine the types and distribution of rocks beneath the earth's surface. They also identify rocks and minerals, conduct geological surveys, draw maps, take measurements, and record data. Geological research helps to determine the structure and history of the earth, and may result in significant advances, such as in the ability to predict earthquakes. An important application of geologists' work is locating oil and other natural and mineral resources. Geologists usually specialize in one or a combination of general areas: earth materials, earth processes, and earth history.

Geophysicists study the composition and physical aspects of the earth and its electric, magnetic and gravitational fields. Geophysicists usually specialize in one of three general phases of the science—solid earth, fluid earth, and upper atmosphere. Some may also study other planets.

A bachelor's degree in geology or geophysics is adequate for entry to some lower level geology jobs, but better jobs with good advancement potential usually require at least a master's degree in geology or geophysics. Persons with strong backgrounds in physics, mathematics, or computer science also may qualify for some geophysics jobs. A PhD is essential for most research positions.

HOTEL MANAGER/ASSISTANT MANAGER

Hotel managers are responsible for operating their establishments profitably and satisfying guests. They determine room rates and credit policy, direct the operation of the food science operation, and manage the housekeeping, accounting, security, and maintenance departments of the hotel. Handling problems and coping with the unexpected are important parts of the job. A small hotel or motel requires only a limited staff, and the manager may have to fill various front office duties, such as taking reservations or assigning rooms. When management is combined with ownership, these activities may expand to include all aspects of the business.

General managers of large hotels usually have several assistants or department heads who manage various parts of the operation. Because hotel restaurant and cocktail lounges are important to the success of the entire establishment, they are almost always operated by managers with experience in the restaurant field.

Other areas that are usually handled separately include advertising, rental of banquet and meeting facilities, marketing and sales, personnel and accounting. Large hotel and motel chains often centralize some activities, such as purchasing and advertising, so that individual hotels in the chain may not need managers for these departments. Managers who work for chains may be assigned to organize a newly-built or purchased hotel, or to reorganize an existing hotel or motel that is not operating successfully.

Experience is the most important consideration in selecting hotel managers. However, employers are increasingly emphasizing college education. A BA in hotel/restaurant administration provides particularly strong preparation for a career in hotel management. Most hotels promote employees who have proven their ability, usually front office clerks, to assistant manager, and eventually to general manager. Hotel and motel chains may offer better employment opportunities because employees can transfer to another hotel or motel in the chain, or to the central office if an opening occurs.

INDUSTRIAL DESIGNER

Industrial designers combine artistic talent with a knowledge of marketing, materials, and methods of production to improve the appearance and functional design of products so that they compete favorably with similar goods on the market. Although most industrial designers are engaged in product design, others are involved in different facets of design. To create favorable public images for companies and for government service, some designers develop trademarks or symbols that appear on the firm's products, advertising, brochures, and stationery. Some design containers and packages that both protect and promote their contents.

Others prepare small display exhibits or the entire layout for industrial fairs. Some design the interior layout of special purpose commercial buildings such as restaurants and supermarkets.

Corporate designers usually work only on products made by their employer. This may involve filling the day-to-day design needs of the company, or long-range planning of new products. Independent consultants who serve more than one industrial firm often plan and design a great variety of products. Most designers work for large manufacturing companies designing either consumer or industrial products, or for design consulting firms. Others do freelance work, or are on the staffs of architectural and interior design firms.

The normal requirement for entering this field of work involves completing a course of study in industrial design at an art school, university, or technical college. Most large manufacturing firms hire only industrial designers who have a bachelor's degree in the field. Beginning industrial designers frequently do simple assignments. As they gain experience, they may work on their own, and many become supervisors with major responsibility for the design of a product or group of products. Those who have an established reputation and the necessary funds may start their own consulting firms.

INSURANCE AGENT/BROKER

Agents and brokers usually sell one or more of the three basic types of insurance: life, casualty, and health. Underwriters offer various policies that, besides providing health benefits, may also provide retirement income, funds for education, or other benefits. Casualty insurance agents sell policies that protect individual policyholders from financial losses resulting from automobile accidents, fire, or theft. They also sell industrial or commercial lines, such as workers' compensation, product liability, or medical malpractice insurance. Health insurance policies offer protection against the high costs of hospital and medical care, or loss of income due to illness or injury. Many agents also offer securities, such as mutual fund shares or variable annuities.

An insurance agent may be either an insurance company employee or an independent who is authorized to represent one or more insurance companies. Brokers are not under exclusive contract with any single company, instead, they place policies directly with the company that best meets a company's needs.

Insurance agents spend most of their time discussing insurance needs with prospective and existing clients. Some time must be spent in office work to prepare reports, maintain records, plan insurance programs that are tailored to prospects' needs, and draw up lists of prospective customers. Specialists in group policies may help an employer's accountant set up a system of payroll deductions for employees covered by the policy.

All insurance agents and most insurance brokers must obtain a license in the state where they plan to sell insurance. In most states, licenses are issued only to applicants who pass written examinations covering insurance fundamentals and the state insurance laws. Agents who plan to sell mutual fund shares and other securities also must be licensed by the state. New agents usually receive training at the agencies where they will work, and frequently at the insurance company's home office. Beginners sometimes attend company-sponsored classes to prepare for the examination. Others study on their own and accompany experienced sales workers when they call on prospective clients.

MANAGER

Managers supervise employees and are accountable for the overall success of the operation which they direct. The scope and nature of a manager's responsibilities depend greatly upon the position and the size of his or her organization.

A department manager at a retail store, for example, may actually spend most of his or her time waiting on customers, and his or her managerial duties may be limited to scheduling employees' work shifts to properly staff the department, or to training new employees in such simple tasks as operating the check-out terminal, processing credit card purchases, and displaying merchandise.

A branch manager, even in a small store or service operation, might have considerably broader duties and responsibilities. He or she might, in addition to supervising and training employees, be responsible for hiring and firing decisions. He or she might have a limited ability to purchase items, and might have some control over a local advertising budget. He or she might also deal with local suppliers of goods and services. Some organizations, however, prefer to delegate rather limited responsibility to branch managers, and instead rely upon a strong network of regional managers who travel from branch to branch, making key operating decisions.

Factories or service firms with extensive processing requirements employ operations and production managers. While these managers typically supervise many people, their primary responsibility is the overall success of the operation, which may be dependent upon equipment, raw material, purchased goods, or outside vendors. The operations manager at a bank, for example, remains heavily dependent upon data processing equipment, and usually will have an extensive background in this area. The production manager at a petroleum refinery, for another example, remains heavily dependent upon a large variety of specialized equipment, and will usually have a background in engineering or chemistry.

The general manager is responsible for the overall day-to-day operations of the firm or operating unit. He or she must be acquainted with each part of the operation. In a small store, the general manager may spend most of his or her time performing non-managerial tasks such as making purchases, or even waiting on customers. In a large corporation, on the other hand, the general manager (who is often the executive vice president) will spend much of his or her time meeting with key executives in each department to ensure that company operations are being conducted successfully.

The educational background of managers and top executives varies as widely as the nature of their diverse responsibilities. Most general managers and top executives have a bachelor's degree in liberal arts or business administration. Graduate and professional degrees are common. Many managers in administrative, marketing, financial, and manufacturing activities have a master's degree in business administration. Larger firms usually have some form of management training program, usually open to recent college graduates. While such programs are usually competitive, they generally offer an excellent opportunity to quickly familiarize oneself with many different aspects of a firm's business. Also, such programs are often open to a broad range of candidates, including both candidates with a BS in business administration, and liberal arts graduates as well.

MATHEMATICIAN

Mathematics is one of the oldest and most fundamental sciences. Mathematicians today are engaged in activities ranging from the creation of new theories and techniques to the translation of economic, scientific, engineering, and managerial problems into mathematical terms.

Mathematical work falls into two broad classes: theoretical (pure) and applied. However, these classes are not sharply defined and often overlap.

Theoretical mathematicians advance mathematical science by developing new principles and new relationships between existing principles of mathematics. Although they seek to increase basic knowledge without necessarily considering its practical use, this pure and abstract knowledge has been instrumental in producing many scientific and engineering achievements.

Applied mathematicians, on the other hand, use mathematics to develop theories and techniques, such as mathematical modeling and computational methods, to solve practical problems in business, government, engineering, and the physical, life, and social sciences. For example, applied mathematicians may analyze the mathematical aspects of launching communications satellites, the effects of new drugs on disease, the aerodynamic characteristics of objects, and the distribution costs of businesses. Some mathematicians, called cryptanalysts, analyze and decipher encryption systems designed to transmit national security-related information.

Mathematicians use computers extensively in many phases of their work—analyzing relationships among variables, solving complex problems, developing models, and processing large amounts of data.

Much work in applied mathematics, however, is carried on by persons other than mathematicians. In fact, because mathematics is the foundation upon which many other academic disciplines are built, the number of workers using mathematical techniques is many times greater than the number actually designated as mathematicians. Engineers, computer scientists, and economists are among those who use mathematics extensively but have job titles other than mathematician. Some workers, such as statisticians, actuaries, and operations research analysts, actually are specialists in a particular branch of mathematics.

Most mathematicians work in the government and in service and manufacturing industries. The Department of Defense is the primary Federal employer of mathematicians. Smaller numbers work for the National Aeronautics and Space Administration and the Department of Commerce. Major employers within the services sector include educational services; computer and data processing services; research and testing services; and management and public relations firms. Within manufacturing, the aircraft and chemicals industries are key employers. Some mathematicians also work for banks, insurance companies, and public utilities.

A bachelor's degree in mathematics is the minimum education needed for prospective mathematicians. In the Federal Government, job candidates must have a four-year degree with a major in mathematics or a four-year degree with the equivalent of a mathematics major—twenty-four semester hours of mathematics courses.

It is helpful for mathematics majors to take several courses in a field that uses or is closely related to mathematics, such as computer science, statistics, or one of the sciences. Mathematicians should have substantial knowledge of computer programming since most complex mathematical computation and much mathematical modeling is done by computer. Mathematicians need good reasoning ability and persistence in order to identify, analyze, and apply basic principles to technical problems. Communication skills are also important, as mathematicians must be able to interact with others, including non-mathematicians, and discuss proposed solutions to problems.

In private industry, job candidates generally need a master's degree to obtain jobs as mathematicians. The majority of bachelor's and master's degree holders in private industry work, not as mathematicians, but in related fields as computer programmers, systems analysts, systems engineers, actuaries, statisticians, and operations research analyst. In addition, a strong background in mathematics facilitates employment in fields such as engineering, economics, finance, and physics.

PERSONNEL AND LABOR RELATIONS SPECIALIST

Personnel and labor relations specialists provide the necessary link between management and employees which helps management make effective use of employees' skills, and helps employees find satisfaction in their jobs and working conditions. Personnel specialists interview, select, and recommend applicants to fill job openings. They handle wage and salary administration, training and career development, and employee benefits. Labor relations specialists usually deal in union-management relations, and people who specialize in this field work primarily in unionized businesses and government agencies. They help management officials prepare for collective bargaining sessions, participate in contract negotiations with the union, and handle day-to-day matters of labor relations agreements.

In a small company, personnel work consists mostly of interviewing and hiring, and one person usually handles all phases. By contrast, a large organization needs an entire staff, which might include recruiters, interviewers, counselors, job analysts, wage and salary analysts, education and training specialists, as well as technical and clerical workers. Personnel work often begins with the personnel recruiter or employment interviewer who travels around the country, often to college campuses, in the search for promising job applicants. These specialists talk to applicants, and then select and recommend those who appear qualified to fill vacancies. They often administer tests to applicants and interpret the results. Job analysts and salary and wage administrators examine detailed information on jobs, including job qualifications and worker characteristics, in order to prepare manuals and other materials for these courses, and look into new methods of training. They also counsel employees participating in training opportunities, which may include on-the-job, apprentice, supervisory, or management training.

Employee benefits supervisors and other personnel specialists handle the employer's benefits programs, which often include health insurance, life insurance, disability insurance, and pension plans. These specialists also coordinate a wide range of employee services, including cafeterias and snack bars, health rooms, recreational facilities, newsletters and communications, and counseling for worker-related personal problems. Counseling employees who are reaching retirement age is a particularly important part of the job. Labor relations specialists give advice on labor management relations. Nearly three out of four work in private industry, for manufacturers, banks, insurance companies, airlines, department stores, and virtually every other business concern.

The educational backgrounds of personnel training, and labor relations specialists and managers vary considerably due to the diversity of duties and level of responsibility. While some employers look for graduates with degrees in personnel administration or industrial and labor relations, others prefer graduates with a general business background. Still others feel that a well-rounded liberal arts education is the best preparation. A college degree in personnel administration, political science, or public administration can be an asset in looking for personnel work with a government agency. Graduate study in industrial or labor relations is often required for work in labor relations. Although a law degree is often required for entry-level jobs, most of the people who are responsible for contract negotiations are lawyers, and a combination of industrial relations courses and a law degree is becoming highly desirable.

New personnel specialists usually enter formal or on-the-job training programs to learn how to classify jobs, interview applicants, or administer employee benefits. Next, new workers are assigned to specific areas in the employee relations department to gain experience. Later, they may advance within their own company, transfer to another employer, or move from personnel to labor relations work. Workers in the middle ranks of a large organization often transfer to a top job in a smaller company. Employees with exceptional ability may be promoted to executive positions, such as director of personnel or director of labor relations.

PHYSICIST

Through systematic observation and experimentation, physicists describe the structure of the universe and the interaction of matter and energy in fundamental terms. Physicists develop theories that describe the fundamental forces and laws of nature. The majority of physicists work in research and development. Some do basic research to increase scientific knowledge. Some engineering-oriented physicists do applied research and help develop new products. Many physicists teach and do research in colleges and universities. A small number work in inspection, quality control and other production-related jobs in industry, while others do consulting work.

Most physicists specialize in one or more branches of the science. A growing number of physicists are specializing in fields that combine physics and a related science. Furthermore, the practical applications of a physicist's work have become increasingly merged with engineering. Private industry employs more than one half of all physicists, primarily in companies manufacturing chemicals, electrical equipment, and aircraft and missiles. Many others work in hospitals, commercial laboratories, and independent research organizations.

Graduate training in physics or a closely related field is almost essential for most entry-level jobs in physics, and for advancement into all types of work. A PhD is normally required for faculty status at colleges and universities, and for industrial or government jobs administering research and development programs. Those with a Master's Degree qualify for many research jobs in private industry and in the Federal Government. In colleges and universities, some teach and assist in research while studying for their PhD degrees. However, those with a BA may qualify for some applied research and development positions in private industry and in government, and some holding bachelor's degrees are employed as research assistants in colleges and universities while studying for advanced degrees. Many also work in engineering and other scientific fields.

Physicists often begin their careers performing routine laboratory tasks. After gaining some experience, they are assigned more complex tasks and may advance to work as project leaders or research directors. Some work in top management jobs. Physicists who develop new products sometimes form their own companies or join new firms to exploit their own ideas.

PSYCHOLOGIST

Psychologists study human behavior and mental processes to understand, explain, and modify people's behavior. They may study the way a person thinks, feels, or behaves. Research psychologists investigate the physical, cognitive, emotional, or social aspects of human behavior. Psychologists in applied fields counsel and conduct training programs; do market research; or provide mental health services in hospitals, clinics, or private settings.

Since psychology deals with human behavior, psychologists apply their knowledge and techniques to a wide range of endeavors including human services, management, education, law, and sports. In addition to the variety of work settings, psychologists specialize in many different areas. Clinical psychologists—who constitute the largest specialty—generally work in hospitals or clinics, or maintain their own practices. They may help the mentally or emotionally disturbed adjust to life. Others help people deal with life stresses such as divorce or aging. Clinical psychologists interview patients; give diagnostic tests; provide individual, family, and group psychotherapy; and design and implement behavior modification programs. They may collaborate with physicians and other specialists in developing treatment programs. Some clinical psychologists work in universities, where they train graduate students in the delivery of mental health services. Others administer community mental health programs.

Counseling psychologists use several techniques, including interviewing and testing, to advise people on how to deal with problems of everyday living—personal, social, educational, or vocational. Developmental psychologists study the patterns and causes of behavioral change as people progress through life from infancy to adulthood. Some concern themselves with behavior during infancy, childhood, and adolescence, while others study changes that take place during maturity and old age. Educational psychologists design, develop, and evaluate educational programs. Experimental psychologists study behavior processes and work with human beings and animals such as rats, monkeys, and pigeons. Prominent areas of experimental research include motivation, thinking, attention, learning and retention, sensory and perceptual processes, effects of substance use and abuse, and genetic and neurological factors in behavior.

Industrial and organizational psychologists apply psychological techniques to personnel administration, management, and marketing problems. They are involved in policy planning, applicant screening, training and development, psychological test research, counseling, and organizational development and analysis, among other activities. For example, an industrial psychologist may work with management to develop better training programs and to reorganize the work setting to improve worker productivity or quality of worklife. School psychologists work with teachers, parents, and administrators to resolve students' learning and behavior problems. Social psychologists examine people's interactions with others and with the social environment. Prominent areas of study include group behavior, leadership, attitudes, and interpersonal perception.

Other areas of specialization include cognitive psychology, community psychology, comparative psychology, consumer psychology, engineering psychology, environmental psychology, family psychology, forensic psychology, health psychology, neuropsychology, psychometrics, population psychology, psychopharmacology, and military and rehabilitation psychology.

Although a doctoral or a master's degree is generally required for employment as a psychologist, a college grad with a degree in psychology is qualified to assist psychologists and other professionals in community mental health centers, vocational rehabilitation offices, and correctional programs; to work as research or administrative assistants; and to take jobs as trainees in government or business. However, without additional academic training, their advancement possibilities are limited. In the Federal Government, candidates having at least 24 semester hours in psychology and one course in statistics qualify for entry-level positions. Competition for these jobs is keen, however.

PUBLIC RELATIONS WORKER

Public relations workers aid businesses, government, universities, and other organizations to build and maintain a positive public image. They apply their talents and skills in a variety of different areas, including press, community, or consumer relations, political campaigning, interest-group representation, fund-raising, or employee recruitment. Public relations is more than telling the employer's story, however. Understanding the attitudes and concerns of customers, employees, and various other public groups, and effectively communicating this information to management to help formulate policy is an important part of the job.

Public relations staffs in very large firms may number 200 or more, but in most firms the staff is much smaller. The director of public relations, who is often a vice-president of the company, may develop overall plans and policies with a top management executive. In addition, large public relations departments employ writers, research workers, and other specialists who prepare material for the different media, stockholders, and other groups the company wishes to reach.

Manufacturing firms, public utilities, transportation companies, insurance companies, and trade and professional associations employ many public relations workers. A sizeable number work for government agencies, schools, colleges, museums, and other educational, religious, human service and other organizations. The rapidly expanding health field also offers opportunities for public relations work. A number of workers are employed by public relations consulting firms which furnish services to clients for a fee. Others work for advertising agencies.

A college education combined with public relations experience is excellent preparation for public relations work. Although most beginners in the field have a college degree in communications, public relations, or journalism, some employers prefer a background in a field related to the firm's business. Other firms want college graduates who have worked for the news media. In fact, many editors, reporters, and workers in closely related fields enter public relations work. Some companies, particularly those with large public relations staffs, have formal training programs for new workers. In other firms, new employers work under the guidance of experienced staff members.

Promotion to supervisory jobs may come as workers demonstrate their ability to handle more demanding and creative assignments. Some experienced public relations workers start their own consulting firms. The Public Relations Society accredits public relations officers who have at least five years of experience in the field and have passed a comprehensive six-hour examination.

PURCHASING AGENT

Purchasing agents, also called industrial buyers, obtain goods and services of the quality required at the lowest possible cost, and see that adequate supplies are always available. Agents who work for manufacturing companies may purchase maintenance and repair supplies; those working for government agencies may purchase such items as office supplies, furniture, business machines, or vehicles, to name some.

Purchasing agents usually specialize in one or more specific groups of commodities. Agents are assigned to sections, headed by assistant purchasing managers, who are responsible for a group of related commodities. In smaller organizations, purchasing agents generally are assigned certain categories of goods. About half of all purchasing agents work for manufacturing firms.

Most large organizations now require a college degree, and many prefer applicants who have an MBA degree. Familiarity with the computer and its uses is desirable in understanding the systems aspect of the purchasing profession. Following the initial training period, junior purchasing agents usually are given the responsibility of purchasing standard and catalog items. As they gain experience and develop expertise in their assigned areas, they may be promoted to purchasing agent and then senior purchasing agent. Continuing education is essential for purchasing agents who want to advance their careers. Purchasing agents are encouraged to participate in frequent seminars offered by professional societies, and to take courses in the field at local colleges and universities.

The recognized mark of experience and professional competence is the designation certified purchasing manager (CPM). This designation is conferred by the National Association of Purchasing Management, Inc. upon candidates who have passed four examinations and who meet educational and professional experience requirements.

QUALITY CONTROL SUPERVISOR

A quality control supervisor may either be involved in the spot checking of items being manufactured or processed or in assuring that the proper processes are being followed. A quality control system involves selection and training of personnel, product design, the establishment of specifications, procedures and tests, the design and maintenance of facilities and equipment, the selection of materials, and recordkeeping. In an effective quality control system, all these aspects are evaluated on a regular basis, and modified and improved when appropriate.

While some quality control positions involved with the supervision of the production of simpler items might require little background besides on-the-job training, many require a specialized degree in engineering, chemistry, or biology. While all manufacturing firms require some degree of quality control, this is especially important in the chemistry, food and drug industries. Some drug manufacturers for example, may assign one out of six production workers to quality assurance functions alone.

REPORTER/EDITOR

Newspaper reporters gather information on current events and use it to write stories for daily or weekly newspapers. Large dailies frequently assign teams of reporters to investigate social, economic, or political conditions, and reporters are often assigned to beats, such as police stations, courthouses, or governmental agencies, to gather news originating in these places. General assignment reporters write local news stories on a wide range of topics, from public meetings to human interest stories.

Reporters with a specialized background or interest in a particular area write, interpret, and analyze the news in fields such as medicine, politics, foreign affairs, sports, fashion, art, theater, consumer affairs, travel, finance, social events, science, education, business, labor, religion, and other areas. Critics review literary, artistic, and musical works and performances while editorial writers present viewpoints on topics of interest. Reporters on small newspapers cover all aspects of local news, and may also take photographs, write headlines, lay out pages, and write editorials. On some small weeklies, they may also solicit advertisements, sell subscriptions, and perform general office work. Reporters must be highly motivated, and are expected to work long hours.

Most newspapers will only consider applicants with a degree in journalism, which includes training in the liberal arts in addition to professional training in journalism. Others prefer applicants who have a bachelor's degree in one of the liberal arts and a master's degree in journalism. Experience as a part-time "stringer" is very helpful in finding full time employment as a reporter. Most beginning reporters start on weekly or small daily newspapers, with a small number of outstanding journalism graduates finding work with large daily newspapers, although this is a rare exception. Large dailies generally look for at least three years of reporting experience, acquired on smaller newspapers.

Beginning reporters are assigned duties such as reporting on civic and community meetings, summarizing speeches, writing obituaries, interviewing important community leaders or visitors, and covering police, government, or courthouse proceedings. As they gain experience, they may report on more important events, cover an assigned beat, or specialize in a particular field. Newspaper reporters may advance to large daily newspapers or state and national newswire services. However, competition for such positions is fierce, and news executives are flooded with applications from highly qualified reporters every year. Some experienced reporters become columnists, correspondents, editorial writers, editors, or top executives; these people represent the top of the field, and competition for these positions is extremely keen. Other reporters transfer to related fields, such as public relations, writing for magazines, or preparing copy for radio or television news programs.

SALES REPRESENTATIVES FOR MANUFACTURERS/WHOLESALERS

Sales representatives market their company's products to manufacturers, wholesale and retail establishments, government agencies, and other institutions. Regardless of the type of product they sell, the primary job of sales representatives is to interest wholesale and retail buyers and purchasing agents in their merchandise (as opposed to retail sales workers who sell directly to the consumer).

Manufacturers' and wholesale sales representatives spend much of their time traveling to and visiting with prospective buyers. During a sales call, they may show samples or catalogs that describe their company's products. Because the prospective customer is most likely considering products from many competing vendors, the sales rep must use product knowledge and interpersonal skills to persuade the customer that a given product is best. Sales representatives also take orders and help resolve problems or complaints with merchandise. Sometimes, sales representatives promote their company's products at trade shows and conferences. Other duties of a sales rep might include analyzing sales statistics, preparing reports, and handling administrative duties.

A career as a sales representative for a manufacturer or wholesaler has many benefits including high pay, travel, and the opportunity to meet many new people. However, this field is not for the meek or soft-spoken. The most difficult part of the job, referred to as "cold calling", requires the salesperson to call prospective customers who have yet to express any interest in the company's products or services and may have little or no interest in even talking to the sales person, let alone making a purchase.

A sales position is the best way to get into a top management position at many companies. This is because sales work provides a strong overall view of the company's products, an understanding of the nature of the competition, and an appreciation for the needs of the customer base. An entry-level position in sales is the closest thing to a fast-track management training program that many companies offer.

The background needed for sales jobs varies by product line and market; however, a college degree is increasingly desirable. Any summer or part-time experience in sales will also be greatly beneficial to the college student seeking a career in this field.

SECURITIES AND FINANCIAL SERVICES SALES REPRESENTATIVES

Most investors, whether they are individuals with a few hundred dollars or large institutions with millions to invest, use securities sales representatives when buying or selling stocks, bonds, shares in mutual funds, or other financial products. Securities sales representatives also provide many related services for their customers. Depending on a customer's knowledge of the market, the representative may explain the meaning of stock market terms and trading practices, offer financial counseling, devise an individual financial portfolio including securities, corporate and municipal bonds, life insurance, annuities, and other investments, and offer advice on the purchase or sale of particular securities.

Financial services sales representatives call on various businesses to solicit applications for loans and new deposit accounts for banks or savings and loan associations. They also locate and contact prospective customers to present their bank's financial services and to ascertain the customer's banking needs. At most small and medium-sized banks, branch managers and commercial loan officers are responsible for marketing the bank's financial services. As banks offer more and increasingly complex financial services, for example, securities brokerage and financial planning—the job of financial services sales representatives—will assume greater importance.

A college education is becoming increasingly important, as securities sales representatives must be well informed about economic conditions and trends. Although employers seldom require specialized academic training, courses in business administration, economics, and finance are helpful. Securities sales representatives must meet state licensing requirements, which generally include passing an examination and, in some cases, furnishing a personal bond. In addition, sales representatives must register as representatives of their firm according to the regulations of the securities exchanges where they do business or the National Association of Securities Dealers, Inc. (NASD).

Before beginners can qualify as registered representatives, they must pass the General Securities Registered Representative Examination. Banks and other credit institutions prefer to hire college graduates for financial services sales jobs. A business administration degree with a specialization in finance or a liberal arts degree including courses in accounting, economics, and marketing serves as excellent preparation for this job. Financial services sales representatives learn through on-the-job training under the supervision of bank officers. Outstanding performance can lead to promotion to managerial positions.

SOCIOLOGIST

Sociologists study human society and social behavior by examining the groups and social institutions that people form. These include families, tribes, communities, and governments, as well as a variety of social, religious, political, business, and other organizations. Sociologists study the behavior and interaction of groups, trace their origin and growth, and analyze the influence of group activities on individual members. Some sociologists are concerned primarily with the characteristics of social groups, organizations, and institutions. Others are more interested in the ways individuals are affected by each other and by the groups to which they belong. Still others focus on social traits such as gender, age, or race, that make an important difference in how a person experiences life on a daily basis.

As a rule, sociologists work in one or more special fields, such as criminology; racial and ethnic relations; urban studies; group formation; social organization, stratification, and mobility; education; social psychology; urban, rural, political, industrial, and comparative sociology; gender roles and relations; sociological practice; and the family. These subjects have recently been attracting more mainstream attention due to the increase in the number of divorces and changes in living arrangements.

Other specialties include medical sociology—the study of social factors that affect mental and public health; gerontology—the study of aging and the special problems of aged persons; environmental sociology—the study of the effects of the physical environment and technology on people; clinical sociology—therapy and intervention in social systems for assessment and change; demography—the study of the size, characteristics, and movement of populations; criminology—the study of factors producing deviance form accepted legal and cultural norms; and industrial sociology—the study of work and organizations. For example, an industrial sociologist may work as an arbitrator helping settle disputes arising in the workplace.

Other sociologists specialize in research design and data analysis. Sociologists usually conduct surveys or engage in direct observation to gather data. For example, an organizational sociologist might study the effects of leadership on individuals in a small work group and a medical sociologist may study the effects of terminal illness on family interaction. Sociological researchers also evaluate the efficacy of different kinds of social programs. They might examine and evaluate particular programs of income assistance, job training, or remedial education. Increasingly, sociologists use statistical and computer techniques in their research.

The results of sociological research aid educators, lawmakers, administrators, and others interested in resolving social problems and formulating public policy. For example, in recent years sociologists have devoted more time to studying issues related to abortion rights, AIDS disease, high school dropouts, homeless, and latch-key children. Some sociologists are primarily administrators. They may, for example, administer social service programs in family and child welfare agencies or develop social policies and programs for government, community, youth, or religious organizations. A number of sociologists also work as consultants in the government evaluating social and welfare programs or in private business, advising on the management of complex organizations and conducting market research.

Although a PhD or a master's degree is usually the minimum requirement for employment as a sociologist, bachelor's degree holders in sociology often get jobs in related fields. Their training in research, statistics, and human behavior qualifies them for entry-level positions in social services, management, sales, personnel, and marketing. Many work in social service agencies as counselors or child care, juvenile, or recreation workers. Others are employed as interviewers or as administrative or research assistants. Sociology majors with sufficient training in statistical and survey methods may qualify for positions as junior analysts or statisticians in business or research firms or government agencies. Regardless of a sociologist's level of educational attainment, completion of an internship while in school can prove invaluable in finding a position in this field.

In the Federal Government, candidates generally need a college degree with 24 semester hours in sociology, including coursework in theory and methods of social research. However, since competition for the limited number of positions is keen, advanced study of the field is highly recommended.

STATISTICIAN

Statisticians devise, carry out, and interpret the numerical results of surveys and experiments. In doing so, they apply their knowledge of statistical methods to a particular subject area, such as economics, human behavior, the natural sciences, or engineering. They may use statistical techniques to predict population growth or economic conditions, develop quality control tests for manufactured products, or help business managers and government officials make decisions and evaluate the results of new programs. Over half of all statisticians are in private industry, primarily in manufacturing, finance, and insurance firms.

A bachelor's degree in statistics or mathematics is the minimum educational requirement for many beginning jobs in statistics. For other entry-level jobs in the field, however, a BA with a major in an applied field of study such as economics or a natural science, and a minor in statistics is preferable. A graduate degree in mathematics or statistics is essential for college and university teaching. Most mathematics statisticians have at least a BA in mathematics and an advanced degree in statistics. Beginning statisticians who have a BA often spend their time performing routine work under the supervision of an experienced statistician. Through experience, they may advance to positions of greater technical and supervisory responsibility. However, opportunities for promotion are best for those with advanced degrees.

SYSTEMS ANALYST

Systems analysts plan efficient methods of processing data and handling the results. Analysts use various techniques, such as cost accounting, sampling, and mathematical model building to analyze a problem and devise a new system. The problems that systems analysts solve range from monitoring nuclear fission in a powerplant to forecasting sales for an appliance manufacturing firm. Because the work is so varied and complex, analysts usually specialize in either business or scientific and engineering applications. Most systems analysts work in manufacturing firms, banks, insurance companies, and data processing service organizations. In addition, large numbers work for wholesale and retail businesses and government agencies.

College graduates are almost always sought for the position of systems analyst. For some of the more complex positions, persons with graduate degrees are preferred. Employers usually seek analysts with a background in accounting, business management, or economics for work in a business environment, while a background in the physical sciences, mathematics, or engineering is preferred for work in scientifically oriented organizations. A growing number of employers seek applicants who have a degree in computer science, information systems, or data processing. Regardless of the college major, employers seek those who are familiar with programming languages.

In order to advance, systems analysts must continue their technical education. Technological advances come so rapidly in the computer field that continuous study is necessary to keep computer skills up to date. Training usually takes the form of one and two-week courses offered by employers and software vendors. Additional training may come from professional development seminars offered by professional computing societies. An indication of experience and professional competence is the Certificate in Data Processing (CDP). This designation is conferred by the Institute for Certification of Computer Professionals, and is granted to candidates who have five years experience and have passed a five-part examination.

TECHNICAL WRITER/EDITOR

Technical writers and technical editors research, write, and edit technical materials, and also may produce publications and audiovisual materials. To ensure that their work is accurate, technical writers must be expert in the subject area in which they are writing. Editors are also responsible for the accuracy of material on which they work. Some organizations use job titles other than technical writer/editor, such as staff writer, publications engineer, communications specialist, industrial writer, industrial materials developer, and others. Technical writers set out either to instruct or inform, and in many instances they do both. They prepare manuals, catalogs, parts lists, and instructional materials needed by sales representatives who sell machinery or scientific equipment and by the technicians who install, maintain, and service it.

Technical writers are often part of a team, working closely with scientists, engineers, accountants, and others. Technical editors take the material technical writers produce and further polish it for final publication and use. Many writers and editors work for large firms in the electronics, aviation, aerospace, ordinance, chemical, pharmaceutical, and computer manufacturing industries. Firms in the energy, communications, and computer software fields also employ many technical writers, and research laboratories employ significant numbers.

Employers seek people whose educational background, work experience, and personal pursuits indicate they possess both writing skills and appropriate scientific knowledge. Knowledge of graphics and other aspects of publication production may be helpful in landing a job in the field. An understanding of current trends in communication technology is an asset, and familiarity with computer operations and terminology is increasingly important.

Many employers prefer candidates with a degree in science or engineering, plus a minor in English, journalism, or technical communications. Other employers emphasize writing ability and look for candidates whose major field of study was journalism, English, or the liberal arts. Depending on their line of business, these employers almost always require course work or practical experience in a specific subject as well, computer science, for example. People with a solid background in science or engineering are at an advantage in competing for such jobs. Those with BA's or MA's in technical writing are often preferred over candidates with little or no technical background.

Beginning technical writers often assist experienced writers by doing library research work and preparing drafts of reports. Experienced technical writers in companies with large writing staffs may eventually move to the job of technical editor, or shift to an administrative position in the publication or technical information departments. The top job is usually that of publications manager (and other titles), who normally supervises the people directly involved in producing the company's technical documents. The manager supervises not only the technical writers and editors, but also staff members responsible for illustrations, photography, reproduction, and distribution.

UNDERWRITER

Underwriters appraise and select the risks their company will insure. Underwriters decide whether their insurance company will accept risks after analyzing information in insurance applications, reports from loss control consultants, medical reports, and actuarial studies. Most underwriters specialize in one of the three major categories of insurance: life, casualty, and health. They further specialize in group or individual policies.

For beginning underwriters, most large insurance companies seek college graduates with degrees in liberal arts or business administration. Underwriter trainees begin by evaluating routine applicants under the close supervision of an experienced risk appraiser. Continuing education is a necessity if the underwriter expects to advance to senior level positions.

Insurance companies generally place great emphasis on completion of one or more of the many recognized independent study programs. Many companies pay tuition and the cost of books for those who successfully complete underwriting courses; some offer salary increases as an additional incentive. Independent study programs are available through the American Institute of Property and Liability Underwriters, the Health Insurance Association of America, and the Life Office Management Association.

As underwriters gain experience, they can qualify as a "Fellow" of the Academy of Life Underwriters by passing a series of examinations and completing a research paper on a topic in the field. Exams are given by the Institute of Home Office Underwriters and the Home Office Life Underwriters Association. The designation of "Fellow" is recognized as a mark of achievement in the underwriting field. Experienced underwriters who complete a course of study may advance to chief underwriter or underwriting manager. Some underwriting managers are promoted to senior managerial positions after several years.

About the Author

Bob Adams is president of Bob Adams, Inc., the nation's leading publisher of career guides. He publishes the *JobBank* series of local job search books, each of which features information on hundreds of area employers in major U.S. metropolitan areas.

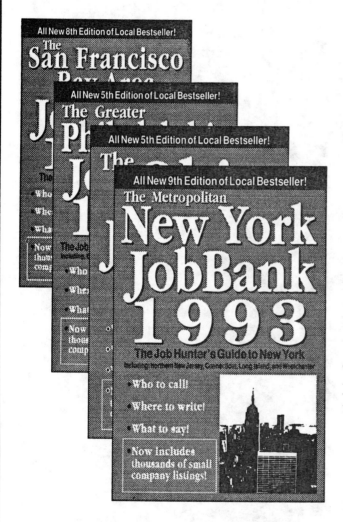